About the author

Liz Harfull is passionate about telling the stories of Australia's quiet voices—the extraordinary, everyday people who make up our communities. An award-winning journalist and rural communicator, she grew up on a farm near Mount Gambier, discovering her love of both writing and cooking at a young age.

In 2006, Liz walked away from corporate life to write books. Her leap of faith was rewarded two years later with *The Blue Ribbon Cookbook*, which captured the stories and traditions of South Australian country shows and show cooks, and became a surprise bestseller. It even took the author to Paris after winning a Gourmand World Cookbook Award.

Since then Liz has written two national bestsellers, *Women of the Land* and *The Australian Blue Ribbon Cookbook*. Inspired by her mother, her most recent book, *City Girl Country Girl*, explored the adventures of women from the city and overseas as they made new lives in rural Australia.

Today Liz lives in the Adelaide Hills, occasionally finding time to bake scones and make jam, while juggling a business writing career.

TRIED, TESTED *and* TRUE

Presented for the
6th Edition
of
The
SUTTONTOWN
Recipe Book
800 Selected Recipes
1983 $2.50

Sounds Delicious
Sydney Philharmonia Cookbook

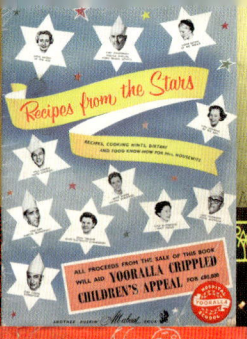

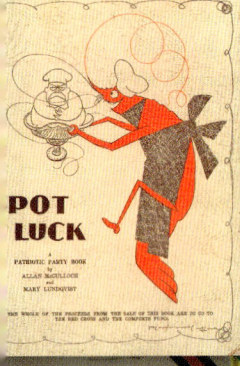

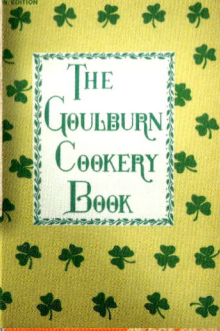

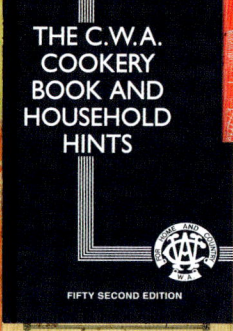

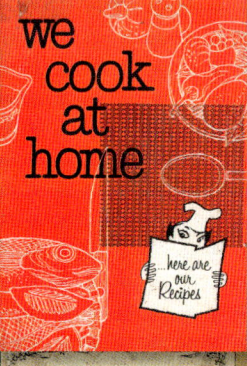

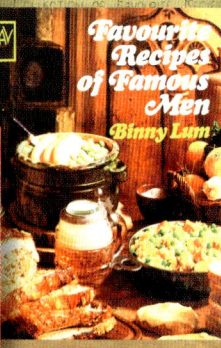

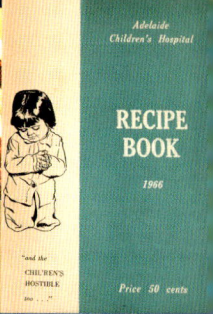

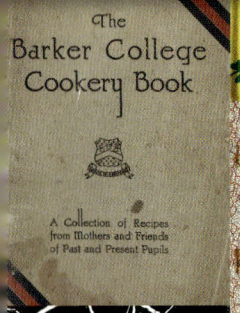

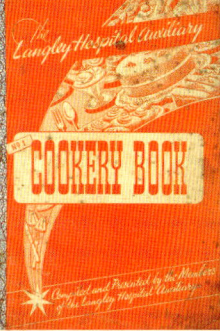

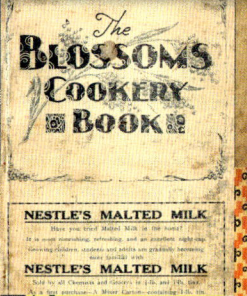

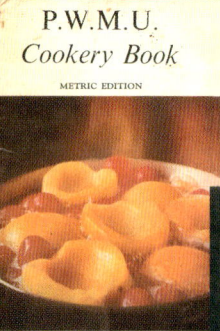

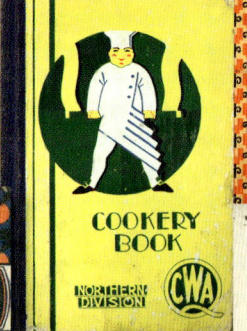

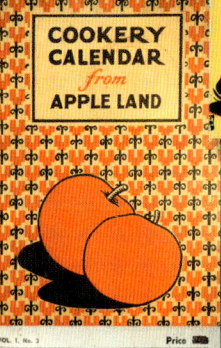

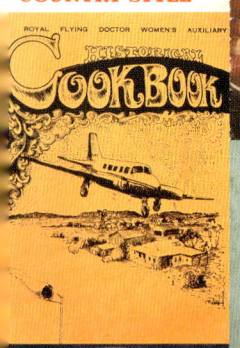

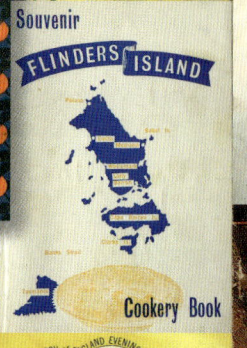

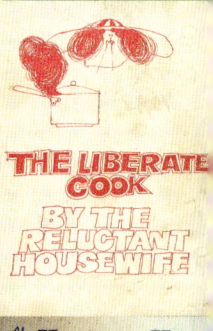

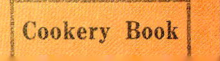

THE MELBOURNE CHORALE
CHRISTMAS BOOK

Recipes from the Stars
RECIPES, COOKING HINTS, DIETARY
AND FOOD-KNOW HOW FOR ALL HOUSEWIVES
ALL PROCEEDS FROM THE SALE OF THIS BOOK
WILL AID YOORALLA CRIPPLED
CHILDREN'S APPEAL FOR £10,000

JEAN HORAN KINDERGARTEN
FLINDERS PARK

SELECTED
RECIPES
SOUTH SANDRINGHAM
METHODIST
LADIES GUILD

POT
LUCK
PATRIOTIC PARTY BOOK
by
ALLAN McCULLOCH
and
MARY LINDSAY
THE WHOLE OF THE PROCEEDS FROM THE SALE OF THIS BOOK ARE TO GO TO
THE RED CROSS and THE COMFORTS FUND

THE
GOULBURN
COOKERY
BOOK

Junior Red Cross
COOKERY
BOOK.

we
cook
at
home
here are
our Recipes

Favourite
Recipes
of Famous
Men
Binny Lum

Adelaide
Children's Hospital
RECIPE
BOOK
1966
Price 50 cents

The
Barker College
Cookery Book
A Collection of Recipes
from Mothers and Friends
of Past and Present Pupils

The Langley Hospital Auxiliary
No. 1
COOKERY BOOK
Compiled and Presented by the Members of
the Langley Hospital Auxiliary

THE C.W.A.
COOKERY
BOOK AND
HOUSEHOLD
HINTS
FIFTY SECOND EDITION

The
BLOSSOMS
COOKERY
BOOK Ltd.

Methodist Church of Australasia
NEW SOUTH WALES CONFERENCE
FAR WEST MISSION
500 Contributed
RECIPES
also
Interesting Articles
By Members of Mission Staff

LOOK WHO'S
COOKING!

COOKING
COUNTRY STYLE

P.W.M.U.
Cookery Book
METRIC EDITION

Kayser SLIPPER HEEL
SLENDERISES THE ANKLE
NESTLE'S MALTED MILK
NESTLE'S MALTED MILK
HOME COOKERY
AND JEWISH RECIPES
Kayser Chamoisette
Gloves
Kayser SILK GLOVES
FOR ALL OCCASIONS

COOKERY
CALENDAR
from
APPLE LAND

GREEN
GOLD
Cookery Book

ROYAL FLYING DOCTOR WOMEN'S AUXILIARY
HISTORIC
Cook BOOK

THE MITCHELL VALLEY
Recipe
Book

The ORANGE
RECIPE
GIFT BOOK

COOKERY
BOOK
NORTHERN
DIVISION
CWA

VOL. 1. No. 2   Price
Good
Sense
COOK
BOOK
WITH
RECIPES
TO
SUIT
ALL
OCCASIONS
IN AID OF THE
EASTLAKES SUB-NORMAL SCHOOL APPEAL

LIMITED EDITION

Miss Australia
Cookbook

THE PROCEEDS OF THIS BOOK ARE FOR THE OLYMPIC SWIMMING POOL
APPEAL AND THE AUXILIARY WISH TO THANK THE DISTRICT HOUSEWIVES
WHO HAVE CONTRIBUTED THEIR FAVOURITE RECIPES
PRICE 4/-
Cookery Book

"BETHANY"
Cookery Book
700 TESTED RECIPES.

Souvenir
FLINDERS ISLAND
Cookery Book

The
Red Cross
Recipe Book

THE LIBERATED
COOK
BY THE
RELUCTANT
HOUSEWIFE

The
HELPING HAND
Cookery Book

ST. JAMES CHURCH OF ENGLAND EVENING GUILD
ENTREES
AND
CASSEROLES

TRIED
TESTED
and TRUE

Treasured recipes and untold stories
from Australia's community cookbooks

~~~~~~~~~~

Liz Harfull

ALLEN&UNWIN
SYDNEY·MELBOURNE·AUCKLAND·LONDON

Dedication

To the keepers of community stories—
history group volunteers, librarians, archivists
and magical Trove—without whom this book
would have been impossible.

Contents

INTRODUCTION

Among my most treasured possessions is a small bundle of cookbooks that belonged to my grandmother, Amy Harfull. She died before I was born, but they give me a strong sense of connection with her, and my bachelor uncle, Ross, who cooked from them too.

The collection includes one of my father's primary-school dictation workbooks, which has been used like a scrapbook, with recipes cut out of newspapers and magazines pasted over his neat, blue cursive writing; a farm machinery catalogue receives the same treatment, recipes from neighbours and friends crowding out the latest models of Caterpillar diesel tractors.

There are a few conventional cookbooks but they also turn out to be more than the covers promise. The "Back to Suttontown" Recipe Book, which Amy wrote her name on in 1933, has so many additional bits of paper squeezed or stapled between its pages, that it is bursting at the seams. There is a tonic for poultry alongside a recipe for orange and lemon tart, a jubilee cake recipe from Roma Clarke who lived on the dairy farm next door, a pudding recipe from a church friend Ilie Kuhl, and my sister-in-law Anne's sultana cake. Towards the back of the book is a typed recipe for bread, sent all the way from Tanna Island in the South Pacific, where my adopted Uncle Charlie and his wife, Jean, were serving as Presbyterian missionaries.

Filling out my grandmother's collection is the Spare Corner series of cookbooks, featuring readers' recipes published in The Leader, a town and country weekly that was popular in the Mount Gambier area, where my family farm. And there is a very precious copy of The Blossoms Cookery Book, published in 1931 to raise money for a soup kitchen that fed thousands of underprivileged children in Adelaide during the Depression.

What the items in this motley collection have in common is that they are all made up of recipes that came from everyday cooks—usually with their names affixed, and shared with a generous spirit. These are the sources that my grandmother, my mother, and generations of Australian women trusted to guide them in a world before celebrity chefs and television cooking shows dominated the scene.

In fact, the books that best reflect what many Australians cooked and ate at home for most of the twentieth century were put together by people

Killara Steam Pudding.

3/4 in off 1b butter.

ab.spoons butter
cup brown sugar
x together   add   1 cup milk
1 cup fruit
1 cupS.R.Flour
2 cups bread crumbs
spice to taste   about 1 teaspoon.

steam for 2½ hours

Sponge. Nell Connell.

3 eggs
½ cup sugar
2 heaped tabsp cornflour
1 heaped tabsp plain flour
1 rounded sm teaspn cr tartar
1 bare xx level teaspn c. soda.

Beat white of eggs stiff(about minute or frothy)
beat yolks,add to whites,add sugar,give few whiskes
prepare flour etc,& sift twice grease tins & paper in
bottom whisk mixture up few minutes add dry ingredients
fold in with spoon.Cook 15 to 20 mins.

Ice Cream.MrsLindner.

8 tabspns powdered milk
¾ cup sugar
3 teasps gelatine dissolved in 3 tabsps boiling water
4 cups fresh milk
1½ teasp vanilla.

Method. Freeze,then beat and freeze again.

ix p.milk o sugar with 1 cup mi...
to paste   then add gel.   later

Remove starch from an iron,
carb. soda which has be...
some paper.

Alison St bread

7 oz butter
4 oz ic sugar
cream togethe
dash salt
add ☐ 10 oz
plain flour
mix together
roll out to ½ in
or ¼ in & bake
3.50 oven about
20 mins.

Right: My grandmother, Amy Harfull,
with her sons, Lyall (my father, on the
left) and Ross, 1923. Above: Pages
from her 1933 edition of The "Back to
Suttontown" Recipe Book.

you have never heard of, usually in the name of helping others. Known as community cookbooks, these publications have raised what is likely to amount to millions of dollars for Australian charities and causes, ranging from cash-strapped local schools and churches to sports teams and the scout movement, hospitals and medical research, and even political parties and international peace movements.

Many of these books were humble publications, hand-printed and stapled together by volunteers. But some, like the iconic *Green and Gold Cookery Book* from South Australia, the *PWMU Cookbook* from Victoria and *The C.W.A. Cookery Book and Household Hints* from Western Australia, have outlived fleeting food fads, and are still in print and much used by cooks whose grand-mothers weren't even born when they were first compiled.

The first community cookbook

The concept of community cookbooks seems to have begun in the United States in the 1860s, during the American Civil War. In 1864, Maria J. Moss donated proceeds from *A Poetical Cook-book* to benefit northern soldiers. Her book is recognised by historians as the first community cookbook published in America. Canada followed in 1877 with *The Home Cook Book*, which benefited the Hospital for Sick Children in Toronto. In less than ten years it sold 100,000 copies, making it the best-selling English language cookbook in Canada in the nineteenth century.

An edition was even published in Sydney sometime around 1890, which may in turn have inspired antipodean charity workers. According to Adelaide academic Sarah Black, who wrote a thesis about community cookbooks for her PhD, the first recorded Australian example was put out by the Queensland Presbyterian Women's Missionary Union in 1894. The *W.M.U. Cookery Book* eventually sold more than 225,000 copies, with the final and 22nd edition published almost 90 years later, in 1981.

Evidence has been swept away by floods, however the WMU may have been pipped at the post by the wife of a pastoralist in central Queensland. Sydney-born Helen Moffitt married Henry Coldham in 1887 and moved to Wolfang station, where she gave birth to a daughter in October 1888. Sometime between then and leaving the district in 1903, Mrs Coldham compiled *A Voice from the Bush*, a small collection of 'tested recipes', which raised money for All Saints Church of England at Clermont.

The first few years of the new century saw the release of two of the most successful cookbooks ever published in Australia. The *PWMU Cookbook* is our

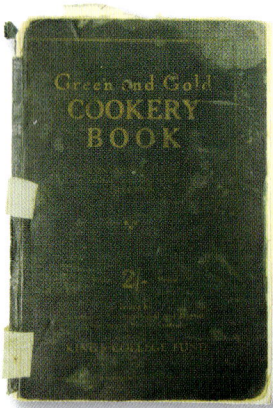

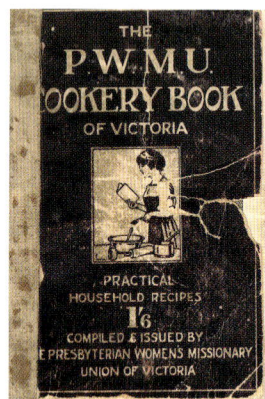

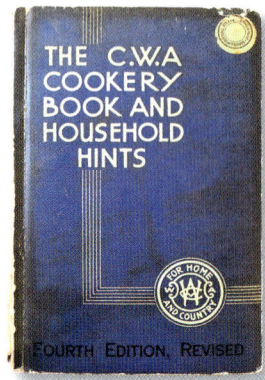

From top: *Green and Gold Cookery Book*, first edition, 1924 (Pembroke School Archives); *The P.W.M.U. Cookery Book*, fifth edition, 1923; *The C.W.A. Cookery Book and Household Hints*, fourth edition, revised (State Library of WA).

oldest continuously published cookbook. Although the title has varied over time, it has been in print for more than 110 years. Since it was released in 1904 by the Presbyterian Women's Missionary Union of Victoria, the book has sold more than 500,000 copies. It has survived two world wars, the Depression, massive social and cultural changes, the emergence of radio, television and the internet, and a veritable tsunami of other books about food and wine—more than 26,000 new titles are published annually around the world—to fix its place firmly in many Victorian homes and hearts.

In the same year that the first edition of the PWMU book came out, a collection of recipes compiled by Jean Rutledge was produced to raise funds for the Church of England's Goulburn diocese. By 1930, a staggering 34 editions and 200,000 copies of *The Goulburn Cookery Book* had been printed. There were yet more editions over the next two decades, with the last copies disappearing from bookshop shelves in the early 1950s. The cookbook was given a new lease of life in 1973, when a facsimile edition was published as a fundraiser for the National Trust.

A focus on fundraising

Since these books, many hundreds of community cookbooks have been produced across Australia. From the beginning of this project, I decided to focus on the first 100 years or so, up to the end of the 1980s. The books I wanted to write about also needed to be fundraisers, rather than mainly educational or promotional exercises. I found almost one thousand books matching those two criteria, tucked away in libraries and archives, op shops and private collections, and I'm fairly sure that I have barely scratched the surface.

The emergence of digital printing techniques and online amateur publishing tools has revived the concept, with hundreds of professionally printed cookbooks coming onto the market in recent years. They are beautiful books, but I find myself particularly drawn to much more modest renditions from the 1950s, '60s and '70s. These books were usually reproduced on roneo or Gestetner machines, with volunteers walking along tables to compile the pages one by one, then staple them together. There seems to be so much heart in these modest books, put together by volunteers with more than a little sweat, maybe some tears and, hopefully, a lot of love and laughter.

Thumbed through one at a time, they are interesting for what they convey about the communities they came from and the kind of food people were cooking. Collectively, they have an unexpected power that draws people in. Time and again, the volunteers and librarians helping me with my research

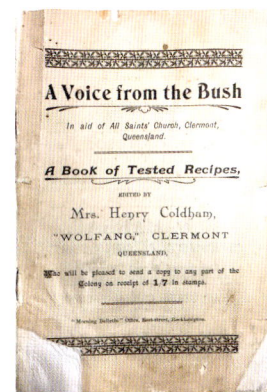

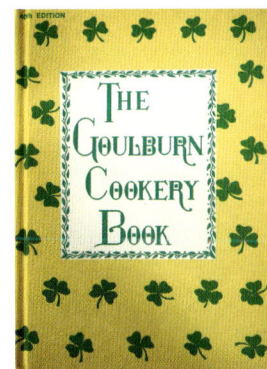

From top: *The W.M.U. Cookery Book*, Queensland, 1976 edition. (Barr Smith Library, University of Adelaide); *A Voice from the Bush*, c. 1890 (courtesy Central Queensland University); *The Goulburn Cookery Book*, facsimile edition, 1973 (State Library of SA).

became fascinated by the little books that were emerging from their archives, many of them unrequested for years.

I knew it was not just me when, one afternoon in a state library, a storeman tasked with retrieving items from the basement, started asking questions. A former train driver, he began flicking through the pages before handing them over. After a few hours he was drawing my attention to the odd recipe that had caught his eye and thought might be worth a try.

Then there were the young librarians who exclaimed over the covers. The covers of community cookbooks tell you so much about the place, the time and the cause. They are incredibly diverse and can be gorgeous or eye-popping, childlike or sophisticated, smile-inducing or laugh-out-loud terrible, retro cool or a time-travelling travesty.

There are the soft and simple covers of the first twenty years of the tradition, with no graphics—just rows of serif fonts matter-of-factly explaining what people will find inside. Next came the bold wartime covers from the 1910s, with silhouettes of battle scenes and flying flags to stir support. In the 1920s and '30s, organisations declared themselves fashionable with rounder typefaces and dynamic Art Deco design elements, while more conservative groups opted for softer graphics of flowers, buildings and smiling women.

The 1950s and '60s boasted a new era of clean, modern kitchens, graced by perfect housewives dressed in high heels and frilly white aprons, as they stood over electric stoves preparing perfect meals for their perfect families. With a more liberated age emerging, designs in the 1970s and '80s moved away from featuring women to featuring the food, or clever cartoons and caricatures, on backgrounds of searing orange and lime green.

Below, from left: A popular Tasmanian CWA cookbook from the 1950s (Special Collections, Deakin University Library); a 1983 preschool fundraiser from Western Australia (State Library of WA); a fundraiser for the Yooralla Hospital School for Crippled Children in Victoria, c. 1960 (State Library of Victoria); a CWA of the Air, Kalgoorlie branch, cookbook, c. 1965 (State Library of WA); a 1969 fundraiser for Perth's Claremont Hospital; also known as the *Excell Cook Book*, a popular Red Cross cookbook from the 1920s, and a 1955 fundraiser for the Kyneton District Hospital, from its Langley auxiliary (both Special Collections, Deakin University Library); and a 1973 South Australian cookbook raising money for an Adelaide kindergarten (State Library of South Australia).

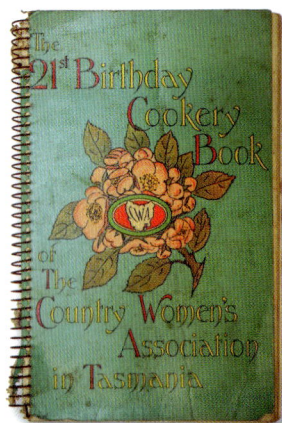

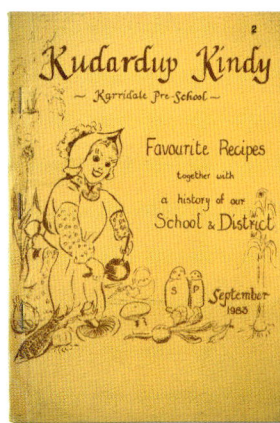

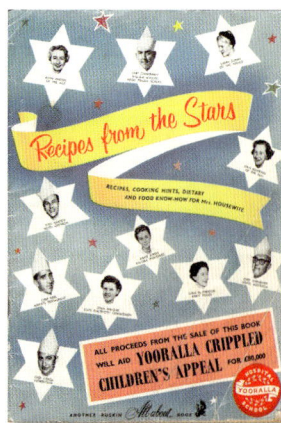

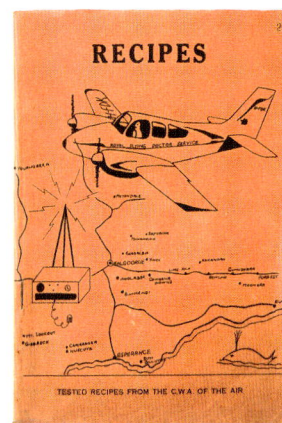

Criteria for selection

Choosing which books to feature was a nightmare, given I could not write about them all. I didn't want to focus on just the bestsellers and best known. Sometimes it was the cover that made me want to know more, but most often it was the glimpses of personal stories that peeked out from behind a recipe or the book's introduction. Most community cookbooks do not carry an author or compiler's name on the cover and, if they do, up until the 1960s it was more likely their husbands' first names, so that the individual identities of the women are obscured.

Then there were the all-important signals giving away that the books had been used. Even in state library collections, many of these cookbooks originally came from private kitchens. I knew that I had struck a winner when there were ticks and comments alongside recipes, or butter stains smearing the page. One day sitting in the State Library of New South Wales I even found a small piece of yellowed meringue clinging to a pavlova recipe.

Once a book gained my attention, the next step was some preliminary research to see what I could find out about it—the beneficiaries, the compilers if they were named, and the recipe donors. Sometimes the organisations were long gone, and their very existence forgotten. Often the school or church still existed but no-one there now knew anything about the cookbook or the names mentioned, and no records had been kept. Many times, but not always, my detective work and perseverance paid off. After days and sometimes weeks and even months of searching, the jigsaw would start to come together, piece by piece, creating a picture of a remarkable woman or moment in history.

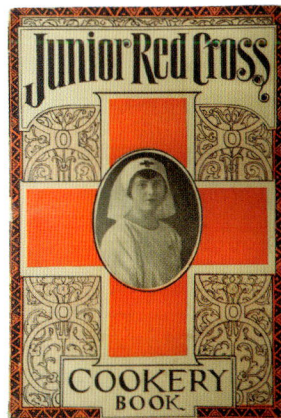

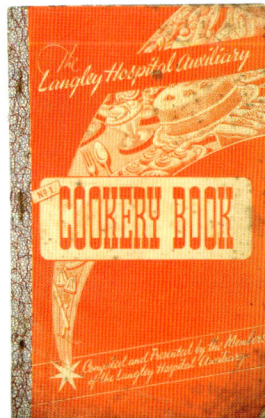

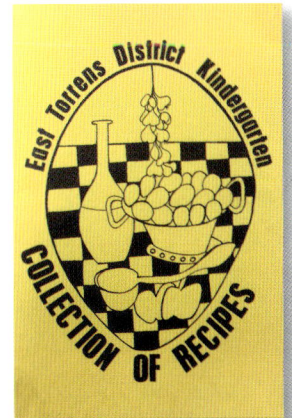

For the older books, I relied heavily on the wonderful gift to our nation that is Trove—the National Library of Australia's website, which provides access to digitised newspapers, images and library catalogues. In country communities, local history groups were an absolute godsend, with volunteers cheerfully digging material out of their archives, often at short notice.

The task of tracking down people actually involved in creating the books, or their descendants, was another challenge altogether. In smaller rural communities where families tend to stay put, local knowledge helped me make connections. And sometimes, with unusual names, I tried pot luck via online search engines, phone directories and social media.

As I tackled books published in the 1960s, '70s and even as recently as the '80s, my work took on a sense of urgency. In some cases there were only one or two older people still alive who helped create the cookbook. Most of them had never been asked about this moment in their lives before, so the story could be recorded, and there was imminent danger of it being lost.

Many of the people I spoke to were astounded to learn that the humble cookbooks they, or their mothers—or, in one case, husband—had put together, had found their way into library collections and that someone was interested. Talking about them sparked wonderful memories for those involved firsthand, and gave family members and friends a chance to reminisce and pay tribute to an important person in their lives.

Selecting the recipes

The other element of writing this book involved selecting and reworking the recipes. Tell-tale markings indicating what had been used and how they rated with the book's original owner gave me a jump start. If there were no such clues, I looked for recipes provided by the women involved in putting the book together, or ones that caught my eye because they were unusual. Conversely, I also looked for recipes popular in their day and indicative of the period, but likely unknown to many modern cooks, and worthy of rediscovering.

For recipes pre-1970, the first step was converting the measurements into metric. For recipes written before the 1930s the challenge was more difficult. Three different cup sizes were used in Australian cookbooks—breakfast, tea and coffee. Tablespoons varied between households—for example, my mother used a very large tablespoon, which was more a serving spoon, to measure many things. There was a similar problem with dessertspoons, which are no longer a standard measurement.

There was also the issue of ingredients no longer existing, or having changed in some way, so that what might appear familiar really wasn't. Or a recipe might stipulate a can, bottle or glass of something, without mentioning the volume or weight.

Then there was the challenge of the method. Early cookbooks contain virtually none—it was assumed that every housewife or cook would know the basic steps for making various types of dishes. Wood ovens had no thermostat, so temperatures and cooking times often weren't mentioned either, let alone precise pan sizes.

The tools available to cooks have changed over the years too. I want the recipes I have revisited to be made by contemporary home cooks, so it was important to update the method to make it as easy as possible without changing the end result. Before blenders came along, cooks mashed things or forced them through sieves. Egg whites, fluffs and cake batter had to be hand-beaten or whisked using beaters with a handle to turn. Early recipes instructed cooks to remove a saucepan from the 'fire', and there was no fridge to speed up setting processes or keep things cool.

Where I could, I asked donors of the original recipes, or their descendants, for insights on how to make them, capturing the knowledge handed down through families. If that wasn't possible I experimented myself, or found a talented home cook who was familiar with the recipe and willing to share some tips. Then every recipe was tested again by a willing band of volunteers with varying degrees of skill, to make sure they worked and were easy to follow.

The end result is, I hope, a collection of practical, updated versions that hold true to the original promise. Almost every cover or foreword or review written for these cookbooks includes at least one of the following three words—tried, tested and true. The promise that goes with them all is that the recipes are favourites, well used by the donor. Most contributors chose carefully. After all, their name was usually printed alongside the recipe and their reputation was at stake, especially in close-knit communities.

As to the stories, the overwhelming majority of them have not been told before. Others have only been told in part, with a focus on the books, not the people behind them. As a writer, it is the human element that fascinates me most. My aim, as always, was to bring out from the shadows the lives and achievements of these 'quiet voices' in our communities. The voices that whisper in my ear and compel me to write.

Liz Harfull

RECIPES

for

SAVING
SOULS

OUR HISTORY *in* RECIPES

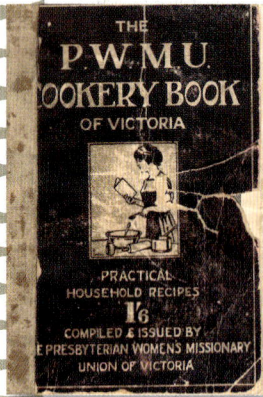

Fiona Bligh was about seven when she made her first recipe from the *PWMU Cookbook* in 1981. A talented baker, she is a little embarrassed now to admit that it was the simple but classic Australian childhood favourite, honey joys. Following a pattern established by her mother, she recorded the outcome by carefully writing a note next to the recipe—'very nice'.

'My Mum had a terrible habit of writing over her recipes. If something was good, she wrote that and if it was bad she put a big cross through it. There are ticks and comments and crosses all through her cookbooks,' Fiona says. Her mother even noted what her children baked and the date they made it, transforming the book into a snapshot of the family's cooking life.

Much to her fascination, Fiona has discovered that the *PWMU Cookbook*, Australia's longest continuously published cookbook, is a surprising reflection of many families' histories. A graduate from the University of Melbourne with honours in history, Fiona became absorbed by the broader context when she wrote *From Suet to Saffron*, a detailed account of the cookbook's story. 'The more you look at it, the more you realise the book is a time capsule that shows a huge amount of change in Australian culture and the lives of women across 100 years,' she says.

The Presbyterian Women's Missionary Union of Victoria was established in 1890, during a period when there was a worldwide evangelical movement to share the gospel, and help the poor and vulnerable in practical ways. Women in Australia were also campaigning hard at the time to win the right to vote. The following year a petition carrying some 30,000 signatures was delivered to the Victorian parliament. It took another seventeen years to sway them, but that did not stop women from looking for ways to contribute outside their own homes, as they started to achieve greater independence.

From the beginning, the PWMU was keen to enable more women to become missionaries, and 'take an active share'. Within a year, 28 branches with 1500 members had raised £617, making it possible to appoint the organisation's first missionary to Korea. The daughter of a Ballarat goldminer, Isabella Menzies served there for more than 30 years, establishing an orphanage and helping to rescue and educate destitute girls.

Left: Fiona Bligh with her collection of PWMU cookery books (image by Vince Brophy). Opposite: *The P.W.M.U. Cookery Book*, fifth edition, 1923.

Mission work in Korea through schools, hospitals and vocational training remained the key focus of the PWMU's efforts for the next 50 years, with additional outreach to India, Vanuatu, China and, within Australia, to Aboriginal, Chinese and Jewish communities. The work was funded by church offerings, bequests and donations, and activities ranging from fetes and stalls to collecting used stamps, running a tea room in Collins Street in Melbourne, selling arts and crafts, and the recipe book.

The first edition was published in 1904 under the title *Home Cookery for Australia*. It was prompted by a letter from a Melbourne printing house, keen to replicate the success of a cookbook published by the union's New South Wales counterpart. Arbuckle, Waddell and Fawckner would produce the book if the PWMU could provide the contents. In return, the firm would give them 25 per cent of the net profit of all copies sold.

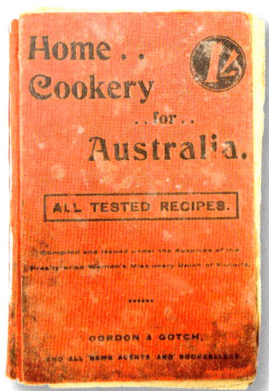

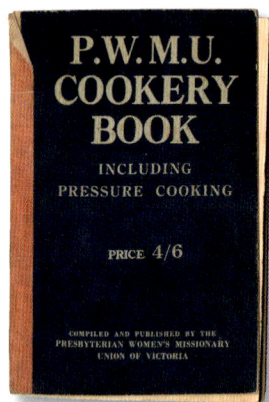

After careful consideration, the organisation agreed and set up a small committee led by Mrs C. Strachan to collect, test and select the recipes and household hints. Fiona says the overall vision was to compile a practical, handy resource, with recipes that were simple, healthy and economical.

The committee quickly gathered up material covering twenty 'classes'. Aside from traditional Scottish favourites, reflecting the cultural heritage of the Presbyterian Church, the selection featured popular recipes of the day, such as kedgeree, suet pudding and nose-to-tail options made with every part of a sheep, including the head. Household advice on the best way to banish flies, clean carpet, use up odd pieces of bread and treat colds were collected in a miscellaneous section. There was also dietary advice and nourishing dishes for invalids, such as calf's foot jelly, beef tea and gruel. Additional 'observations' were provided about food preparation, for instance: 'Frying is at once the quickest and usually the most objectionable way of cooking food . . .'

Initially, copies of the new cookbook were sold through PWMU branches, the main Assembly Hall in Melbourne's city centre, and from Mrs Strachan's private home. The book sold well, but there were problems with branches being slow to gather up the proceeds and return them to head office. To overcome this issue and boost sales, from 1920 the PWMU allowed the books to be sold through newsagents, stationers and bookshops.

By then the publication had transformed into *The P.W.M.U. Cookery Book of Victoria*. The first edition produced under this title in 1916, during the First World War, was amended to remove or rename any recipes with German titles. A new patriotic recipe for Gallipoli tea cakes was introduced, and a vegetarian cookery section was added, with recipes featuring pulses, nuts, and root and leafy vegetables. The book again proved popular, selling 85,000 copies and raising £2000 over the next thirteen years.

Then came *The New P.W.M.U. Cookery Book*. It was given this title because of significant revisions, triggered by a production issue completely foreign in today's digital world. The heavy metal blocks of type created to print the book were worn out after so many copies and needed to be reset.

The committee seized the moment to completely revise the contents, under the guidance of Miss Agnes 'Menie' Campbell. A much-loved figure in the PWMU, Menie went to Korea as a missionary in 1911 and served as principal of a girls' primary school until ill health forced her to return to Australia in 1924. Despite being unwell, she happily took on the role of editor, sending out word that she was looking for new recipes and suggested improvements.

When the new edition came out in 1929, for the first time in its history, an individual's name appeared on the imprint page, which acknowledged Menie's input. It was her final service to the PWMU. She died the following year, after telling a colleague with some pride 'that the users found it good'.

Despite Menie's fine work, sales were affected in the early 1930s by the Depression. A decade later the Second World War brought more challenges, with restrictions of paper supplies holding up a reprint. However, the popular little cookbook kept selling and the women of the PWMU kept working to improve and adapt it to changing times.

After the war ended, the PWMU took note of the latest gadgets in Australian kitchens and added a section about how to use pressure cookers, with specially adapted recipes. This addition was considered so significant that it was promoted on the front cover. Despite the very real danger of early models exploding, pressure cookers were becoming popular because they saved time and money for 'hurry-up' housekeepers with children or paid employment, and busy social lives. The same edition also introduced a section for ice cream recipes, given that many Australian homes were now acquiring American-style refrigerators with freezer compartments. For the first time, there was also a separate section that focused on entertaining, featuring canapés and nibbles that could be served with cocktails and pre-dinner drinks.

Above: PWMU missionary and cookbook editor Agnes 'Menie' Campbell (courtesy Presbyterian Church of Victoria Archives).

Despite these innovations, by 1960 the PWMU realised that the book was seriously outdated and in danger of falling out of favour. Apart from the three new sections introduced in the late 1940s, the contents had essentially not changed for more than 30 years. So a new committee of five was appointed to carry out another major revision, gathering 'in a spirit of light hearted and blissful ignorance' about the scale of the project they had taken on.

After consulting with outside experts, they changed the format of the book, introducing a full-colour washable cover and spiral binding so that the book stayed open flat on the selected page. New sections were introduced for meals in a hurry, luxury with leftovers and entertaining. Capturing a trend that leapt from the pages of women's magazines, garnishes of parsley were introduced to dress up dishes for the dining table.

'During the war, women replaced men in the workforce and they spent less time cooking, but by the end of the 1950s, there was a shift to women being back in the home and becoming the perfect wife and hostess. We saw the rise of the middle classes, and one of the ways that you demonstrated that was showing off your home and entertaining people,' Fiona says.

The next major revision in the early 1970s was triggered by Australia changing to the metric system of measurement. Recognising the important role the book could play in educating home cooks, the committee created a five-page section with tables and information about the new system. Every recipe was converted, then double and triple tested to make sure it still worked. 'One of the husbands I spoke to, said that he had never eaten so much in his life,' says Fiona.

The process took two years, and reflected an attention to detail that has been maintained since the first edition. 'Everything was tested by the committee and that's still how we do it today. The person who oversaw the most recent edition in 2013 tested every single recipe in her own home. It took several years.'

The *P.W.M.U. Cookery Book: metric edition* was one of the most successful editions in the book's history. Launched in 1974, by the following year it was selling 2000 copies per month, and had been adopted by some Victorian high schools to teach domestic science. Within three years, 60,000 copies had been sold. 'It sells because it's practical,' one of the hardworking committee members, Val Howatt, told *The Age*.

In 1977, a wider change came, which might have finally brought an end to the cookbook's remarkable endurance. The Presbyterian, Congregational and Methodist churches decided to amalgamate and form the Uniting Church in Australia. But some individual Presbyterian churches voted against the union, the PWMU continued, and a joint committee was formed with the new church's Adult Fellowship group to keep the cookbook going and share the profits.

Now known as the *PWMU Cookbook*, the publication has sold well over 500,000 copies since the first edition and is still in print. Having joined the legions of mothers who taught their children how to cook from it, Fiona puts its success down to the PWMU Cookbook Committee holding true to the original vision, without being afraid to embrace new trends and changing technology. 'But most importantly, the cookbook is a sincere expression of their faith and a practical way to support Christian missions, and particularly women missionaries. The faith of the women who have contributed to the book is actually the foundation of the endeavour, which helps to explain both the book's longevity and the tireless commitment of PWMU women over the years to keep producing it. It is about far more than raising money.'

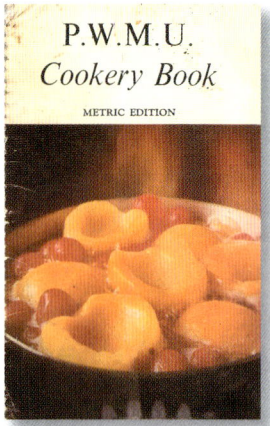

Above: The first metric edition of the *P.W.M.U. Cookery Book* (courtesy Special Collections, Deakin University Library). Opposite: Robinson's Barley advertisement, 1923 edition.

Scotch broth

The PWMU Cookbook and this recipe have a close personal connection for me. My father, Lyall Harfull, was of Scottish descent and raised in the Presbyterian church at Mount Gambier, which he supported throughout his long life. One of the family's dearest friends was Reverend Charles MacLeod from Melbourne, who boarded with the Harfulls during the 1930s while he was training to become a minister. After the Second World War, Uncle Charlie was posted to the island of Tanna in the South Pacific, with his wife, Jean, to serve as missionaries. During their return visits to Australia, they were popular speakers at PWMU gatherings, talking about their work on the island in Vanuatu, then known as the New Hebrides.

The following recipe is based on a combination of the Scotch broth found in the first edition of the cookbook made unusually, with beef, a more recent version in the 1974 metric edition, and my mother's Scotch broth, which was a family favourite. In the colder months of the year, a huge pot of it was usually simmering away on the back of the slow combustion stove. Dad and my brother Roger would grab a mug after milking the cows, or sitting for hours on an open tractor sowing oat crops. I liked it too, after coming inside from riding my horse in the winter chill, ruddy cheeked and nose dripping.

INGREDIENTS

1 kg lamb neck, soup bones
  or shanks
2 litres (8 cups) water
100 g (½ cup) pearl barley
3 carrots, diced small
2 turnips, diced small
1 large onion, finely diced
½ leek, white part only,
  chopped
salt
freshly ground black pepper
2 tablespoons finely chopped
  curly-leaf parsley

METHOD

Remove as much fat from the lamb as possible. Put the lamb, including the bones, in a large saucepan with the water, and bring it to the boil over medium heat. Remove any scum as it rises to the top.

Rinse the pearl barley in cold water and add it to the saucepan with the carrots, turnips, onion and leek. Season with salt and pepper and boil, covered, for 1½ hours, stirring occasionally.

Remove the bones and meat from the saucepan. Discard the bones. Chop the meat into small pieces and return it to the saucepan. Add the parsley and adjust the seasoning.

- Mum would often boil the lamb on its own for about 30 minutes, then let the stock sit overnight. Any fat rises to the top and solidifies, which makes it easy to remove. Alternatively, complete cooking the soup, then let it sit overnight before removing the fat.

- The secret to this soup is the turnips. For true Scotch broth, you really cannot substitute anything else.

- As the cooking time draws to an end, keep a close eye on the soup to make sure it isn't sticking to the bottom of the saucepan and burning.

Opposite: *The Goulburn Cookery Book*, 1906 edition (State Library of NSW).

MORE *than* SHE KNEW

One of the most successful cookbooks in Australian history came from the kitchen of a gracious stone homestead in the Bungendore district of New South Wales. *The Goulburn Cookery Book* sold more than 250,000 copies across 40 editions, and provided a source of culinary inspiration and guidance for generations of Australian women.

The collection of more than 800 recipes and hints was the work of Jane Rutledge, known as Jean, who lived on Gidleigh station where she raised four children with her husband, William Forster Rutledge. Born at Braidwood in 1853, Jean was the daughter of Major Richard Morphy, an Irish soldier who came to Australia after serving with the British Army in India. Her mother, Mary Styles, grew up on a large holding at Bungonia, which had been taken up by her pioneering English father in the 1820s.

William was also of Irish descent. His father was a well-known pastoralist in the Queanbeyan district, noted for breeding champion racehorses. Interested in music and golf, William obtained an arts degree from the University of Sydney before taking over management of Gidleigh for his father.

Jean was 34 years old when they married in 1887. A gushing profile piece published in the *Sydney Mail* when she was about 70, painted a picture of a vibrant, witty woman with bright black eyes and rosy cheeks. It praised her sunny disposition and the warm hospitality she showed guests, with the doors of Gidleigh always open to the district and Sydney visitors weary of city life.

No mention is made of her cooking prowess; however the house at Gidleigh was built only five years before Jean arrived as a newlywed and its large kitchen boasted all the latest mod cons. There was a hot and cold water 'apparatus', a fine range, a baking oven, and separate butler's pantry, scullery and store fitted with every convenience.

There is some confusion about when the first edition of *The Goulburn Cookery Book* appeared, potentially the result of an inadvertent error in a church history book, which mentions 1899, and then the apparent insertion of this date in the preface of the cookbook when it was reproduced in 1973. However, paperwork that signed over copyright to the Church of England in January 1905, records that the date of first publication was 2 October 1904.

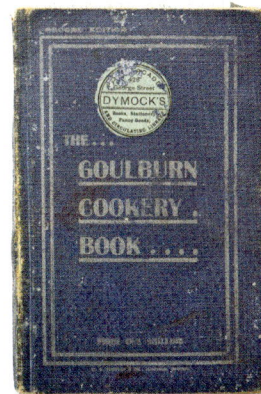

It is possible that Jean began compiling the cookbook sometime around the turn of the century, perhaps to keep her mind busy after her youngest son, Philip, was killed in a tragic riding accident in November 1899. He was only six years old.

The official gazette for the Diocese of Goulburn reported in July 1904 that, after some years collecting and experimenting with various valuable recipes, Jean was now working with the Church Society organising secretary, Reverend Frederick McDonnell, to bring the work to a 'successful climax'. Publishers had been interviewed and advertisements secured to help cover the costs.

The response to *The Goulburn Cookery Book* was phenomenal, with glowing reviews in the lead-up to Christmas and a sustained rush in sales. The *Goulburn Evening Penny Post* thought it 'one of the best publications dealing with the culinary art that we have ever seen. It is packed with recipes, which have the merit of being set forth plainly and which deal, for the most part, with materials that are readily obtainable. It is doubtful whether a better shilling's worth of the kind has ever been offered to the public.'

The Sydney Mail and New South Wales Advertiser believed the cookbook demonstrated that Mrs Rutledge thoroughly understood the needs of the Australian housewife, drawing particular attention to a specific section for cold summer puddings suited to hot local conditions. It contained no less than 67 recipes.

'Although there hardly seems any necessity for another Cookery Book, yet I cannot but think that this collection of recipes will meet a want, especially among the women in the bush,' Jean explained in the preface, thanking friends who had contributed recipes to supplement her own. 'I have tried to leave nothing to chance, and the vague counsels to "make a nice light crust for a pie," or a "batter as thick as cream," find no place here.'

Above, from top: Jean Rutledge with her sons, Tom and Pat; and Gidleigh homestead (courtesy National Trust of Australia, NSW). Opposite: Advertisement from the 28th edition, 1921 (State Library of SA).

The cookbook certainly found instant favour with a broad audience. The first edition of 5000 copies sold out by May 1905, so a second edition of 10,000 was quickly ordered. In November the diocese began what turned out to be a 45-year relationship with Edwards Dunlop and Company, a Sydney business that became sole distributors of the book across Australia and New Zealand.

One and sometimes two editions then appeared every year until 1923, generating an average profit of more than £230 per year between 1911 and the start of the Depression in 1929. Even though sales slowed because of the tough economic times, the book kept selling, reaching the milestone of 200,000 copies with the publication of the 34th edition in 1930.

That same edition saw the first change in the book's contents since it was released, when Jean added a 28-page supplement of health recipes. William had died in 1912, leaving her to bear her grief alone after their second son, Patrick, was killed on the Western Front in 1917. There was also the constant worry about her oldest son, Thomas, who was wounded at Gallipoli and served with distinction in France before returning home to take over Gidleigh. But Jean was still living there and taking an active interest in her book in her late seventies.

Jean died in August 1932, at the age of 79. In paying tribute, Bishop Lewis Radford praised her wider vision of aiding the church and its work: 'Whatever other memories and memorials keep her name before the minds of those who knew her at home and at Church, the *Goulburn Cookery Book* will be her best monument. It was once said of a woman's offering, "She hath done what she could." That was true of Mrs Rutledge, but what she did was far more than she knew.'

In 1935, the church revised the cookbook, which was republished in 1937 as *The New Goulburn Cookery Book*. Sales were sluggish until 1942, when the diocese was surprised to discover that the military was buying copies in large numbers to train their cooks during the Second World War. But after the war, with print costs rising and demand falling, the diocese decided there would be no more editions. By that stage the cookbook had produced a net profit of between £6000 and £7000 for the church, making an enormous difference to the work of the diocese, particularly in its poorer parishes.

The last copies disappeared from bookshop shelves in the early 1950s, until a facsimile edition of the original book was published with the church's permission in 1973, as a fundraiser for the National Trust in New South Wales.

Excellent beefsteak pie

INGREDIENTS

Suet paste (pastry, enough for 2 or 3 large pies):

450 g (3 cups) plain flour, plus 1 tablespoon extra

½ teaspoon salt

90 g butter, chopped

juice of ½ lemon

185 ml (¾ cup) cold water

230 g fresh suet

Filling:

600 g topside steak, thinly sliced

3 tablespoons plain flour

20 g butter

¼ teaspoon salt

1 medium tomato, chopped

1 tablespoon finely chopped curly-leaf parsley

1 teaspoon thyme leaves

1 teaspoon finely chopped marjoram or oregano

80 ml (⅓ cup) beef stock (approximately)

freshly ground black pepper

1 egg, lightly beaten

Like many home cooks today, I had never cooked with suet (a type of beef fat) until I made this recipe. But suet is making a comeback, and it can be sourced from most quality butchers if you give them a day or two's notice. Experts agree it is worth the effort because neither butter nor lard works quite the same way in pastry. Apparently they have different melting points, which changes the texture and lightness of the end result, not to mention the flavour.

Both the filling and the 'paste' recipe, or pastry as we call it now, come from The Goulburn Cookery Book. *However, I've combined the methods of two different pie recipes from the book, which use the unusual technique of rolling thin strips of beef to make the filling. The end result is a pie packed with moist, tender meat; gravy is served as an accompaniment.*

METHOD

To make the suet paste (pastry), sift the flour (450 g) and salt into a large bowl. Rub in the butter with your fingertips.

Combine the lemon juice and cold water in a cup. Make a well in the centre of the dry ingredients and add the liquid, a little at a time, stirring with a knife until the mixture starts to cling together. Work it with your hands to form a soft, slightly sticky dough.

Turn the dough out onto a lightly floured work surface and knead it lightly with the heel of your hand until it is smooth. Roll it out to form a long rectangle.

Remove any skin from the suet, and chop it finely or shred it in a food processor or blender. Toss it in the extra tablespoon of flour to help prevent it forming clumps. Scatter a handful of the suet over the surface of the pastry.

Fold the pastry in three, folding the bottom third up and the top third down. Give the pastry a quarter turn (90 degrees), then repeat the process, rolling it out to form a rectangle again, scattering more suet, then folding the same way. Repeat this two more times (a total of four times), until you have used all the suet. Cut the pastry into three pieces, wrap them in plastic wrap and rest them in the fridge for 1 hour.

To make the pie, preheat the oven to moderately hot (200°C). Grease a 22 cm pie dish.

To make the filling, cut the steak into slices about 5 cm wide and 8–10 cm long.

In a small bowl, rub together the flour, butter and salt. In another small bowl, combine the tomato, parsley, thyme and marjoram.

Dip each piece of steak in the flour mixture, coating both sides. Place a small amount (about ½ teaspoon) of the tomato mixture at one end of each piece of steak, then roll up.

Pack the rolls tightly into the pie dish. Pour over the beef stock, adding just enough to come within 1 cm of the rim of the dish. Season with pepper to taste.

Roll out one piece of pastry until it is about 5 mm thick. Place it over the top of the pie dish. Trim the edge of the pastry around the dish, using a sharp knife, then cut several small slits in the pastry to allow the steam to escape. Brush the pastry with the beaten egg.

Bake the pie in the oven for 30 minutes, keeping a close eye on the crust. Turn the oven down to moderately slow (170°C) and cook for another 30 minutes, covering the crust with foil when it starts to become too brown.

Serve with creamy mashed potatoes and your favourite brown gravy.

Below: Australian army cooking school recruits learning how to cook, c. 1941 (Argus Newspaper Collection of Photographs, State Library of Victoria).

LIZ'S TIPS

- The suet paste recipe makes enough for two or three large pies. Wrap any uncooked pastry and freeze for future use.

- You can buy pre-packaged suet, but avoid brands that process it into small, hard pellets, which are not really suitable for this pastry-making technique. Try to source fresh suet from a butcher who breaks down their own beef carcases.

- Once you start working the pastry with your hands, if there are still dry ingredients in the bottom of the bowl, sprinkle in a little more water and keep working the ball of pastry around the bowl until it is clean.

- Ask your butcher to cut the steak so it is about 2 mm thick, as for beef olives. If you can't buy it that way, put the steak between sheets of greaseproof paper and beat it with a rolling pin before you cut.

- When adding the stock, make sure you trickle it around all the pieces of meat and give it time to settle before you cover it with pastry, just in case you can top the level up a little more.

- Use some of the trimmed pastry to create decorations for the top of the pie.

- To help reduce the risk of the pastry shrinking during cooking, rest the pie in the fridge for 30 minutes before you brush on the beaten egg.

- Place the pie dish on a baking tray to catch any spills, and to make it easier to remove from the oven without damaging the crust.

- An alternative technique for making pies from this era was to pour cold gravy over the meat, instead of beef stock. Some recipes also suggested adding hot gravy after the pie was cooked, by pouring it through a hole in the centre of the pastry. The hole was usually covered by a small ceramic decoration, or a circle of pastry during cooking.

Below: Advertisement from *The Goulburn Cookery Book*, 1921 edition (State Library of SA). Opposite: *The Rodney Cookery Book*, second edition, c. 1912 (State Library of NSW).

NO *mere* TRIFLE

The Rodney Cookery Book is a bit of a mystery. Copies are very rare, and the year of publication and details of how it came about seem to be lost in the mists of time.

Named after a shire centred around the Goulburn Valley town of Tatura, the cookbook was published under the auspices of the All Saints Church of England Ladies Guild. What appears to be the only surviving first edition copy held in a public collection at the local museum, is inscribed with the date 'Xmas 1907'.

The cookbook was obviously a success, because an expanded edition of 600 'carefully selected and tested recipes bearing the signatures of well known ladies of the district' was published about four years later.

Both versions include contributions from Mrs C.H. Zercho, whose charismatic husband, Charles, was inducted as the local minister in September 1903. Margaret Zercho, known as Maggie, was the daughter of long-serving Eaglehawk councillor Frederick Clark, an English builder who emigrated to Australia in the 1850s and entered the mining industry.

The son of a German stonemason, Charles Zercho was also born on the central Victorian goldfields. He was educated at the University of Melbourne and ordained as a priest in 1897, at the age of about 30. When he married Maggie in 1900, he was serving as minister at the small parish church of St John's at Malmsbury, about 30 kilometres south-east of Castlemaine, where he grew up.

Charles was obviously quite a catch. A talented cricketer and footballer, who played a season for Essendon in 1890 and also excelled at track events, he was described as being handsome, tall and athletic, with a 'dynamic' personality. At Malmsbury he was credited with recruiting more than 100 candidates for confirmation in the church, including 40 adults, exceeding any other parish. Within months of settling into the vicarage at Tatura, the ladies of his congregation were so impressed that they surprised him with a handsome new buggy and set of harness, expressing the hope that he would stay long enough to wear them out.

Charles rewarded them by harnessing his passion for education to establish a new Church of England grammar school for boys and a high school for girls, as alternatives to the Catholic schools that had recently opened in Tatura. The development in 1904 was encouraged by the Bishop of Bendigo, who was concerned about the dangers of exposing Protestant children to education in a Roman Catholic institution, at a time when there were deep divisions in the community between the two faiths.

The tensions were highlighted in an amusing incident in 1908, when Charles appeared before the Tatura police court, charged with using insulting language—a shocking misdemeanour for a cleric, who was also responsible for shaping young minds. Apparently his ire had been aroused by the local senior constable, a Catholic by the name of Dwyer, when he was served with a summons for not having his seven-year-old son, Harry, vaccinated. Charles considered that he had been treated unfairly because he was Anglican. According to Dwyer, the reverend accused him of contemptible action, claiming that he would never have summoned a clergyman from his own church. To much laughter in the court, Charles said the remark was an unfortunate 'slip' and the charge was dismissed.

Described as a born teacher, Charles juggled his parish duties with being headmaster of the Tatura schools. By 1908 he had also opened the vicarage to boarders, who were cared for by Maggie while she fulfilled her other duties as a busy parson's wife and mother. Apart from Harry, she had a baby daughter, Marjorie. The Zerchos were also grieving the loss of a son who died the day he was born in 1905, and a daughter who had died in 1903 when she was just six months old.

In 1910, the Zerchos headed to Melbourne where Charles served as chaplain and resident master at Brighton Grammar School. He was later headmaster at a series of grammar schools, including All Saints at St Kilda where he attracted significantly more students because of his vision and drive, and his reputation as a strict disciplinarian. His brother Frederick was no slouch in the education sector either. He established Zercho's Business College in Melbourne, which became the largest business college in Australia.

In later life Charles returned to working as a parish priest. Maggie died in 1940, and her husband died 22 years later at the age of 95.

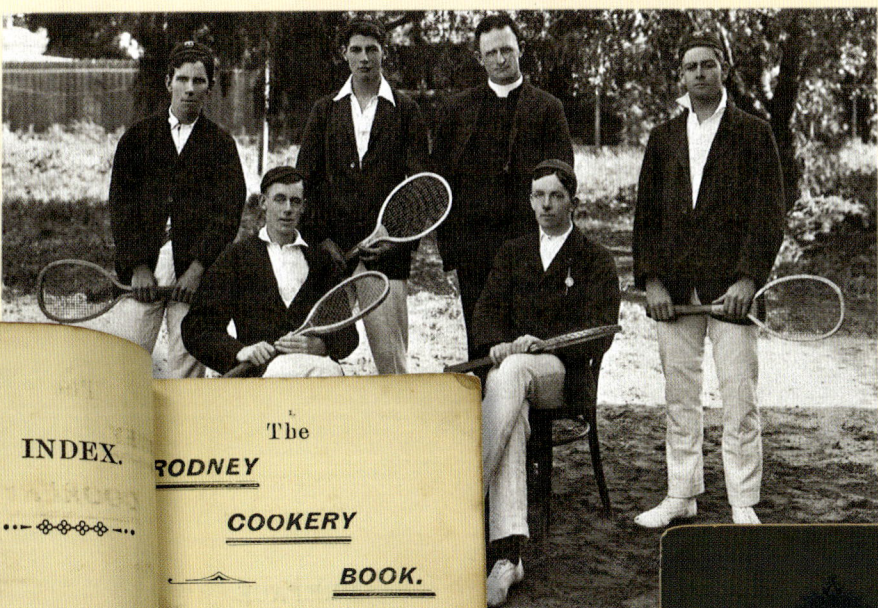

Clockwise from top: All Saints Anglican Church, Tatura (courtesy Tatura Anglican Parish); Reverend Charles Zercho (courtesy Kingswood College); title and index pages of *The Rodney Cookery Book*'s second edition (State Library of NSW); Reverend Zercho with Brighton Grammar School's winning tennis team in the 1911 Schools' Amateur Athletic Association of Victoria competition (courtesy Brighton Grammar School Archives).

INDEX.

...·❖❖❖❖·...

Cakes ... ...
Bread ... ...
Biscuits ... ...
Confectionery ... ...
Puddings, etc. ... ...
Meats ... ...
Various Dishes, etc. ...
Soups ... ...
Jams and Preserves ...
Jellies, Trifles, etc. ...
Pickles and Sauces ...
Summer Drinks ... ...
Miscellaneous ... ...
Useful Hints ... ...
Stray Notes ... ...

The
RODNEY
COOKERY
BOOK.

SECOND EDITION.

Containing 600 new & carefully tested
Recipes and a host of useful
information.

Sold by all Leading Stationers.

Price : **ONE SHILLING.**

Wholesale Orders from J. F. JOHNSON,
Newsagent, Tatura, or single copy
posted, 1s 1d.

Published by Church of England Ladies
Guild, Tatura.

Trifle

INGREDIENTS

½ plain double sponge cake, cut into 3 cm thick slices

12 macaroons (see below)

24 small amaretti biscuits

125 ml (½ cup) sherry or sweet wine

3 tablespoons brandy

60 g flaked almonds, toasted, plus extra for decorating

finely grated zest of 1 lemon

115 g (⅓ cup) raspberry or strawberry jam (approximately)

500 ml (2 cups) good-quality vanilla custard

250 ml (1 cup) cream

2 teaspoons icing sugar

Macaroons:

2 egg whites

1 cup caster sugar

110 g almond meal

1 teaspoon rosewater

This recipe makes one of the best trifles I have ever tasted, which is astounding given the very high benchmark in my family—thanks to Bob Davis, a long-standing friend from the Mount Gambier district, who is a trifle-making genius. It is not credited in The Rodney Cookery Book *but it comes from the famous* Mrs Beeton's Every Day Cookery and Housekeeping Book, *first published in Britain in 1865.*

I have simplified the original recipe to use a good-quality shop-bought custard and sponge, and amaretti instead of ratafia biscuits. But I strongly advise taking time to make the almond macaroons, which are based on a separate recipe contributed by Maggie. Not to be confused with the French-style macarons so popular today, they incorporate a splash of rosewater to add another layer of flavour.

METHOD

To make the macaroons, preheat the oven to slow (160°C). Line a baking tray with baking paper.

Place the egg whites in a large bowl and beat with an electric mixer on high speed until soft peaks form. Gradually add the sugar and beat on high speed for about 5 minutes, until the sugar is dissolved, the mixture is thick and glossy, and stiff peaks form. Fold in the almond meal and rosewater.

Place heaped teaspoonfuls of the mixture on the tray, about 5 cm apart, and bake for 5 minutes. Reduce the heat to 140°C and bake for another 20 minutes, until lightly golden. Leave the macaroons to cool on the tray until they are set, then remove them to a wire rack to cool completely. (Makes about 24.)

To make the trifle, cover the entire base of a deep, glass bowl (approximately 20 cm diameter), with the sponge. Break the macaroons into large pieces and scatter over the sponge with the amaretti biscuits.

Mix together the sherry and brandy, then slowly pour or spoon the mixture over the sponge and biscuits, making sure the sponge is soaked thoroughly.

Sprinkle over the flaked almonds and grated lemon zest, then spread a thin layer of jam over the top. Pour over the custard. Cover the trifle with plastic wrap and place in the fridge overnight to set. Before serving, whip the cream with the icing sugar and spread over the top. Decorate with the extra flaked almonds.

LIZ'S TIPS

- The macaroons will keep for weeks in a tightly-sealed plastic container in a cool, dry place.

- This trifle is the perfect way to use dry or slightly stale cake. The sponge cake recipe on page 192 makes an ideal base if you would prefer not to buy one.

- The original recipe was definitely not teetotal. It used twice as much alcohol, and even recommended adding a 'little more' to make sure the cakes were well soaked.

- The trifle is much better left overnight, allowing time for the alcohol to absorb and the flavours to develop.

- You can use your own favourite custard recipe instead of buying custard. When hot it should be thick enough to coat the back of a metal spoon. Cover the surface with plastic wrap to help prevent a skin forming, and leave it to cool before adding it to the trifle.

Left: Advertisement from *Home Cookery and Jewish Recipes*, c. 1920s (State Library of NSW).

EINSTEIN AND THE ECLIPSE

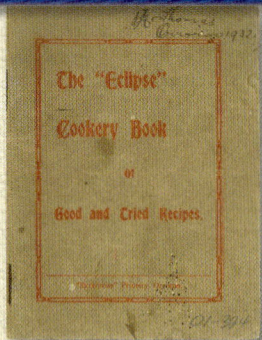

Community groups have come up with all sorts of themes for cookbooks over the years, but surely the little bush town of Orroroo in South Australia is the only one to find motivation in an astronomical event.

The *"Eclipse" Cookery Book of Good and Tried Recipes* was produced for sale at a bazaar held in the local Town Hall on 22 September 1922—the day after a total eclipse of the sun. The solar eclipse excited worldwide interest because scientists hoped it would provide the perfect opportunity to confirm Einstein's radical new theory of relativity, testing his prediction that light passing near massive bodies such as the sun would appear to bend. Normally, the sun was too bright to see this happen, but a solar eclipse and recent breakthroughs in camera technology meant that it should not only be possible to see it, but to photograph it.

The hopes of ladies in Orroroo were not so grand. They just wanted to raise money for St Paul's Anglican Church, built two years earlier to replace an older building damaged in a severe storm.

Above, from top: *The "Eclipse" Cookery Book of Good and Tried Recipes*, 1922 (courtesy Orroroo Historical Society); and St Paul's Anglican Church (State Library of SA, B 8648). Right: Loading camels en route to Cordillo Downs station, north of Innamincka, where a special 'Einstein' camera was erected to photograph the eclipse, after being transported to the site by pack camels, 1922 (National Library of Australia). Opposite: *St Andrew's Modern Recipe Book*, c. 1930 (State Library of Tasmania).

A DIFFERENT WAY to READ PAPERS

St Andrew's Modern Recipe Book contains some priceless information if the thermostat in your oven ever stops working. Just use the paper index.

'If a sheet of writing paper burns whenever it is put in, it is too hot,' the cookbook recommends. 'If the paper becomes dark brown, it is suitable for pastry, scones, muffins, little dinner loaves etc. . . . If light brown, it does for small cakes and buns, pies and tarts . . . If dark yellow for cakes . . . If light yellow, for biscuits, puddings etc.'

The cookbook was published around 1930 by the women's guild of St Andrew's Presbyterian Church in Launceston. The modest publication features a foreword by the then minister, Reverend John Lewis Hurse, who hoped it would prove useful to members of the culinary department. Besides about 70 pages of unattributed recipes, the book features a section of miscellaneous useful hints.

Among the recipes is a selection using Cadbury's Bournville Cocoa, which was then being made at the British company's new Hobart factory, opened with great fanfare in 1922. Australia had become an important market for Cadbury, after placing the company's first overseas order about 40 years earlier. Cadbury selected Tasmania above Sydney and Melbourne as the preferred location for a new manufacturing base, because of the cool climate, access to cheap hydro-electricity, and a plentiful supply of quality milk.

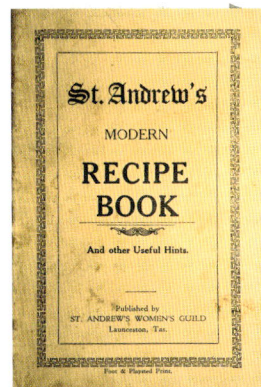

Chocolate shortcake   SERVES 4

The recipes provided to the St Andrew's women by Cadbury included this very simple but tasty chocolate shortcake. I've made it more chocolatey than the original by adding extra cocoa powder, and updated it to use a pre-made pastry case so it can be whipped up in just a few minutes.

METHOD

Preheat the oven to moderate (180°C).

Spread the jam thinly over the base of the pastry case.

2 tablespoons raspberry jam

1 x shortcrust pastry flan case
(approximately 18 cm in
diameter)

3 tablespoons caster sugar

1 egg

3 tablespoons self-raising
flour

3 heaped teaspoons cocoa
powder

30 g butter, melted

icing sugar for dusting

Beat the caster sugar and egg together until thick and creamy and the sugar is dissolved. Sift in the flour and cocoa powder and beat until combined. Lastly, stir in the melted butter. Pour the mixture over the jam and spread evenly in the pastry case.

Bake in the oven for 15–20 minutes, until the filling is firm and slightly springy to the touch. Cool and dust with icing sugar.

LIZ'S TIPS

- If you prefer, use your favourite shortcrust pastry recipe to make the flan case, and blind-bake before adding the filling.
- Use a good-quality cocoa powder, with a rich, dark flavour.
- The tart keeps well for several days. It is delicious served with thick cream and fresh raspberries or poached pears.

Opposite: Advertisement from
Let's Cook with Chocolate, 1955.

A Health-Building Food

**Created in the famous Cadbury factory at Claremont, Tasmania,
by mountain and sea**

In these ideal surroundings—away from the dust and smoke of the cities—famous Bournville Cocoa is made in Cadbury's modern, hygienic factory. As nourishing as it is delicious—Cadbury's Bournville Cocoa is a real food—rich in calories and minerals, full of wholesome goodness.

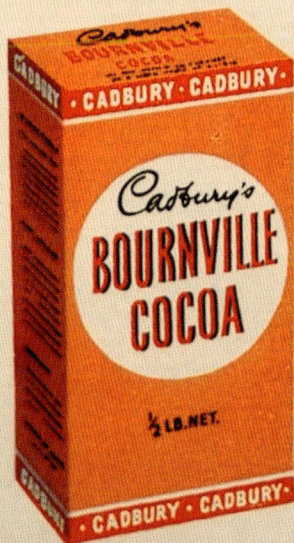

By using this world-famed Cadbury product for cooking as well as for drinking, you are assured of the purest, high quality ingredient. You have the satisfaction of knowing that it is economical, too.

Cadbury's
by Mountain and Sea

FATHER'S *delight*

High-profile Anglican archbishop, Dr Felix Arnott, loved cooking and fine dining so much that one of his final acts was to plan a special lunch for family and friends to share after his funeral.

The former Archbishop of Brisbane died in 1988 after a long and illustrious career in the Anglican Church, where he was recognised as a leading theological scholar by his supporters, and a dangerous liberal by his critics. On the other hand, he was also known as a kind and generous man who people quickly liked, with one parishioner describing him as the 'cuddliest bishop I have ever seen' because he looked so approachable. After interviewing him in 1978 over a cup of tea and a delicious cream sponge, *The Australian Women's Weekly* journalist Rosemary Munday described him as the 'very model of a storybook gas-and-gaiters cleric', with an impish grin, birdlike concentration and a pullover stuffed loosely with letters, memos and papers.

Born in England in 1911, Felix Arnott studied the classics and gained first-class honours in theology at Oxford. He was ordained as a priest in 1935 and served his first curacy in a small market town in Yorkshire, where he fell in love at first sight with his soon-to-be wife, Anne. The couple emigrated to Australia shortly after their wedding in 1938. They settled in Brisbane, where Felix had been invited to take up a position as warden of St John's College, a male-only residential college affiliated with the University of Queensland.

From there, his career took him to Sydney where he served as warden of St Paul's, Australia's oldest university residential college at the University of Sydney, for seventeen years. Well liked by students, he developed a reputation for his ability to explain complex issues in clear and simple language and became a regular participant in a 1950s ABC radio panel discussion program.

In 1963 the Arnotts moved to Melbourne, where Felix was made an assistant bishop, responsible for overseeing church schools. Although he was deeply interested in education, his biographer and church colleague, Bishop Ralph Wicks, wrote, 'If there was a meal prior to a meeting he could be just as concerned about the detail of the food and the wine to be served as with the business agenda'.

Felix apparently took up cooking after he was made Archbishop of Brisbane in 1970, responsible for 377 churches and 60,000 parishioners spread over 34,000 square kilometres. When the Arnotts moved into their designated residence they found an archaic stove that never worked, so Anne asked for a new one. The diocese remodelled the entire kitchen. 'It was then that he started cooking in a very big way,' she told the *Women's Weekly*.

His daughter, Felicity, recalled Felix rushing in from clerical duties one day when Anne was away, to serve his four children an extraordinary feast of stuffed cucumbers topped with prawns and caviar, chicken cooked in an orange sauce, and an immaculate mousse. 'It was a bitter coffee flavour, and father was worried it mightn't turn out properly because he couldn't find a mould,' Felicity explained.

No doubt encouraged by their archbishop, in 1978 the church produced *Fathers' Delights*, to raise money for its Diocesan Development Fund. The spiral-bound cookbook contained a collection of recipes from the 'Wives of Anglican Priests in the Diocese of Brisbane'—and, of course, Felix. 'I have enjoyed the hospitality of most of the Rectories and Vicarages and appreciate what fine cooks most of our clergy wives are, and how skilfully they make best use of their resources,' he wrote in the foreword, warning that the book should not mislead people into thinking that the clergy dined sumptuously every day.

Felix retired in 1980 after an extraordinary career, which included his appointment by the Archbishop of Canterbury to an international commission that spent eleven years exploring what might be involved in reuniting the Roman Catholic and Anglican churches. During the 1970s he also served on the panel of the controversial Royal Commission on Human Relationships, with author and social rights activist Anne Deveson and the eminent reformist lawyer and jurist Elizabeth Evatt. The commission helped to change public discussion around families, gender and sexuality. Felix courted controversy again when he spoke out in defence of civil liberties during a notorious period in Queensland's history, when Premier Joh Bjelke-Petersen clamped down on public demonstrations.

Immediately after retiring, Felix moved to Italy—a country he loved—and took up an honorary chaplaincy in Venice. Five years later, when the city's famous bridges became too much for him, the Arnotts moved to England. With Felix's health continuing to decline, they returned to Queensland to be closer to their family. Felix died in July 1988 at the age of 77.

Above, from top: Dr Felix Arnott (courtesy Anglican Church Southern Queensland, Records and Archives Centre); and an illustration from the cookbook. Opposite: *Fathers' Delights*, 1978.

Paying tribute to him after his death, the then Dean of Brisbane, the Very Reverend Arthur Grimshaw, said that while Felix could be irascible, determined and downright difficult when not getting his own way, he was also 'able to enter a rectory and be completely at home with the family, helping with reading stories to the children, or helping in the kitchen—not expecting to be waited on or treated as a high dignitary'.

Felix's funeral was held at St Mary's at Kangaroo Point, following detailed plans, which he had carefully prepared, down to the list of about twenty people who were invited to attend. Afterwards, guests adjourned to a splendid luncheon at the Brisbane Club. 'Normally when one goes to a funeral of an Archbishop, one comes away with a memento order of service. On this occasion we came away with a menu—typical of Felix in his humanity and his perceptive care of others,' said Grimshaw.

Cold salmon mousse

SERVES 8

This is Dr Felix Arnott's own recipe—one of two he contributed to Fathers' Delights. *It is featured in the entree section of the book. Dr Arnott recommends using the best-quality salmon, and serving the mousse with a cucumber salad.*

INGREDIENTS

415 g tinned red salmon, drained, skin and bones removed

60 ml (¼ cup) white-wine vinegar

60 ml (¼ cup) water

1 tablespoon powdered gelatine

1 tablespoon caster sugar

1 teaspoon mustard powder

½ teaspoon salt

1 tablespoon horseradish cream

1 tablespoon mayonnaise

freshly ground black pepper

140 g (1 cup) finely diced celery

2 teaspoons chopped capers

4 spring onions, finely chopped

125 ml (½ cup) thickened cream, lightly whipped

METHOD

Lightly oil a 1 litre (4 cup) mould, or a small loaf pan (approximately 22 x 11 cm).

Put the salmon in a food processor with a tablespoon of the vinegar and process lightly.

Put the water in a small metal bowl. Sprinkle the gelatine over the cold water, place the bowl over hot water and stir until the gelatine is dissolved. Stir in the sugar, mustard, salt, horseradish, mayonnaise, pepper and the remaining vinegar.

Add the gelatine mixture to the salmon and blend briefly, until combined. Add the celery, capers, and spring onions, then blend briefly until combined. Lastly, fold through the cream.

Pour the mousse into the mould or loaf pan. Cover with plastic wrap and refrigerate until set.

To serve the mousse, stand the mould or pan in hot water for just a few seconds, then turn the mousse out onto a platter.

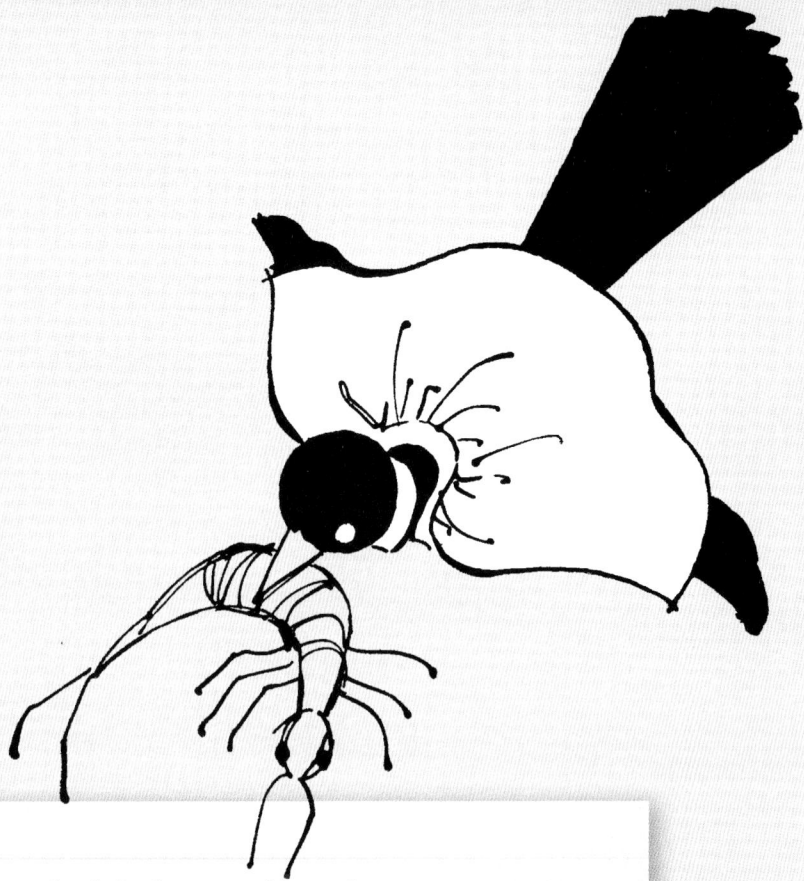

LIZ'S TIPS

- Use red salmon, not pink, because it produces a mousse with a much nicer colour.

- To save time, use a food processor to chop the celery before you start making the mousse.

- The original recipe had a very sharp flavour, so I have reduced the amount of vinegar and suggested horseradish cream instead of pure horseradish.

- After filling the mould, tap it on the benchtop to help the mousse settle.

- The mousse will take at least 2 hours to set, or you can leave it overnight for the flavours to further develop.

- Depending on whether you are using a metal or ceramic mould, you may need to dip the mould in hot water more than once, for no more than 10 seconds each time, until the mousse loosens.

- For the full retro experience, use a fish-shaped mould, decorate the turned-out mousse with thin slices of cucumber, and serve it with triangles of wholegrain or rye toast.

- Try the mousse on toast for breakfast with smashed avocado.

RECIPES

with an

ARTISTIC FLOURISH

Taking POT LUCK

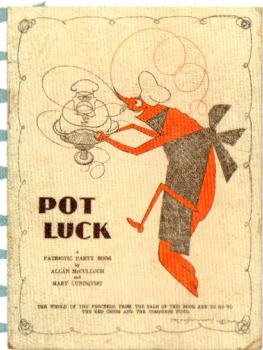

The humorous and distinctive line drawings of a bank teller by day and an artist by night, bring to life a cookbook published in Melbourne during the Second World War.

Alan McCulloch worked for the Commonwealth Bank for almost twenty years, but apparently hated every minute of it. Far more interested in becoming an artist, like his charismatic brother Wilfred, he took evening classes at the National Gallery of Victoria Art School. On holidays and weekends in the mid-1930s, he joined Wilfred and a young painter by the name of Arthur Boyd at an artists' camp at Gunnamatta Beach on the Mornington Peninsula.

McCulloch left the bank behind him in 1944 and eventually became a prominent figure in the art world. Described on his death in 1992 as the most influential art critic to have practised in Australia, he wrote for the Melbourne *Herald* for 30 years and compiled the *Encyclopedia of Australian Art*, which is still recognised as the 'bible' on Australian art. He also drew cartoons for various newspapers and magazines, illustrated several books, exhibited his own work and founded the Mornington Peninsula Arts Centre.

In early 1941, McCulloch worked alongside Melbourne society hostess Mary Lundqvist (nee Sharp) to create *Pot Luck: a patriotic party book*. The small book of exotic recipes for entertaining was part of Mary's campaign to win the Lord Mayor's Queen Carnival, which aimed to raise £50,000 for the Red Cross and the Australian Comforts Fund. Women were selected to represent various public services, standing as their 'queen' and competing for votes over several weeks, while organising an intensive number of fund-raising activities. People paid to vote and the crown went to the woman who raised the most money. The campaign was a staggering success. Attracting more than 22 million votes, it raised double its target, including an unknown amount from the sales of *Pot Luck*.

Among the newspaper clippings tracking the book's release, is a small snippet published by the *Argus* on 20 March 1941. Apparently on the day the book came out, Alan went to the military camp at Royal Park to enlist. He was in the mess hut when he bumped into Wilfred, who had also decided to enlist, without his family knowing. Realising that one of them should stay behind to care for their widowed mother, they agreed that Alan would go home.

Clockwise from top: Alan McCulloch and his wife, Ellen, with artist Albert Tucker (right) at Whistlewood, the McCulloch's home on the Mornington Peninsula, c. 1962 (courtesy McCulloch family); an illustration from the cookbook; Mary Lundqvist participating in the procession held as part of the Lord Mayor's Queen Carnival, March 1941 (Harold Paynting collection, State Library of Victoria); Alan and Ellen McCulloch in Paris, 1948 and Wilfred McCulloch in uniform, c. 1941 (courtesy McCulloch family). Opposite: *Pot Luck: a patriotic party book*, 1941.

Below and following pages:
Illustrations by Alan McCulloch
from the cookbook.

It was a fateful decision for Wilfred. He became a stretcher bearer in the Australian Army Medical Corps and died in the fall of Singapore less than a year later, in February 1942.

~~~~~~

Skinklada

SERVES 1

This recipe is from the Swedish section of Pot Luck. *In April 1934, Mary sailed for Cairo to marry Ragner Lundqvist, the Swedish vice consul in Egypt, whom she met while he was visiting Australia on business. Lundqvist died about eighteen months after their wedding and Mary returned to Melbourne. In the book she writes about visiting Sweden and her experiences attending a smorgasbord party in a little coastal town near the Lapland border, where she was faced with a meal of gargantuan proportions. 'There is no doubt about it, the Swedes seem to be the fortunate possessors of special stomachs, developed by centuries of training,' she wrote.*

Among the hors d'oeuvres she suggests is skinklada, a very simple, traditional Swedish kind of baked omelette.

INGREDIENTS

60 g good-quality ham or
  bacon, diced
2 eggs
250 ml (1 cup) full-cream milk
salt
freshly ground black pepper

METHOD

Preheat the oven to moderate (180°C). Grease a 23 cm pie dish.

Scatter the ham or bacon over the bottom of the dish.

In a medium bowl, whisk together the eggs and milk. Season with salt and pepper to taste. Pour the mixture over the bacon and cook for 30 minutes, until set.

LIZ AND MARY'S TIPS

- Mary suggested making skinklada with smoked salmon or anchovies as an alternative to ham or bacon.
- Serve for breakfast, or with a green salad for lunch.

RECIPES *with* HARMONY

Some internationally famous musical names came to the aid of the Sydney Philharmonia when it published a cookbook leading up to its 60th anniversary.

Australia's largest choral organisation started life modestly enough in 1920 as a suburban choral society based at Hurlstone Park in Sydney's inner west. By 1979, when *Sounds Delicious* was released, it was the ABC's choir of choice to perform with the Sydney Symphony Orchestra, and was presenting its own annual subscription series of concerts.

The organisation's 150 amateur singers were rewarded for devoting about 200 hours each year to rehearsing and performing, by having the opportunity to work with some of the world's most highly regarded professional conductors, musicians and solo singers. They included British conductor and composer Sir David Willcocks, who agreed to become patron. Particularly well known for his association with the Choir of King's College, Cambridge, where he was Director of Music for almost twenty years, Sir David fulfilled his duty by providing recipes for spiced apricot lamb and a baked custard.

The cookbook project was initiated to support the increasing costs of presenting high-quality performances to the Australian public. It was led by

Above: *Sounds Delicious*, 1979 (courtesy Sydney Philharmonia). Right: The Sydney Philharmonia on the steps of the Sydney Opera House (image by Keith Saunders).

convenor Rosemary Sage, who also secured recipes from operatic sopranos Dame Joan Sutherland and Marilyn Richardson, as well as Australian-born conductor Sir Charles Mackerras, then chief guest conductor of the BBC Symphony Orchestra.

A highlight of the book's design is the witty line drawings by illustrator Vicki McKenzie.

Chicken Valencia

SERVES 6

This recipe was contributed by Patrick Thomas. Thomas set his sights on becoming a conductor at the age of twelve, after seeing the legendary Eugene Ormandy conduct at Brisbane City Hall in 1944. In a diverse career stretching over almost 35 years, he conducted hundreds of performances across Australia and overseas. At the time the cookbook came out, he was conductor in residence with the ABC, based in Sydney. This recipe is a beautiful, delicately balanced combination of flavours, redolent of Spain.

METHOD

To make the stuffing, soak the raisins in the sherry for 30 minutes. Chop one-third of the raisins and combine them in a bowl with the ham, butter, parsley and orange zest. Set aside.

Place the chicken breasts between two sheets of baking paper, then use a rolling pin to flatten the breasts until they are about 1 cm thick. Place some stuffing in the centre of each breast, then fold the breast over to enclose the stuffing. Secure with small skewers or toothpicks, or use butcher's twine.

Combine the flour and paprika on a plate, then coat the chicken in the combined flour and paprika.

Heat the butter in a large frying pan over medium heat and cook the chicken until it is golden brown. Remove the chicken from the pan and drain off any excess fat.

Cook the onion in the same pan until soft, add the garlic and cook for 1 minute. Return the chicken to the pan with the orange juice, chicken stock and cinnamon stick. Season with salt and pepper to taste. Cover and simmer gently until cooked through and tender—about 30 minutes. Remove the chicken from the pan and set aside to keep warm. Remove the cinnamon stick and add the remaining raisins.

INGREDIENTS

6 single chicken breasts

30 g plain flour

1 teaspoon paprika

60 g butter

1 small onion, finely chopped

2 garlic cloves, crushed

juice of 1 large orange

500 ml (2 cups) chicken stock

1 cinnamon stick

salt

freshly ground black pepper

2 teaspoons cornflour

6 slices of orange

Stuffing:

120 g (2/3 cup) raisins

2 tablespoons sherry or orange juice

30 g cooked ham, finely diced

30 g butter, softened

1 tablespoon chopped flat-leaf parsley

grated zest of 1/2 orange

Mix the cornflour to a smooth paste with a little cold water, then stir into the sauce. Stir continuously until the mixture boils, then simmer gently for 3 minutes, stirring occasionally.

To serve, remove the skewers, toothpicks or twine from the chicken. Place each breast on a slice of orange and pour over the sauce.

```
LIZ'S TIPS

•   I've modified the original recipe, which left the skin on the
    chicken. I've also used fresh garlic instead of incorporating
    1 teaspoon garlic salt with the flour and paprika.

•   Serve with steamed vegetables or a fennel salad.
```

Above and previous page: Illustrations by Vicki McKenzie from *Sounds Delicious* (Barr Smith Library, University of Adelaide). Opposite: *The Melbourne Chorale Christmas Book*, 1980.

SINGING *for* THEIR SUPPER

Ann James was a young art teacher working for the Victorian Ministry of Education in 1980 when she offered to come up with a few simple line drawings for a cookbook being put together by The Melbourne Chorale.

She was roped into the task by choir member Nola Ryan, one of her colleagues in the department's publications section. Employed to design and illustrate educational materials for primary and secondary schools, both women were happy to contribute to the fundraising exercise. 'It was a lovely gathering of talents and friendship,' says Nola.

Responsible for the overall design of the book, Nola created the cover while Ann focused her energies on highlighting selected recipes and the title page for each section. Even though she was not a choir member, Ann donated her time. The choir's well-known founder and musical director, Val Pyers, was delighted with the end result, describing her drawings as whimsical, witty and charming.

Within months of *The Melbourne Chorale Christmas Book* being released, Ann's first picture book was published following exposure in a competition for unpublished work. Written by Gwenda Smyth, *A Pet for Mrs Arbuckle* was the first of more than 60 children's books that Ann has since illustrated, and sometimes written, in an award-winning career spanning almost 40 years.

Now one of Australia's most celebrated children's book illustrators, she has been honoured for her significant contributions to children's literature in Australia, particularly through her work with Books Illustrated, which she co-founded in 1988. The venture started off as a gallery for picture-book illustrations and their creators, expanding to run workshops and curate major exhibitions, which have toured Australia and overseas.

Like most of the choir's performances, the cookbook was a resounding success. With recipes carefully reviewed by a professional recipe editor called in by Val, the first edition of 3000 copies quickly sold out, leading to calls for an encore. After continual requests, a second edition was produced in time for Christmas in 1983.

In perhaps a first for a community cookbook, in addition to recipes, the *Christmas Book* incorporates 26 original carol settings by Sydney-born composer Christopher Willcock, now regarded as one of the world's leading Catholic composers of liturgical music. Produced to celebrate the choir's fifteenth anniversary, the book also captures key moments in the company's transformation from an exuberant conglomeration of eighteen voices into one of Australia's 'finest and most adventurous choral organisations'.

Reflecting on some of the less conventional fundraising activities members took on to supplement income from grants and performances, founding member Jim Dooley recalled singers selling frozen turkeys, stuffed toys, encyclopedias and car stickers.

In 2008, the choir integrated with the Melbourne Symphony Orchestra to become the MSO Chorus. It is made up of 120 singers from all walks of life, who volunteer their time to rehearse and perform at everything from concerts and arts festivals, to the AFL Grand Final and Anzac Day services.

Above: An illustration by Ann James from *The Melbourne Chorale Christmas Book.* Right: Today's MSO Chorus (courtesy Melbourne Symphony Orchestra).

Ice cream Christmas pudding

This recipe was contributed by Joan Cooke, who described it as somewhat extravagant, but delicious. 'It is so rich no-one can eat too much so it goes a long way,' she explained. 'A treasured memory of mine is the sight of my twenty-month old nephew with this sweet smeared all over his face and in his hair. On his face was a smile that said all was right with the world. From his lips came just one word: Yum.'

Obviously other members of the choir agreed. The cookbook editors received five slightly different versions to choose from, including submissions from Val Gregory, Susan Barclay, Christine Dart and Marjorie Mathers.

METHOD

Coarsely chop the raisins, sultanas, citrus peel and cherries. Combine them in a small bowl. Add the cinnamon, nutmeg and mixed spice, then stir in the rum. Cover with plastic wrap and leave overnight to marinate at room temperature.

The next day, dissolve the cocoa in the hot water and set aside to cool.

Line a 2 litre (8 cup) pudding basin or bowl with plastic wrap.

Put the egg whites in a large bowl and beat until soft peaks form. Add half the icing sugar and beat until stiff.

In a separate bowl, beat the cream and remaining icing sugar until thick.

Gently fold the egg white mixture into the cream mixture, then fold in the fruit and spice mixture, almonds and the cocoa mixture.

Spoon the mixture into the basin. Cover with foil and freeze overnight, or until firm.

Let the pudding stand at room temperature for about 10 minutes to soften slightly before turning out onto a large plate and serving.

INGREDIENTS

85 g (½ cup) raisins

85 g (½ cup) sultanas

60 g mixed citrus peel

60 g (¼ cup) glacé cherries

1 teaspoon ground cinnamon

1 teaspoon ground nutmeg

2 teaspoons mixed spice

2 teaspoons rum or brandy

2 teaspoons cocoa powder

1 tablespoon hot water

4 egg whites

125–185 g (1–1½ cups) icing sugar

600 ml thickened cream

60 g toasted slivered almonds

LIZ'S TIPS

- If you prefer a stronger flavour, double the amount of rum or brandy.

- A 2 litre (8 cup) metal pudding basin with a lid is ideal for making this recipe. You do not need to line it. To remove the ice cream before serving, stand the basin in hot water for a few seconds.

WIND BENEATH *their* WINGS

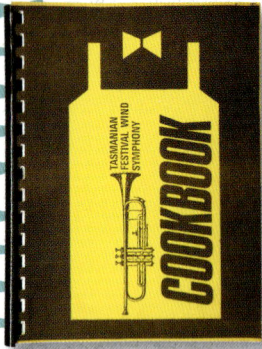

They were known as the Cross Quintet—five siblings from a non-musical background, all part of a concert band that started out as a transitory clutch of young musicians and ended up lasting for more than 20 years.

Carolyn, Kate, Janine, Andrew and Deb Cross were members of the Tasmanian Festival Wind Symphony, which featured wind instruments, playing everything from classic concert band pieces to jazz and special arrangements of pop music and classical works.

Based in Devonport, the Wind Symphony came out of a youth camp held in 1984, under the auspices of the Mersey Valley Festival of Music. Among the teachers at the camp was Melbourne music educator and conductor Russell Hammond. 'He had a brainwave that it shouldn't be over after the camp, but that students from all over Tasmania should continue to meet once a month,' explains Carolyn.

Everyone thought it was a splendid idea, so Russell became the musical director, flying in to take rehearsals. So did highly respected Adelaide teacher and conductor Bruce Raymond, who worked with the group for six years, nurturing and encouraging the 70 to 80 mostly high-school students who made up the Wind Symphony at any given time. Many were studying music at school, or through private tuition, but connections made through Russell, Bruce and Mersey Valley festival administrator, Shirley McCarron, and her husband, Max, opened doors to experiences they might otherwise have only dreamt about.

'It had a huge impact,' says Carolyn, who was the inaugural band leader. 'We got to work with people like James Morrison, Don Burrows and Graham Lyle, and Peter Clinch who ran the music department at Melbourne University. The opportunities it afforded us were just enormous.'

The Wind Symphony became so proficient that it went on several tours to the mainland, playing at festivals and schools. In 1988, the group made a two-week Bicentennial tour to play gigs in Sydney, Canberra, Albury-Wodonga, Shepparton and Melbourne. The contingent included all five Cross siblings, with Kate on saxophone, Janine on oboe, Andrew playing trumpet, and Carolyn and Deb on clarinet.

Given that neither of them played a musical instrument, this development must have been slightly perplexing to their parents, Christine and Peter Cross, as it swept up the whole family. Their musical odyssey began when Carolyn, the eldest child, decided to learn the clarinet in year seven at Latrobe High School. Following her example, Kate and Janine also started learning instruments when they reached high school. Andrew decided to play a brass instrument while he was still in primary school, as a result of a membership drive by the Latrobe Federal Band, the oldest continuous serving brass band in Australia. Deb also started clarinet in primary school, taking lessons from Carolyn.

From the beginning, generating enough funding to cover the costs of taking a large contingent of players on the road was a challenge. They relied mostly on Arts Council grants and corporate sponsorship but, when the Wind Symphony decided to make its first visit to the mainland in 1987 to attend Adelaide's Come Out Festival, someone hit on the idea of putting together a recipe book.

The *Tasmanian Wind Symphony Cookbook* is a stylish publication featuring recipes handwritten by calligrapher Melinda Risby, and original artwork by Rod Taylor. In a clever play on words, the titles for ingredients and method are replaced with 'Instrumentation' and 'Composer's Notes'.

Shirley and Max also used their contacts to secure recipes from musical high flyers, such as soprano Dame Joan Sutherland and concert pianist Geoffrey Tozer, but most come from orchestra mums like Christine Cross.

From the beginning, Christine and Peter billeted students from Hobart and Launceston, when they travelled north for the monthly rehearsals. They also regularly travelled with the band to help with logistics and act as chaperones, while Peter often took on the duties of stage manager. Christine did her bit too, feeding band members during rehearsals. 'Everyone would travel up on the Friday and then rehearse all day Saturday and we would always have a casserole lunch,' Carolyn says.

The Tasmanian Festival Wind Symphony unfortunately folded in about 2009, after it became too difficult to generate enough funding. Since then life has taken the Cross siblings in different directions, but Carolyn's career remains firmly rooted in music. In 2017, she was teaching 23 classes a week to students at Bellerive and Risdon Vale Primary schools, and directing no fewer than eight ensembles.

Above: An illustration by Rod Taylor from the cookbook. Below: Carolyn Cross teaching music at Risdon Vale Primary School, Tasmania (courtesy Carolyn Cross). Opposite: *Tasmanian Wind Symphony Cookbook*, 1986 (State Library of Tasmania).

Bach-erole à la fish (Tuna bake)

SERVES 4

INGREDIENTS

1 x 45 g packet low-salt
chicken noodle soup

375 ml (1½ cups) water

500 ml (2 cups) milk

60 g butter, plus extra for
finishing

½ medium onion, finely
chopped

⅓ cup chopped capsicum or
½ cup chopped celery

3 tablespoons plain flour

425 g tinned tuna, drained

310 g (1¼ cups) tinned
creamed corn

1 tablespoon lemon juice
(optional)

100 g (1 cup) grated cheddar
cheese

30 g (½ cup) fresh
breadcrumbs

Tuna casserole was a big favourite with band members, as well as the Cross family. Three versions were included in the cookbook, including a recipe provided by Christine, which she made regularly for the rehearsal sessions. Carolyn doesn't remember it including capsicum, which she did not like as a child, but she does recall that her mum would often make it extra special by incorporating crushed potato chips into the topping. When she revisited this childhood favourite for a 1970s-themed dinner party with friends, they heartily approved.

METHOD

Preheat the oven to moderate (180°C). Grease a 2 litre (8 cup) capacity casserole dish.

Cook the chicken noodle soup according to the directions on the packet, using the water and 125 ml (½ cup) of the milk.

Melt the butter in a large saucepan over medium heat. Sauté the onion and capsicum in the butter until tender. Stir in the flour and allow to cook over low heat for 2–3 minutes, stirring frequently.

Remove from the heat and gradually blend in the soup and the remaining milk. Cook, stirring continuously over medium heat, until thick and smooth. Stir in the tuna and corn, and the lemon juice, if desired.

Tip the tuna mixture into the casserole dish. Top with the cheese and breadcrumbs and dot with the extra butter. Bake for 30 minutes, until golden.

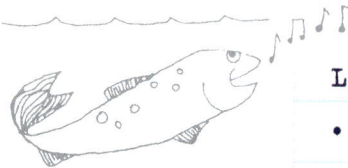

LIZ AND CAROLYN'S TIPS

- You need the family-sized soup mix packet for this recipe, not a single-serve cup packet.

- It's best to make the breadcrumbs from stale bread, and use a generous amount with plenty of cheese so it creates a thick, crunchy topping.

- You might prefer to use a combination of cheeses such as cheddar, mozzarella and parmesan, which melt well together and produce a golden topping.

- If you want the full Cross experience, crush a generous handful of plain potato chips, then mix them with the cheese and breadcrumbs before sprinkling over the casserole.

Opposite: Afternoon Tea with the "P.H.E.", 1987.

THREADING *the* NATION

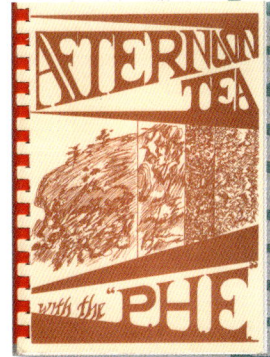

Dorothy Hyslop was met with stunned silence one day in 1980, when she proposed an ambitious plan to create a commemorative work for Canberra's new Parliament House. She wanted embroidery guilds around Australia to collaborate on a frieze in the grand scale of the famous Bayeux Tapestry, and present it to the nation as a gift to celebrate its 200th birthday.

The artistic and logistical challenges were formidable. The Canberra-based guild, of which Dorothy was a member, was relatively small and there were no regular, formal connections with other state or territory guilds. But the idea was embraced by parliamentary leaders, as well as the construction authority working to make sure the new building was ready in time for the country's Bicentenary celebrations in 1988. They even gave the guilds funding to run a design competition, engage the chosen artist and employ a national coordinator to bring it all together.

The project took eight years, more than 1000 volunteers and 12,000 hours to make happen, from negotiations to involve all the guilds and develop the concept, to testing and selecting materials, stitching samplers, preparing the backing linen, building frames, creating the embroidered panels, then putting them together and mounting the final completed work.

Six artists were invited to provide designs exploring the 'Australian land and its impact upon the human values and lives of its inhabitants'. The winner was Kay Lawrence, a textile artist then based in South Australia.

Over the next five years about 500 embroiderers pushed their skills to the limit, creating a work of art that is sixteen metres long. To complete their designated panels, members of what is now known as the Embroiderers' Guild ACT were rostered into groups of four over an intensive six-month period, working together in a member's home at Red Hill. 'We had a flat on the ground floor with its own entrance and a separate little kitchen,' says Libby Fenwick-Williams, who was one of the volunteers.

While they worked, people often dropped in to check on progress and bring food, particularly baked treats, which could be enjoyed with a cuppa during the many short breaks that were essential to recharge tired hands and minds. The food shared during these sessions inspired Lois Evans to propose a cookbook to raise money towards the cost of materials.

Above: Libby Fenwick-Williams working on a panel of the embroidery, May 1986. Below: Dorothy Hyslop making the first stitch, 3 May 1986 (courtesy Embroiderers' Guild ACT).

Below: Stitchers from the Canberra-based guild who worked on the embroidery: standing (from left), June Weatherstone, Ellestan Dusting, Liz Evans, Jeanette Fowler, Anne Mussett, Helene Phillips and Elva Oakley; and seated (from left), patron Lady Stephen and Dorothy Hyslop (courtesy Embroiderers' Guild ACT).

..... Manoo mainaa arganangam Wangudanjama arganangama nan

Published in 1987, *Afternoon Tea with the "P.H.E."* features members' favourite biscuit, cake, slice, scone and bread recipes, as well as some savoury treats. Libby was on maternity leave, so she volunteered to edit it, drawing on her experience working in the publications section of a small government agency. 'I had all these pages of people's handwritten recipes. I don't recall it being at all difficult extracting them from people, but there was a lot of difficulty reading some of the handwriting,' she laughs.

Libby is not certain how many copies were printed or how much money the cookbook raised, but it sold out, and ten years later the tiny but tenacious Dorothy convinced the guild to publish an anniversary edition. 'She worked very hard for the guild over the years. She was small, not bird-like, but trim, and always well dressed. She had a strong intellect and she got a lot done in a very minimalist way. She just worked quietly and constantly, and made things happen,' Libby recalls.

Dorothy was made a Member of the Order of Australia in 1989 for her contribution to the project, and appointed a Life Member of the guild in 1992. She died in 2011, at the age of 95. The embroidery still hangs in the Great Hall at Parliament House where it has been admired by millions of visitors.

Below: Panels stitched by the ACT guild, from Kay Lawrence (born 1947) *Parliament House Embroidery*, 1984–1988, Gifts Collection, Parliament House Art Collection, Canberra, ACT

Chocolate nut bars

INGREDIENTS

Base:

110 g (¾ cup) wholemeal
plain flour

1½ tablespoons cocoa
powder

3 tablespoons raw caster
sugar

90 g butter, chopped

Topping:

2 eggs

150 g (¾ cup) raw caster
sugar

3 tablespoons plain flour

1 teaspoon baking powder

60 g (½ cup) walnuts,
chopped

45 g (½ cup) desiccated
coconut

110 g (½ cup) chopped glacé
ginger

1 teaspoon natural vanilla
extract

90 g dark chocolate

I've chosen to include Afternoon Tea with the "P.H.E.", *not just in celebration of the extraordinary volunteer effort that the Parliament House Embroidery represents, but because of a personal connection. I write in a room that once was Kay Lawrence's work space, with a tall ceiling to accommodate a loom, and beautiful natural light, particularly in the morning.*

This delicious slice, cut into fingers or bars, is one of three chocolate recipes that Dorothy contributed to the cookbook. Despite having three components, it's easy to make, and time-efficient too because you mix together the topping while the base is baking. 'Dorothy was certainly a good cook,' says Libby.

METHOD

Preheat the oven to moderate (180°C). Grease and line a 20 cm square, shallow cake pan or slab pan.

To make the base, sift the flour and cocoa into a bowl, then stir in the sugar. Rub in the butter until the mixture resembles fine breadcrumbs. Work the mixture together with your hands and then press it into the prepared pan, using the back of a spoon. Bake for 15 minutes.

While the base is cooking, make the topping. In a large bowl, beat the eggs well. Add the sugar and beat until the mixture is thick and light.

Sift together the flour and baking powder, then fold them into the egg mixture with the walnuts, coconut, ginger and vanilla. Fold gently until thoroughly combined. Pour the mixture over the base while it is still hot, then return it to the oven for 30 minutes, until golden brown and firm to the touch.

When the slice is cool, melt the chocolate and spread it evenly over the top. Once the chocolate starts to set, cut the slice into small bars.

LIZ'S TIPS

- You can use a food processor to incorporate the butter into the base.
- You don't have to beat the topping mixture until the sugar dissolves.
- Use good-quality cocoa powder and chocolate.
- Because the chocolate topping is made with just chocolate, it can be tricky to cut without the chocolate cracking. Use a sharp knife dipped in hot water, and do it before the chocolate is completely set. Alternatively, melt 20 g butter with the chocolate.

Recipe Book

BUILDING

with

RECIPES

SEA of HEARTBREAK

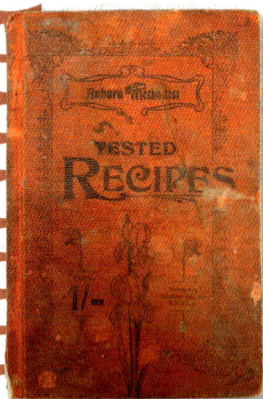

Alice Shaw had every reason to fear ships and the sea. Her father, William Rout, a high-profile pioneer from Nelson in New Zealand, was lucky to escape with his life when he was caught in a violent storm while sailing off the coast in a small, unseaworthy ship. However, Alice's husband, Henry Wharton Shaw, and her mother, Harriette, were not so fortunate.

Harriette died at sea in 1888, after suffering a heart attack while travelling to England accompanied by William and Alice. Harriette appeared to be in perfect health when she farewelled family and friends, so the loss came as a terrible shock. Then, in February 1909, Henry drowned when the SS *Penguin* struck rocks and sank in Cook Strait. Known affectionately as Harry, the Englishman was travelling on business as Australasian manager of his family's wire rope manufacturing company, based in Sheffield.

Henry and Alice had married in 1892 and settled in Melbourne. At the time of the shipwreck, they were living in a fine brick villa in the inner suburb of Hawthorn, with their three surviving children—fifteen-year-old Adelaide, John who had just turned twelve, and Muriel who was only three. Distressingly for Harry's family, they were initially told that he had survived the shipwreck, but the rescued man turned out to be another Mr Shaw.

Tragedy struck again just a few months later, when Henry's father, John Wharton Shaw, also died at sea while sailing home to England. Less than a month after that, Alice's own father died too. This time there were no ships involved; William passed away after undergoing surgery for an 'internal complaint'. But given the preceding events in her life, it is small wonder that Alice refused to let her son sail to England, where he was enrolled at Eton college and meant to join the family business.

After her heartbreaking series of losses, Alice moved temporarily to Nelson so she had the support of her family. Described by her descendants as a woman with a strong character, she returned after a year to the villa in Melbourne, where she lived just a short walk from the Auburn Methodist Church.

Set on a prominent hill, the church was constructed in the late 1880s to an eye-popping design by Alfred Dunn, one of the city's most exciting young architects. It formed part of a large complex, built at a cost of more than £20,000. Despite becoming a powerful symbol of the growing influence of the

PREFACE.

IN offering this handbook to the public, we desire to express our thanks to those ladies of the Church who have supplied the Recipes, and we hope it will meet with approbation. The proceeds of the sale of the books are intended to assist the Trust Funds of the

Auburn Methodist Church

METHODIST LADIES' GUILD.

Auburn, 1906.

Clockwise from top left: A pencil and colour-wash drawing of Auburn church by the architect, Alfred Dunn, 1888 (State Library of Victoria); Alice Shaw with her children, John, Adelaide and Muriel (courtesy Kerry Rooney); the cookbook's original preface; interior of the church today, during a wedding (courtesy Auburn Uniting Church). Opposite: *600 Tested Recipes*, 1906 (State Library of NSW).

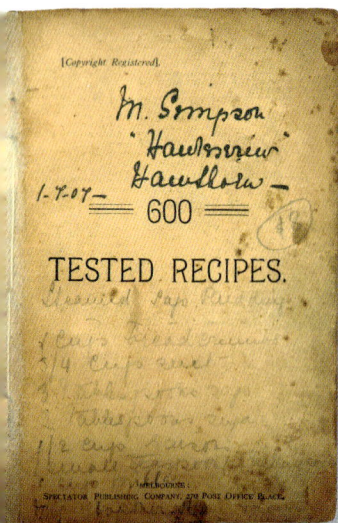

Above: Title page of *600 Tested Recipes*, 1906. Opposite: Advertisement from the 1906 edition of the cookbook.

Wesleyan Methodists and the increasing affluence of its congregation, it took almost 40 years to pay off the debt.

When the Methodist Ladies Guild decided to publish a cookbook in 1906 to help, Alice served as the official compiler. Originally bound in red leather and priced at one shilling, *600 Tested Recipes* proved such a success that it was still in print twenty years later when the ninth edition was released to favourable reviews. Combining 'simplicity with utility', the collection included separate sections for breakfast and supper dishes, entrees and savouries, confectionery and household hints 'supplied by a number of ladies and proven by thousands more'.

Alice passed away in 1956 at the age of 88. However, the church remains a local landmark. Considered to be one of the finest example of its architectural style in Australia, it is now heritage listed and part of the Uniting Church. In 2014, the tradition of sharing recipes continued when the congregation released a new cookbook to celebrate the building's 125th anniversary.

Kidney bean soup   SERVES 4

This soup recipe was donated to 600 Tested Recipes *by a Mrs Atcherley. A hearty and healthy blend of legumes, leeks and tomatoes, it seems surprisingly modern because it uses olive oil. This now everyday ingredient was practically never found in Australian cookbooks at the time and usually had to be sourced in small bottles from a chemist. The original method also called for mashing the cooked ingredients, given there were no blenders in the early 1900s. The resulting colour may be muted, but the flavours are vibrant with the final addition of lemon juice and a generous sprinkling of parsley.*

INGREDIENTS

2 leeks, white part only, sliced

1 tablespoon olive oil, plus extra for drizzling

2 large tomatoes, peeled and chopped

1 teaspoon thyme leaves

840 g tinned kidney beans, rinsed in cold water and drained

1 litre (4 cups) water

1 tablespoon sago or seed tapioca

large handful of flat-leaf parsley, chopped

salt

freshly ground black pepper

juice of ½ lemon

METHOD

Put the sliced leeks in a large saucepan with the tablespoon of olive oil and sauté gently for a few minutes, stirring occasionally to prevent the leeks from browning. Add the tomatoes and thyme and continue to sauté until the tomatoes start to turn to pulp, stirring occasionally.

Add the kidney beans, water, sago, and the parsley, keeping aside some of the parsley for serving. Season to taste with salt and pepper.

Bring the soup to the boil, then cover and allow it to simmer gently for about 15 minutes, until the sago becomes clear.

68

Remove the soup from the heat and blend to a coarse puree. If necessary, return it to medium heat and bring to serving temperature. Adjust the seasoning if necessary, then stir in the lemon juice.

Ladle the soup into serving bowls and sprinkle with the remaining parsley and generous drizzles of olive oil.

LIZ'S TIPS

- For a smoother soup, most likely truer to the original version, pass the blended mixture through a coarse sieve, or colander.
- Mrs Atcherley warned cooks not to let the soup boil after adding the lemon juice.
- You can substitute 200 g tinned crushed tomatoes for the fresh tomatoes.

A HALL FULL of MEMORIES

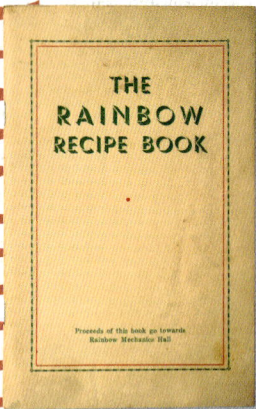

Fayisse Clarke remembers every detail of the beautiful white dress she wore to her first ball, more than 60 years ago. Sewn in the latest flock nylon, it had a very full skirt over layers of tulle that reached to the floor, a wrapped off-the-shoulder bodice, and mother-of-pearl flowers hand-stitched around the neckline.

Fayisse designed and made the garment herself as part of the two-year dressmaking course she completed at the Ballarat School of Mines. It was one of her final projects, scoring her good marks. She chose to make the dress, knowing that she was about to take part in a tradition that is honoured to this day in the Victorian Mallee town of Rainbow.

Along with most of her friends, Fayisse celebrated turning eighteen by making her formal entry into adult society at a debutante ball. It was 1956 and the event was held in the Mechanics' Institute, which played host to just about every community gathering in the town in those days, as well as accommodating the town's library and a room where men played billiards.

For this occasion, the public hall within the red-brick building was filled with fresh flowers, and there was a special carpet for the young women to walk down before being presented. Wearing long white gloves, and a corsage of fresh flowers tied to one wrist, Fayisse curtsied in front of the official party, before being led onto the dance floor by a friend from school, resplendent in a dark suit, white shirt, and bow tie. 'It was really something special,' she says.

Not long after, Fayisse returned to the hall in another ball dress, which she made with yet more layers of tulle, to win a Belle of the Ball competition sponsored by the *Sun News Pictorial* newspaper in Melbourne. Fayisse isn't too sure what the judges were looking for, but it definitely included points for her dress. 'I just loved making ball gowns and evening frocks,' she says.

Then in 1958, Fayisse was back with a different young man in tow. This time it was John, the boy from the farm next door, and the occasion was a 'kitchen tea', leading up to their wedding. These days such events usually involve female relatives and friends of the bride coming together in someone's home for a few party games, coffee and cake, and the presentation of gifts that will be handy in the kitchen. But, in Rainbow in the 1950s, they were much larger affairs held in the institute. The men came too, and there was dancing.

THE RAINBOW RECIPE BOOK

Proceeds of this book go towards Rainbow Mechanics Hall

Clockwise from top: Debutante ball in the Rainbow civic centre, formerly the Mecca Theatre, April 1991 (image by Bill Bachman, National Library of Australia); the Mechanics' Institute and a wedding reception in its main hall, c. late 1950s (courtesy Rainbow Archive and Historical Society); Fayisse Clarke, making her debut, 1956 (courtesy Fayisse Clarke). Opposite: *The Rainbow Recipe Book*, replica edition, 2016.

'People would put a notice in the paper, and everyone would come along with presents for a kitchen—spoons and sandwich plates, and lots of tea towels,' Fayisse says. The netball club made sandwiches, and people brought a plate of supper to share. A local band with piano, saxophone and drums supplied the music for foxtrots and waltzes, and old-time dances like the Pride of Erin.

For another Rainbow woman, memories of the institute revolve around the Digger's Ball, organised by the local Returned Servicemen's League branch for quite a few years after the Second World War. The ball itself was held in the Mecca Theatre, but part-way through the evening, everyone would walk down the street in their finery to the Mechanics' Institute for a sit-down supper. 'It was mainly organised by the RSL ladies and they would canvas the town for help,' says Margery Wallis. 'Different people would make trifles, and there would be cold meat and salads, and fruit salad.'

Margery was often rostered on to help prepare and serve the meal from the institute kitchen. Known as the 'dugout', it was housed in a surprisingly spacious area under the main stage. 'You could enter it from outside the building, at the side, and the stage was quite high so it was quite roomy,' says Margery.

The Mechanics' Institute was so important to Rainbow that, when its predecessor burnt down in the early hours of New Year's Day 1912, it took the town less than a week to appoint an architect and call tenders to build a replacement. The fire happened on a Monday. By Friday of the same week, Lewis Stansfield Smith of Horsham was working on plans for the new building. By the end of January a tender from Rainbow builder Herbert Nicholson Ismay had been accepted to construct it on a more central site, for a cost of £1062. The foundation stone was laid in early March and the building was finished by May.

Until the late 1960s, the institute hosted all sorts of public gatherings and community meetings, lantern shows and movie screenings, the library and even an elementary school. So it's not surprising that more than a few local women answered the call, when the Mechanics' Hall Auxiliary decided to publish *The Rainbow Recipe Book* as a fundraiser, sometime in the early 1960s.

A considerable number of recipes came from the late Esme Roberts, a highly regarded show cook, and Gladys Monssen, who was known for her cake-decorating skills. Margery was approached by her sister-in-law, who was on the committee and desperate for more savoury recipes. She contributed a mince and rice dish popular with her young sons. Dorothy Gosling, who lived east of the town on a farm at Kenmare, provided a lemon slice recipe, which had been shared with her by a neighbour.

Fayisse did not actually donate a recipe herself, but she has one in the cookbook anyway, for a savoury luncheon puff made with cold meat and mashed potatoes, fried in hot fat. It was written out and sent in by her mother, Mollie McLean. 'I don't think we fry anything in fat any more, but on the farm we used to slaughter our own sheep and mum used to render all the fat down,' Fayisse says.

Mollie didn't like cooking all that much, but John's mother, Dorrie, was a prize-winning show cook who took Fayisse under her wing, sharing her knowledge and recipes. 'Her Sunday night teas were a real spread. Salads, cold meat and all the goodies—éclairs and sponges, fruit salads and trifles. And she used to take case fulls to the show.'

Fayisse was soon entering the show too. She has been a steward for a long time, and encouraged her own children to take part. 'We have had great fun over the years,' she says.

The Mechanics' Institute eventually closed in the late 1960s, with the Mecca becoming the main civic centre, and a preschool taking over the old building. It was eventually knocked down, but is still remembered via a mural, which greets people as they drive into Rainbow's main street.

Below: Original contributors to *The Rainbow Recipe Book* at the launch of the replica edition in 2016 (from left), Cynthia Harberger, Fayisse Clarke, Dorothy Gosling, Margery Wallis and Dorothy Christian (courtesy Rainbow Archive and Historical Society).

Cornflake biscuits

MAKES ABOUT 20

INGREDIENTS

120 g butter, softened

110 g (½ cup) caster sugar

1 egg

2 teaspoons golden syrup

150 g (1 cup) self-raising flour

60 g (½ cup) chopped
  walnuts

80 g (½ cup) chopped dates

45 g (1½ cups) cornflakes,
  lightly crushed

This was one of the regular baking standbys when I was growing up, because everyone liked them so much—another quick and easy option, which can be adapted to make use of whatever dried fruit or nuts are available. This version was contributed to The Rainbow Recipe Book *by Mrs Russell.*

METHOD

Preheat the oven to moderate (180°C). Line a baking tray with baking paper.

Cream the butter and sugar in a large bowl until light and fluffy. Beat in the egg, then the golden syrup. Sift in the flour, then stir in the walnuts and dates to form a stiff mixture.

Roll heaped teaspoonfuls of the mixture in the crushed cornflakes. Place them on the tray about 5 cm apart, then flatten them slightly. Bake for 10–12 minutes, until golden.

Allow to cool slightly on the tray, before removing them to a wire rack to cool completely.

LIZ'S TIPS

- The mixture needs to be stiff so you can roll it easily. Add a little more flour if necessary.
- Crush the cornflakes with your hands until they are in relatively small pieces.
- This recipe is a great way to use up slightly stale cereal, or the smaller broken remnants usually found at the bottom of a box.
- The biscuits burn easily, so keep a close eye on them towards the end of baking time.

Below: Advertisement from *Courier Mail*, 1942.

NEVER JUDGE *a* BOOK *by its* COVER

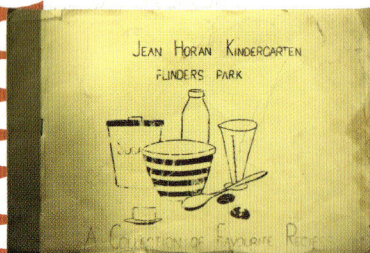

Jean Horan was not the sort of person who took no for an answer, even if it led her down a slightly unconventional path. In 1948, the quiet but determined mother of two was put in charge of a committee that drove planning and fundraising for a new preschool at Flinders Park in Adelaide. In the boom post-war years, the western suburbs were home to a rapidly increasing number of young children, but there were no educational facilities anywhere nearby.

The committee quickly settled on a preferred site—a triangle of vacant land owned by the local council. Council agreed to make the land available, providing the community could prove it had access to enough money to build the kindergarten and then run it.

Led by Jean, volunteers set to work raising funds. Her son, Kerry, and daughter, Sue, remember their mother baking almost every day over several years for street stalls, afternoon teas, card nights and fetes. She also cajoled local businesses into donating prizes for raffles and bingo nights. Only 157 centimetres tall, with dark, curly hair and a broad smile, she was capable of charming support out of almost anyone she approached. 'She would go into the local butchers and come out with 500 sausages that he had been persuaded to give her for free for the fete barbecue,' Kerry recalls.

When the total money raised fell short of the initial target, Jean hit on a creative solution to speed things up. She went to see a bookmaker. He lived around the corner from the proposed site and thought the kindergarten was a good idea, so he agreed to lend the committee some money. Jean banked it just long enough to convince the council, paid it straight back and then refocused her energies on rounding up building materials and volunteer labour.

It wasn't the first time that Jean had taken an unorthodox approach to make something happen. Her marriage took similar determination. Jean met her future husband one night at a dance in Adelaide, organised by the Wireless Institute. Ken Horan had been expected to follow family tradition and work in the hotel trade, but from the time he was a young boy he had been fascinated with radio.

'He was a radio man his whole life,' says Kerry. 'He built a crystal set when he was 10 or 12, and applied for an amateur radio broadcast licence as soon as he was old enough, when he turned 16.' Ken was still only a teenager when he started giving expert talks to gatherings of the Wireless Institute and local amateur radio clubs in Adelaide.

After they met at the Institute dance, the tall, shy but equally determined Ken soon fell in love with the diminutive Jean. His parents did not approve. 'Dad's family were very strict Catholics and Mum's family were Church of England,' says Sue. 'Dad's parents said, "Sorry, she's not suitable," so they eloped to Broken Hill. They got married in the registry office, which the Catholic church didn't recognise, so we were never legitimate as far as our paternal grandparents were concerned.'

The Horans stayed in the mining town until 1941, when Ken was offered a job as a radio engineer at Philips Electrical Industries in Sydney. The Second World War was raging and he was keen to enlist, but authorities considered his skills of more use helping the company to develop top-secret telecommunication systems for the military. After the war, Philips consolidated its Australian operations in an old munitions factory in Adelaide where, by the end of the 1950s, 3500 people were employed, manufacturing radios and televisions. Ken returned to his hometown to take up a senior role, and settled into Flinders Park with Jean and their four-year-old son, Kerry. Sue was born shortly after.

The siblings are not sure why Jean focused her energies on the kindergarten project, and other later volunteer efforts at their primary and secondary schools, although Kerry recalls his mother saying, 'We can't just sit around playing bridge all the time, can we?'

But it's likely Jean was influenced by pioneering educationalist Adelaide Miethke. During a remarkable career, which began as a student teacher in 1899, this extraordinary woman pushed for greater opportunities for girls and women teachers, and drove campaigns that mobilised school children to raise many thousands of pounds during the two world wars. She was South Australia's first female high-school inspector and, in 1944, created the world's first school of the air, at Alice Springs.

Adelaide was also founding president of a child welfare association set up in 1942 to establish preschools and playgrounds in the Woodville district, which encompassed Flinders Park. Jean's committee fell under its umbrella, and Jean later served as the association's secretary, working alongside Adelaide. 'She was great friends with her,' says Sue.

The new kindergarten at Flinders Park was officially opened in 1953, after operating for three years out of a local church hall. Building the facility involved a mammoth volunteer effort, which saw all the materials and labour donated for nothing, chiefly thanks to Jean's charm and persistence. Two professional builders even gave their time at weekends to supervise.

Jean went on to serve as president, secretary and treasurer of the governing council, devoting more than twenty years of her life to the facility. Her fundraising efforts never stopped. Sometime in the early 1960s, they involved helping to put together *A Collection of Favourite Recipes*. Jean typed up most of the 240 contributions from parents and staff and then volunteers gathered

at her house to churn out thousands of pages on a Gestetner duplicating machine, before collating and stapling them together by hand. Like many community cookbooks, its low production values by today's standards do not reflect the quality of the recipes inside.

Jean died of cancer in 1966, aged just 54. The year before her death, she was invited to a very special ceremony, when the place that absorbed so much of her energy was officially renamed the Jean Horan Kindergarten in her honour.

Caramel sauce

MAKES ABOUT 2 CUPS

Sue still refers to the kindergarten cookbook to make her mother's caramel sauce recipe, which Jean served with home-made ice cream. 'You can't beat that caramel sauce,' says Sue. 'Mum was a very good cook. We grew up on meat and three veg, but she was a great cake cook and she made everything from scratch, even ice cream.'

INGREDIENTS

90 g butter, chopped

180 g brown sugar

105 ml (⅓ cup) sweetened condensed milk

1½ tablespoons golden syrup

185 ml (¾ cup) hot water

METHOD

Place the butter, sugar, sweetened condensed milk and golden syrup in a small saucepan. Stir with a wooden spoon over low heat until the sugar has dissolved and the mixture is thick, a rich caramel colour and starting to leave the side of the saucepan.

Immediately remove the saucepan from the heat and stir in the hot water, a little at a time, stirring well between additions to ensure it is thoroughly combined.

Return the saucepan to the stove and stir continuously over medium heat until the mixture boils. Boil for 1 minute, continuing to stir until the sauce becomes smooth. Pour it into a jug or small basin to cool.

Serve poured over a good-quality vanilla ice cream.

SUE'S TIPS

- It will take about 8-10 minutes for the sauce to reach the right state before you add the hot water. Do not try to rush it by increasing the temperature or it will catch and burn.
- The sauce will thicken as it cools.
- It keeps well in the fridge for 3 or 4 days, and makes an excellent topping for puddings and cakes.

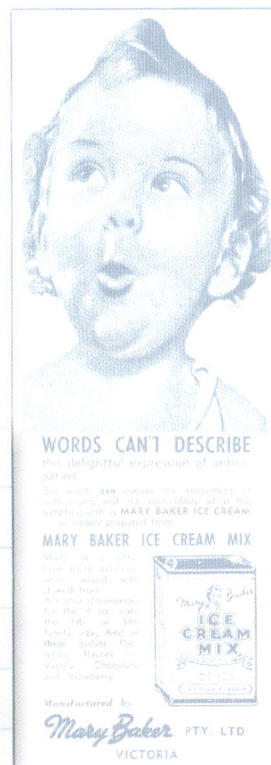

WORDS CAN'T DESCRIBE this delightful expression of anticipation...

MARY BAKER ICE CREAM MIX

Manufactured by

Mary Baker PTY. LTD

VICTORIA

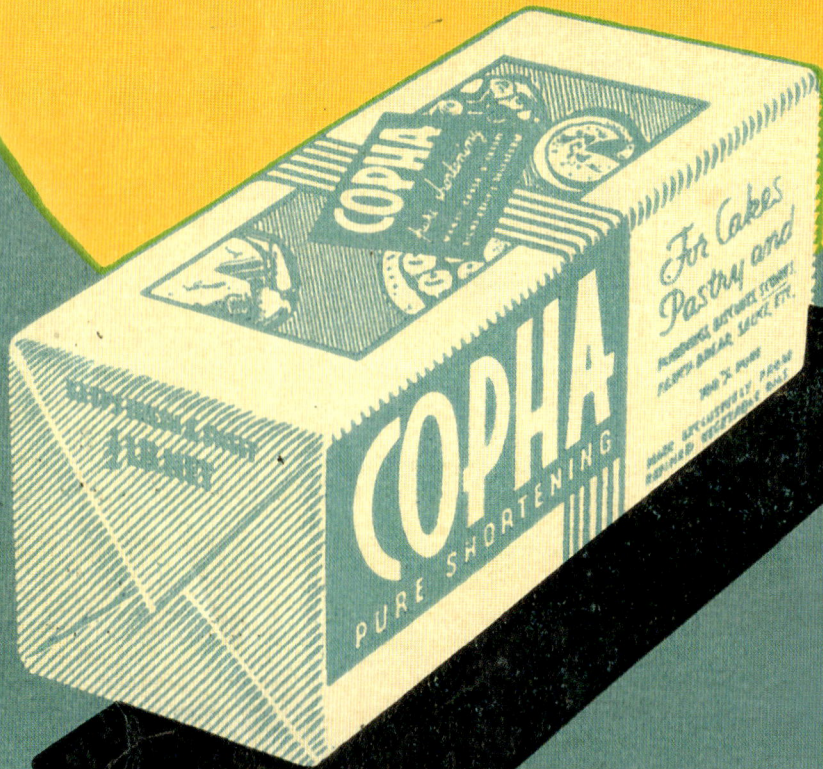

They're Packed with Quality!

Veribest
CHOICE
MIXED
FRUITS
FOR CAKES
AND PUDDINGS

Veribest
SEEDED
RAISINS

Veribest
FRUIT
JELLY CRYSTALS

TOPIC
JAMS
APRICOT JAM

Clockwise from top: Constructing the Bairnsdale Olympic swimming pool in Turnbull Street, c. 1968 (East Gippsland Historical Society, P10277); advertisement from *The Mitchell Valley Recipe Book* (State Library of Victoria); the swimming pool c. 1990 (EGHS P42761); the former swimming pool on the banks of the Mitchell River, c. 1920s–1954 (State Library of Victoria, Rose series P648). Opposite: *The Mitchell Valley Recipe Book*, c. 1960s (State Library of Victoria).

IN *at the* DEEP END

When Australian swimmers Murray Rose and Dawn Fraser won five gold medals between them at the 1956 Olympic Games in Melbourne, they became national heroes and inspired the next generation.

The impact in Victoria's eastern Gippsland region was immediate. The Bairnsdale Swimming Club had been in recess, but by January 1957 it had 350 new members, and a significant problem. The town's only public swimming pool had been cut into the banks of the Mitchell River as part of a relief scheme for the unemployed during the Depression. It was far from ideal.

In 1960, a committee was formed to raise funds for a new Olympic-sized pool in the Botanic Gardens. Community groups soon got behind the campaign to raise £40,000 and, in 1964, the local council voted to make the pool its next major amenities project. By July 1967, in a new era of decimal currency, the Bairnsdale and District Olympic Swimming Pool Committee had raised $32,000 towards the estimated cost of $120,000.

Contributing to that effort was the Ladies' Auxiliary, who put together *The Mitchell Valley Recipe Book*. Led by its president, Mrs A.J. Legg, the group of women rounded up favourite recipes from the district's housewives, and sold the collection for four shillings. Mr Legg, a local plumber, backed the venture by placing an advertisement, promoting the latest Everhot slow combustion stoves, which he sold and installed.

Fundraising was successful enough for tenders to be let and work to begin in early 1968. The pool was finished by the end of the year for about $20,000 more than anticipated.

Today swimmers at Bairnsdale have access to an indoor facility, opened in 1996, but the open-air pool is still in use during summer months. It hosts school carnivals and training sessions for the East Gippsland Waterdragons, a new swimming club formed in 2003, when the Bairnsdale group combined with a club based at Lakes Entrance.

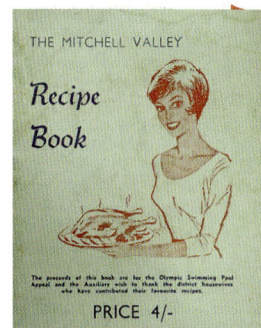

Gingerbread

300 g (2 cups) plain flour

1 teaspoon bicarbonate
 of soda

1 tablespoon ground ginger

¼ teaspoon mixed spice

120 g butter, chopped

120 g dark brown sugar

30 g mixed citrus peel, finely
 chopped

1 egg, lightly beaten

250 ml (1 cup) milk

4 tablespoons golden syrup

Icing:

120 g (1 cup) icing sugar
 mixture

15 g butter, softened

1 tablespoon lemon juice
 (approximately)

If the copy of The Mitchell Valley Recipe Book *held by the State Library of Victoria is any guide, just about every recipe in this collection is a winner. There were so many ticks of approval that it was hard to know where to start. But gingerbread has always been one of my favourite things, and this cake-like version, donated by L. Schmidt of Tambo Upper, is so delicious and quick to make that in the end there was really no choice.*

METHOD

Preheat the oven to moderate (180°C). Grease a 20 cm square cake pan and line it with baking paper.

Sift together the flour, bicarbonate of soda, ginger and mixed spice. Rub in the butter, then stir in the brown sugar and the mixed citrus peel.

In a separate bowl, whisk together the egg and milk, then whisk in the golden syrup. Pour this mixture into the flour mixture, then stir lightly and quickly until the ingredients are just combined.

Pour the batter into the cake pan and bake for 30–40 minutes, or until the gingerbread tests clean when you insert a thin skewer in the centre. Turn the gingerbread out onto a wire rack to cool.

To make the icing, combine the sugar, butter and lemon juice in a small bowl and mix to a smooth consistency. Spread evenly over the gingerbread.

LIZ'S TIPS

- You can use a food processor to incorporate the butter.
- Drop the pan lightly onto the bench before you put it in the oven, to settle the mixture evenly and remove any air pockets.
- This recipe keeps well for several days, stored in an airtight container.

PARTY PRESCRIPTIONS

Party Prescriptions is an odd little book. In fact, I doubt it would make it into print in today's world, no matter the good intentions of its authors.

The small volume of recipes was published in 1963, at a time when licensing laws in most Australian states forced pubs to close in the early evening. The end result was what became known as the 'six o'clock swill', where men fought for a place at overcrowded public bars so they could throw down as much beer as possible before heading home after work. Rather than reducing the amount of alcohol consumed as was originally intended, critics say the laws made drinking an extreme sport, and helped to entrench it as a symbol of Aussie masculinity.

'Beer drinking is the problem and the attack on this Holy Australian Institution must be made with great care,' warned an anonymous Canberra doctor in the foreword to *Party Prescriptions*. To help counteract this social blight, the book set out to create more cultivated palates and showcase alcoholic beverages as an aid to 'finer living'. 'Sophisticated drinking is much more likely to solve the social evils of intoxication than efforts by pressure groups directed towards Abolition or restriction of sale of alcohol,' the good doctor wrote.

The cookbook features information about buying and storing wine, alongside food recipes incorporating wine, and more than 30 pages of drinks for all occasions. A surprising number came from officers serving in the Australian military, on ships and at air force bases around the globe.

The Wardroom on the HMAS *Cerberus* came up with Admiral's Sippers—a cocktail made with one ounce of gin, an equal measure of dry vermouth and a dash of angostura bitters, served over ice. Not to be outdone, the officer's mess at the RAAF base at Williamtown in New South Wales provided a recipe for the Mirage—a cocktail with two-thirds of a measure of brandy, one-sixth of a measure of absinthe and the same of white curaçao, shaken well with ice and served with a maraschino cherry.

But perhaps the oddest aspect of the book, which would never pass muster today, was that all these recipes featuring alcohol were being sold as a fundraiser for a youth movement. Monies made went to the 1st Red Hill Scout Group Building Fund in Canberra.

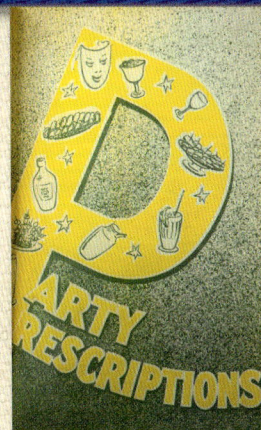

Above: *Party Prescriptions*, 1963 (Barr Smith Library, University of Adelaide).

The Everyday and Everyday and Everyday Recipe

RECIPES

for the

DISABLED

The RECIPE COLLECTOR

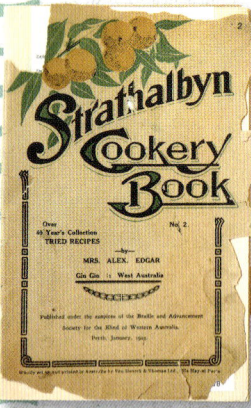

De Grey station was once considered Western Australia's premier pastoral enterprise. Covering about 12,000 square kilometres of the Pilbara, the massive holding ran about 70,000 sheep, 5000 cattle and several hundred horses when Myra Edgar moved there in 1890.

But despite its impressive scale, its fine livestock and its considerable earning capacity, Myra hated it. She hated its isolated location, almost 1800 kilometres from her family. She hated the dust storms that swept in from the east, covering everything with grime. She hated the primitive building that was her first married home, with its unlined iron ceiling and glassless windows. And she hated the extreme heat that stole the life of her baby son.

Myra came from a place very different to the Pilbara. The ninth of thirteen children, she was raised in the thriving port of Fremantle, where her father, John Bateman, was a wealthy shipping merchant. The Batemans were actively involved in the Congregationalist Church and, as an adult, Myra was devoutly religious, reading the Bible every night before going to sleep, and disapproving strongly of alcohol and gambling.

Despite growing up in a large family with an active social life, she was apparently quite shy, once telling a relative that entering a room to find six strangers felt the same as encountering six hundred. At 170 centimetres (five foot seven inches), with big blue eyes, she was tall for a woman of her time and would have stood out.

Myra was 28 years old when she married Alexander Williamson Edgar in July 1890. Originally from western Victoria, where his family owned stations near Harrow, Alex came to the west when he was about 21 to work as a jackaroo on De Grey, which was part-owned by his older brother Jack, and his brother-in-law, a dour Scot named McKenzie Grant. After about four years he became manager, and later part owner of the mammoth enterprise, responsible for its fifteen to twenty overseers and about 300 Aboriginal staff, including 50 shearers.

The newlyweds headed back to the station soon after their wedding at Fremantle. It must have been a shock to Myra, who wrote to one of her sisters a few months later that she was not very much charmed with it yet, but that she expected to get used to it in time. And life did become more comfortable once a new homestead was completed, and a thriving vegetable garden established. She also had a capable cook and two Aboriginal girls to help in the house, and Jack freighted up the piano he gave them as a wedding present, so Myra could play the music she enjoyed.

But nothing would have compensated for losing her first children. Myra was in Fremantle when she gave birth to twins in June 1891. Her daughter Grace was stillborn. The other baby, Alexander, survived and she took him back to De Grey where tragedy struck again three days before Christmas, when he died from the extreme heat.

The Edgars had two more children by the time they left De Grey in 1897 to live in Perth. Alex was planning to retire, but he was still a relatively young man and soon discovered that he did not enjoy city life. In 1899 he purchased his brother's 1200 hectare share in a property at Gingin, about 100 kilometres north of Perth. He named his share Strathalbyn and set about building a large stone house on the side of a hill next to Gingin Brook. Always interested in livestock, he also established a prize-winning stud herd of Shorthorn cattle. Alex claimed the prestigious Governor's Cup five times, after winning the most points across all the livestock sections of the Perth Royal Show, and was elected president of the Royal Agricultural Society of Western Australia, firmly cementing his place in the top echelon of the state's rural community.

Opposite: *Strathalbyn Cookery Book No. 2*, 1925 (State Library of WA). Below: Myra Edgar (courtesy Bateman family). Bottom left: Alexander Edgar with one of his prize-winning bulls at the Perth Royal Show, 1917 (State Library of WA, BA1271/445).

Clockwise from top: De Grey station homestead, 1935 (John K. Ekers collection, State Library of WA 112547PD); image from the 1921 edition of the *Strathalbyn Cookery Book* of a blind student using a book transcribed by members of the Braille and Advancement Society for the Blind of Western Australia; three of Myra's children at the Cheriton flour mill near Gingin (courtesy Gingin Shire); and the first *Strathalbyn Cookery Book*, 1921 (Barr Smith Library, University of Adelaide).

"SILENT FRIENDS."

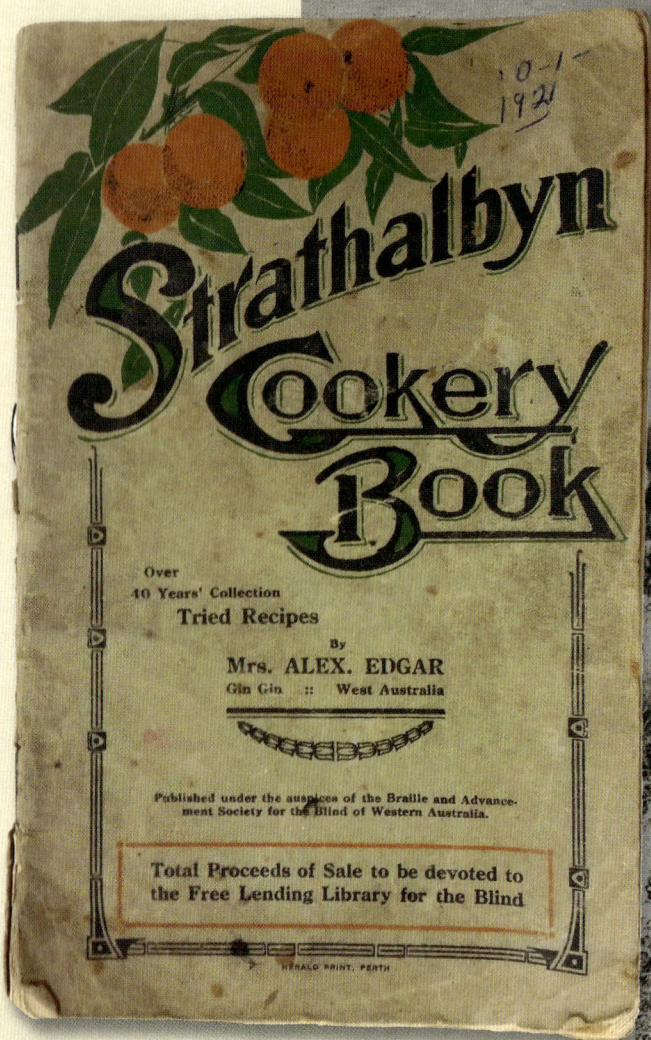

Strathalbyn Cookery Book

Over
40 Years' Collection
Tried Recipes

By
Mrs. ALEX. EDGAR
Gin Gin :: West Australia

Published under the auspices of the Braille and Advancement Society for the Blind of Western Australia.

Total Proceeds of Sale to be devoted to the Free Lending Library for the Blind

HERALD PRINT, PERTH

Meanwhile Myra focused on raising the family; she had five more children after leaving De Grey, including two babies that were stillborn. Alex was no help around the house, and annoyed her by bringing unexpected guests home to stay, or for meals. But she loved to bake and make preserves, even though the Edgars employed a cook. She also loved visiting friends and exchanging recipes, building up a substantial collection over a period of 40 years, which became the basis of two cookbooks.

What turned out to be the first volume of the *Strathalbyn Cookery Book* was published in 1921 under the auspices of the Braille and Advancement Society for the Blind of Western Australia. The author covered most of the production costs with a £25 donation, so that the entire one shilling cover price would go to the society's Free Lending Library for the Blind in Perth.

Seizing the opportunity to raise awareness about its work, the society incorporated several pages about its aims, highlighting the importance of giving the blind community access to quality literature. They sought additional donations to cover the cost of transcribing books into braille, and volunteers to undertake the work. 'The Braille system is very easily mastered, and the work of transcription may be done in one's own home in leisure time. The work is fascinating, and one half-hour a week devoted to writing means one Braille volume a year for the Blind,' the society urged.

The book raised more than £90 within a few months. A second volume with different recipes followed in 1925.

Eccles cakes

MAKES 18 SMALL PASTRIES

This recipe comes from the second volume of the Strathalbyn Cookery Book. *Originally from northern England, these small pastries are hard to find commercially in Australia, but they are easy to make if you use a good-quality, shop-bought pastry. Many versions of this recipe use flaky pastry, but Myra stipulates puff.*

INGREDIENTS

30 g butter, chopped

30 g dark brown sugar

90 g currants

60 g mixed peel

freshly grated nutmeg

2 sheets puff pastry

1 egg white

2 tablespoons white sugar

METHOD

Preheat the oven to moderately hot (200°C). Line a baking tray with baking paper.

Place the butter and dark brown sugar in a small saucepan and stir over medium heat until the butter has melted and the sugar is dissolved. Stir in the currants and mixed peel, then grate in some nutmeg to taste. Remove from the heat and allow to cool.

Cut the pastry into rounds about 8 cm in diameter. Place a teaspoonful of filling in the centre of each round. Wet the edges with a little water and draw them together over the top of the filling. Pinch together to seal well, then turn them upside down and gently work into a round.

Place the Eccles cakes on the baking tray and flatten them gently with your hand, until the fruit just starts to show through the top, without breaking the surface of the pastry. Brush each pastry with egg white and sprinkle generously with white sugar. Use a sharp knife to cut two or three slashes across the top of each.

Bake for 10–12 minutes, until golden. Remove to a wire rack to cool.

LIZ'S TIPS

- Make sure you use good-quality butter puff pastry.
- You can vary the size of the cakes, depending on what size cutter you have available.
- Tempting as it may be, don't eat them straight from the oven as the filling will be very hot.
- The Eccles cakes will keep for quite a few days in an airtight container.

Right: Recipe image by Kay Long. Opposite: *The Everyday and Everyway Recipe Book*, c. 1925 (Special Collections, Deakin University Library).

SECRET RECIPES, PATENT CURES *and* BRUISED REEDS

Thomas Holmes had a contentious message to deliver when he set up the Disabled Men's Association of Australia in the mid-1920s. In the previous decade, thousands of men had returned from the First World War mentally and physically damaged, and they deserved assistance; but so did men who had been permanently incapacitated in civilian life, even though there was no glory attached to their wounds.

'There is a society for the Prevention of Cruelty to Animals, even Homes for stray cats and dogs. But for the man who has lost a limb, or otherwise become incapacitated by accident or disease, there has been no organisation to which he could turn for help towards earning a living,' Holmes wrote in a small book published by the association to promote its work. 'They may be Bruised Reeds, but they are not crushed, nor are they helpless.'

The association held its founding meeting in Melbourne in January 1926, and soon won some high-profile supporters, including two of the war's most outstanding Australian military commanders, Sir John Monash and Brigadier General Thomas Blamey. The primary focus was finding suitable employment for permanently disabled civilians and servicemen who did not qualify to join other organisations or receive pensions. So when the association published a series of books on cooking, household management and popular medicine, it was not just about raising funds. According to Holmes, the books were pro-duced and sold by a trading department employing 24 disabled men.

Most of the publications were written and compiled by Holmes himself, using The Wardmaster as his pen name. Although few details are known about his life, personal references in his books indicate that he served in Britain's Royal Army Medical Corps and, that for some years, he was a wardmaster in charge of male personnel at a hospital for patients with venereal disease. Before coming to Australia, he also wrote pamphlets exposing exploitative practices selling patent remedies at exorbitant prices, when they could be made much more cheaply at home if people knew how.

Holmes emigrated to Australia with his family in 1921, and by 1923 was writing and publishing books from an office in Little Collins Street. Among the publications were two far from conventional 'recipe' books, linked to his earlier interests.

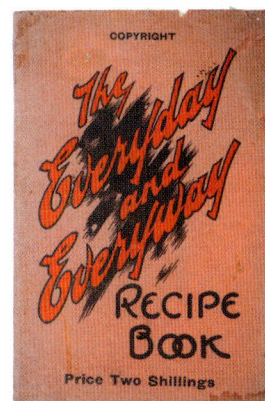

The First Book of Knowledge provided advice to parents on how to educate their children about sex, with a lengthy chapter on the perils of venereal disease. The final section featured home remedies for a variety of ailments, including backache, kidney disorders, indigestion, gout, sore feet, toothache and killing nits. For an outlay of one shilling and sixpence, it promised to tear 'asunder the veil of mystery and ignorance, and focus the light of knowledge on subjects that convention has decreed cannot be discussed'. The association guaranteed that copies would be posted in plain wrapping.

The second book, *Secret Recipes*, was a peculiar combination of more medicinal remedies; recipes for cooking; chemical formulas for items such as cosmetics, tooth powders, hair removal and dandruff cures; and 'private trade' formulas for household chemicals, which promised to remove stains, make linoleum gleam, kill rats and flies, eradicate weeds and cement broken china.

Under the association's banner, Holmes's recipe books became much more conventional. Over a period of about five years he produced at least seven slim cookbooks, including *The Star Recipe Book, The Best of Everything Recipe Book, The All in One Recipe Book and Household Guide, Primary Cookery*, and specific books with recipes for baking and preserving.

Below, from left: *The Star Recipe Book*, c. 1928, and *All the Best Recipe Book*, c. 1930s (Special Collections, Deakin University Library); *All in One Recipe Book and Household Guide*, 1927 (State Library of SA).

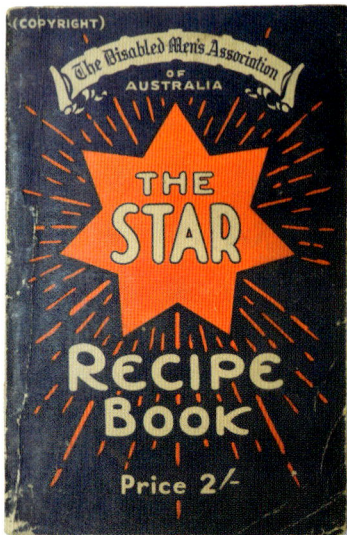

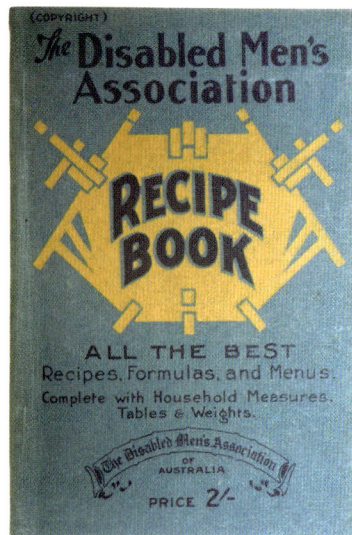

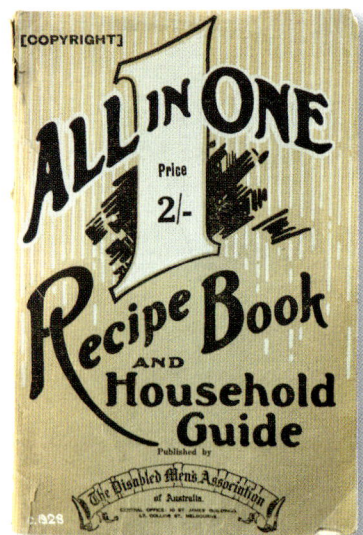

Mandarin marmalade

MAKES ABOUT 5 CUPS

This recipe comes from The Everyday and Everyway Recipe Book, *which appears to have been published by Thomas Holmes before he founded the Disabled Men's Association. The royalties were given to the Australian Red Cross Society to purchase comforts for returned soldiers who were still in hospital. An alternative to the usual orange marmalade, it is a lovely way to make use of an increasingly popular fruit in Australia, which usually comes into season in late autumn. Most mandarin varieties have less pith than oranges, making the preparation easier so, if you have never made marmalade before because it all seems too hard, this might be the recipe for you. But be warned. It is absolutely delicious and seriously addictive, so you might need to make more than one batch.*

INGREDIENTS

12 mandarins

2 lemons

250 ml (1 cup) cold water

1.1 kg (5 cups) white sugar (approximately)

METHOD

Wipe the mandarins and lemons with a damp cloth, then dry them. Set one lemon aside and put the rest of the fruit in a large preserving pan or saucepan with enough cold water to make the mandarins float. Bring to the boil and simmer for about 20 minutes, covered, until the rinds of the mandarins are soft enough to pierce easily with the head of a pin. Drain the fruit.

Once the mandarins are cool, quarter them and remove the pips. Put the pips in a small bowl with the cold water, and leave overnight.

The next day, measure the mandarins in cups. Measure out the same amount of sugar and set aside.

Remove the flesh from the mandarins and blitz it in a food processor. Scrape most of the pith from the mandarin peel and cut the peel into very thin strips. Juice both the cooked and uncooked lemons, then strain the juice.

Strain the soaked pips, keeping the water and discarding the pips. Put the water from the pips and the lemon juice in a large preserving pan or heavy-based saucepan. Add the sugar. Stir over medium heat until the sugar has dissolved and the syrup comes to the boil.

Stir in the mandarin pulp and the sliced peel and continue boiling, uncovered and without stirring, for about 25 minutes, until the marmalade sets when tested.

Remove from the heat and let stand for 15 minutes. Pour into hot sterilised glass jars and seal while hot.

Opposite: *The Biscuit Cook Book*, 1958 (State Library of NSW).

LIZ'S TIPS

- Make sure the fruit is clean, and there is no mould. Remove any brown spots once the mandarins are cooked.

- Soaking the pips overnight helps draw out the pectin which, together with the lemon juice, will set the marmalade. The original recipe used only one lemon, but many modern mandarin varieties have fewer pips, which means less pectin. The extra lemon juice will also give the marmalade a little more tang, offsetting the sweetness.

- To test whether the marmalade has set, keep a saucer in the freezer. Put a small teaspoon of the marmalade on the saucer and leave for a minute or two. If the marmalade is cooked it will wrinkle up when you push it gently with your fingertip.

- Letting the marmalade stand after cooking will help distribute the peel more evenly in the jar, and settle the bubbles.

- To sterilise your jars, wash them in hot soapy water and rinse thoroughly. Place them on a baking tray in a cold oven, making sure they are not touching, then heat the oven to very slow (120°C) and leave for 30 minutes.

STORM *in a* TEACUP

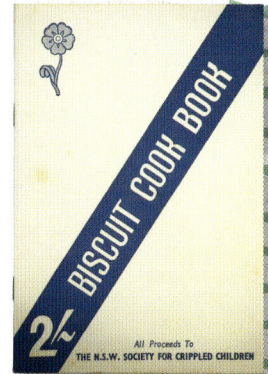

In March 1955, Sydney radio personality Del Cartwright invited listeners on 2CH to join her in a pioneering venture. She wanted to harness the power of the humble cuppa and improve the lives of disabled children.

Within a year the Teamakers' Club of Australia had more than 500 members working hard to raise money for the NSW Society for Crippled Children, and the 2500 disabled children then on its register. By its 40th anniversary in 1995, the club had raised more than $100,000.

While the organisation also ran events such as street stalls and fashion parades, the main focus was selling cups of tea. Encouraged by the motto 'it's the friendship in the pot that makes the difference', people paid five shillings to attend private afternoon tea parties hosted by members in their homes. Occasionally the guests got more than a plate of baked goodies accompanied by a soothing beverage—an unplanned fire disrupted one gathering, and a planned appearance by American singing sensation Johnny Ray caused hearts to flutter at another.

On a grander scale, members also served tea at large functions such as conferences and exhibitions. In 1958, the women excelled themselves, pouring 13,500 cuppas during the nine-day Sydney Homes Exhibition at the showground.

Not content with making cups of tea, the club found an additional way to raise money at the exhibition the following year, which also proved a roaring success. By then it had produced *The Cook's Handbook,* containing more than 120 pages of recipes and household tips. Priced at six shillings and sixpence, the book sold more than 40,000 copies before going out of print, no doubt helped along by Del's endorsement. Not only was Del a trained economist noted for her cooking, since launching the club she had also become a star in the exciting new world of television.

Screened on Sydney's Channel Seven, *Your Home* is attributed as the first program dedicated to women produced for Australian television. Launched within twelve months of the nation's first television broadcast in 1956, it went live to air every weekday for half an hour. At the helm, Del drew admiration for her relaxed style and the sense of genuine friendship she conveyed to viewers. A woman's magazine of the day also found it inspiring that she juggled this

Above: *The Cook's Handbook*,
c. 1950s (State Library of NSW).
Below: *Mrs State's Australian Cook
Book* , 1940 (Barr Smith Library,
University of Adelaide).

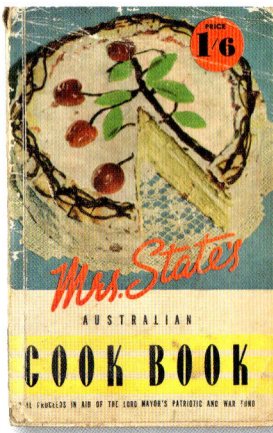

demanding schedule with her ongoing radio commitments and going home every night to cook dinner for her husband, Ken.

The Cook's Handbook also contained recipes provided by New South Wales Department of Technical Education cookery expert Maureen Simpson, as well as another high-profile Sydney woman, who was praised two decades earlier for a similar juggling act. In 1928, Doris State became the first person to graduate with a Bachelor in Domestic Science from the University of Sydney. She was presented with a unique bronze medal struck to celebrate her achievement, which involved three years of theoretical study and two further years' practical work at a technical college.

Doris put her skills to use as the head of a new home management bureau set up in the mid-1930s by the Sydney County Council, responsible for supplying electricity in Sydney. Her duties included presenting practical courses in cooking with electricity, dietetics and home management, giving demonstrations and presenting a regular domestic science segment on radio station 2GB. Doris's sessions proved popular, no doubt enhanced by her skills as an amateur actress and singer—she was a leading light in the Sydney Players Club and, by the age of eighteen, had won 60 medals for her singing and elocution at various eisteddfods.

In the early 1940s, under the auspices of the council, Doris compiled a recipe book that was way ahead of its time, to raise money for the Lord Mayor's Patriotic and War Fund. *Mrs State's Australian Cook Book* featured full-colour plates of the finished dishes in an era when cookbooks rarely had any illustrations at all, let alone high-quality images of food artfully arranged on doilies, with embellishments of curly-leaf parsley.

Another bestseller for the crippled children's society, was a much more modest affair. The *Biscuit Cook Book* was just 31 pages, had a plain blue-and-white cover, and no images of any kind. Also known as the *'Forget-me-not' Biscuit Cook Book*, it was released in March 1958 by the society's Central Council of the Women's Auxiliaries.

The idea was proposed by Miss Margaret Crawford, a well-known and respected auxiliary member who also sat on the board of directors for the Central Council. She thought that it might be a good way of generating some publicity for the society as well as raising money.

The central council agreed, and decided to take it on without seeking any financial support from the society. Instead they sought donations and ran a Christmas raffle to defray the production costs. Meanwhile, circulars were

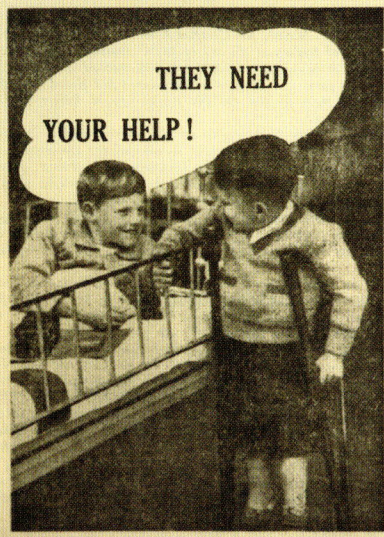

The COOK'S HANDBOOK

Recipes by . . .

Mrs. Doris State, B.Sc., Dom.Sc., Maureen Simpson, Cookery Expert and holder of Certificate for Hotel and Restaurant Cooking of the N.S.W. Department of Technical Education with a foreword by . . .

DEL CARTWRIGHT, Radio and TV Personality and Home Economist.

Del Cartwright

comes to your home
by radio and television

12 BELLEVUE AVENUE, GREENWICH · TEL. JF 3846

THEY NEED YOUR HELP!

Dear Readers,

"The Cook's Handbook" has been designed as a practical help to every housewife. It is the cook book you will want to keep ever at hand.

Apart from the fact that the outright proceeds of the sale of this book will aid the little charges in the care of The N.S.W. Society for Crippled Children, I do most sincerely recommend all the recipes and advice contained in this book.

"The Cook's Handbook" is a tribute to the committee who worked to plan its success and deserves a place in every kitchen.

Del Cartwright

Del Cartwright.

Total proceeds from the sale of this book to The Teamakers' Club which assists The N.S.W. Society for Crippled Children, 136 Chalmers Street, Telephone MX 4392, from whom further copies can be obtained.

THE TEAMAKERS' CLUB

Price **6/6**

The New South Wales Society for Crippled Children

HOUSEHOLD BOOK

1940 Edition

Sold to Aid Funds for the New South Wales Society for Crippled Children.

6d.

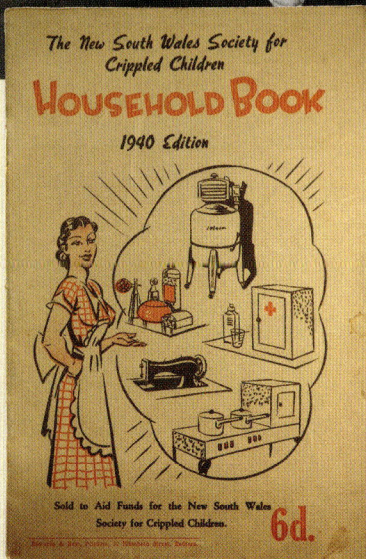

Clockwise from top left: Image from an earlier book published by the NSW Society for Crippled Children, *The Household Book*, 1940 (State Library of NSW); *The Cook's Handbook* title page, c. 1950s (Barr Smith Library, University of Adelaide); society president, Sir Kenneth Coles, presenting life membership to Margaret Crawford (courtesy Northcott); *The Household Book*, 1940; Del Cartwright presenting a cheque to Sir Kenneth for funds raised by the Teamakers' Club, with Mr G.M. Sparkes, Commissioner of the Ceylon Tea Bureau in Sydney, and club patroness Miss Doris Fitton, OBE (courtesy Northcott).

sent out to the network of auxiliaries across New South Wales asking for well-tested biscuit recipes, with Miss Crawford rounding up many more.

Appropriately enough, the book was launched at a special morning tea at the Rex Hotel in Kings Cross. More than 300 auxiliary members and friends enjoyed a program featuring well-known television and radio personalities of the day, and every woman was presented with a small packet of biscuits to celebrate.

Priced at just two shillings, the little cookbook sold like hot cakes. Within three weeks, 10,000 copies had been distributed, including a second edition rushed into print to meet demand. By the end of the financial year, 24,000 copies had sold. By June 1959, sales had topped 35,000.

The money raised by both ventures would have made a significant difference to the society, which was established by the Rotary Club of Sydney in 1929 in response to a polio epidemic. By the end of the 1950s, it was operating three hospitals, three special schools, two social clubs for disabled teenagers, a child-minding centre and six regional diagnostic clinics. Today the organisation is known as The Northcott Society. Almost one thousand staff provide services to more than 13,500 people with disability, as well as their families and carers.

~~~~~~~~~~~~~~~~~~~~~~~~~~~~~~~~~~~~~

Burnt butter biscuits   MAKES ABOUT 25 BISCUITS

This very simple recipe from the Biscuit Cook Book *produces beautiful, rich buttery biscuits best enjoyed with a cuppa. Del and the Teamakers would definitely have approved.*

INGREDIENTS

120 g reduced-salt butter

120 g caster sugar

1 egg, lightly beaten

1 teaspoon natural vanilla extract

150 g (1 cup) self-raising flour

25 blanched whole almonds (approximately)

METHOD

Preheat the oven to moderate (180°C). Line a baking tray with baking paper.

Melt the butter in a large saucepan over medium–low heat, until brown, stirring occasionally. Remove from the heat and allow to cool.

Pour the butter into a mixing bowl. Beat in the sugar, then the egg until the mixture thickens. Stir in the vanilla, then mix in the flour, using a knife, to form a soft dough.

Place small rolled teaspoonfuls of mixture on the baking tray, at least 5 cm apart. Lightly press an almond on the top of each. Bake for 8–10 minutes, until golden.

Leave the biscuits to cool on the tray for a few minutes, before moving them to a wire rack to cool completely.

LIZ'S TIPS

- Pay close attention to the butter as there is a very fine line between rich brown and burnt to the point of bitterness. Remove the butter from the heat as soon as it starts to change colour.

- The butter should be cool, not cold. You don't want it to solidify.

- These biscuits spread considerably during cooking. Don't use too much mixture and allow plenty of space between them. You don't need to flatten them — just press the almond lightly into the top so the ball is only slightly depressed.

- The biscuits cook quickly, so keep an eye on them, and turn the tray part-way through cooking time if one side starts to cook faster than the other.

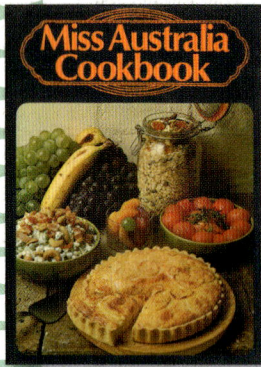

COOKING *with* MISS AUSTRALIA

Winners of the Miss Australia Quest were expected to look glamorous and carry off wearing an ornate pearl crown, but the 'bevy of beauties' who held the title in its heyday were called on for their cooking skills too.

Not to be confused with the Miss Universe or Miss World competitions, the Miss Australia Quest was one of Australia's most successful charity events, raising more than $90 million in 46 years to support people with cerebral palsy. Although there had been national beauty contests before, the version of the quest most people remember began in 1954, when the Australian arm of an American lingerie manufacturer teamed up with the Australian Cerebral Palsy Association.

Every year hundreds of entrants devoted their energies to raising money for what were then known as 'spastic centres', with the proceeds gathered in each state going to the local centre. Finalists were then chosen to represent each state. While appearance was definitely a factor, judges were also looking for 'typical intelligent Australian girls', willing to work hard on behalf of people with cerebral palsy, and who would make ideal ambassadors for their country. Separate Miss Australia Charity Queen titles were also given to the women who raised the most money.

By the 1960s, the quest had become a phenomenon. The final was broadcast nationally on television, and thousands of people gathered in the winner's hometown to greet them afterwards, stopping traffic with street parades, bands and marching girls as the newly crowned titleholder glided past in a luxury car, smiling and waving to the crowds.

Accompanied by chaperones, the Miss Australias then travelled the world promoting their country and raising awareness about cerebral palsy. Along the way they attended glittering social occasions, meeting the rich and famous, such as Prince Charles, Pope John Paul II, United States President Lyndon Johnson, and stars of sport and screen. Many went on to enjoy careers in television and marry high-profile men, such as 1960 winner Rosemary Fenton, from Lord Howe Island, who married National Party politician and federal government minister Ian Sinclair.

A future cookbook author in her own right, Rosemary, and 1959 title-holder Joan Stanbury, who married television journalist Mike Willesee, were among a small group of former Miss Australias who decided in the late 1960s to publish a fundraising cookbook built around the quest. Still actively raising money for the Spastic Centre of New South Wales, the women were concerned that they were always reaching out to the same people for money. 'So we hit on a new idea,' Rosemary told *The Canberra Times* in June 1970.

Released in 1971, the *Miss Australia Cookbook* was edited by Elizabeth Sewell and published by Paul Hamlyn Pty Ltd in Sydney, which donated its profits. Each section featured recipes provided by one of fourteen winners, beginning with the inaugural title-holder, Shirley Bliss, from Narrandera in New South Wales. Shirley chose a gourmet theme, focusing on dishes that she liked to serve at formal dinner parties. Capturing French-influenced food trends popular in Australia during the 1970s, the selection included chateaubriand and crayfish en brochette.

Queenslander Helen Wood, who was crowned by Hollywood legend Elizabeth Taylor in 1957, reflected her origins with food featuring tropical ingredients, such as mango mousse and banana crepes. The 1961 winner, Tania Verstak, drew on her cultural heritage to profile Russian recipes. The first naturalised Australian to win the title, Tania was born in China to Russian parents.

Bachelor girl cooking was the theme selected by Sue Gallie. Fluent in Italian and French, Sue was working as a translator for a Sydney bank when she won the title in 1966. 'For me, "bachelor girl cooking" is one piece of grilled steak and one packet of frozen peas cooked according to the directions on the packet,' Sue wrote. 'Now that isn't cookbook stuff. The recipes I've chosen are my most successful and are also the ones that basically suit my ideas on entertaining. They require no lengthy preparation and many can be prepared well in advance . . . Another thing, they seem to work. If they work for me they'll work for anyone!'

Wiener schnitzel

Opposite: The original recipe image from the *Miss Australia Cookbook*.

INGREDIENTS

4 veal schnitzel steaks

2 heaped tablespoons plain flour

½ teaspoon salt

¼ teaspoon freshly ground black pepper

1 egg, lightly beaten

150 g (1½ cups) dried breadcrumbs (approximately)

125 ml (½ cup) olive oil

60 g butter

1 lemon, sliced

4 black olives

4 anchovy fillets

1 hard-boiled egg, chopped

Marinade:

2 tablespoons vinegar

2 tablespoons tomato sauce

1 teaspoon Worcestershire sauce

1 garlic clove, crushed

juice of 1 lemon

This is one of Sue Gallie's 'bachelor girl' recipes. A perennial favourite in Australia, schnitzels are often bought pre-coated, but the end result is nowhere near as pleasing as schnitzels freshly made at home. This version is different from traditional recipes, in that the meat is marinated before being coated. You don't need to add the suggested garnishes, but they will transport you right back to the 1970s if you want the full experience.

METHOD

To make the marinade, mix all the ingredients together thoroughly. Coat the steaks with the marinade, cover with plastic wrap and refrigerate for 1 hour.

Combine the flour, salt and pepper in a shallow bowl or on a large plate. Remove the meat from the marinade. Dip each steak into the seasoned flour, making sure it is coated evenly. Gently shake off any excess flour and then dip the steak in the beaten egg. Let any excess egg drip off the steak and then coat with the breadcrumbs, using your fingers to gently pat the breadcrumbs down.

Heat the oil and butter in a large, heavy-based frying pan. Cook the schnitzels in batches over medium–high heat for 4–5 minutes each side, until golden brown.

To serve, garnish each schnitzel with a slice of lemon placed in the centre, topped with a black olive wrapped in an anchovy fillet. Decorate with lines of finely chopped egg.

LIZ'S TIPS

- If you can't buy uncoated schnitzel steaks, look for veal or yearling topside, and use a meat mallet to beat the veal until it is about 5 mm thick.
- Put the coating ingredients in shallow containers, then set them up in a line so you can work smoothly through the process.
- Some cooks recommend adding a splash of water or milk to the beaten egg to create an egg wash.
- You can purchase traditional fine dried breadcrumbs, or try panko breadcrumbs, which have a different, lighter texture, absorb less oil and produce a crisper end result.
- Coat and crumb the schnitzels just before cooking, or the crumb mixture will become soggy.

- Cooktops and pans vary, so you may need to experiment a little with how you cook the schnitzels. It's important that the oil and butter are the right temperature before you start. Too hot and the breadcrumbs will burn before the meat is cooked, and too low and they will absorb too much oil. To test whether the oil is hot enough, drop in a few breadcrumbs to see if they start to bubble.
- Sue suggests serving the schnitzels with potato salad and red cabbage.

Right: Sue Gallie pictured visiting the Sydney Opera House under construction, on the front cover of a Coca-Cola company magazine, 1966. (Trademarks of The Coca-Cola Company are used with permission. The Coca-Cola Company is not the producer of this guide, nor does it endorse the contents.)

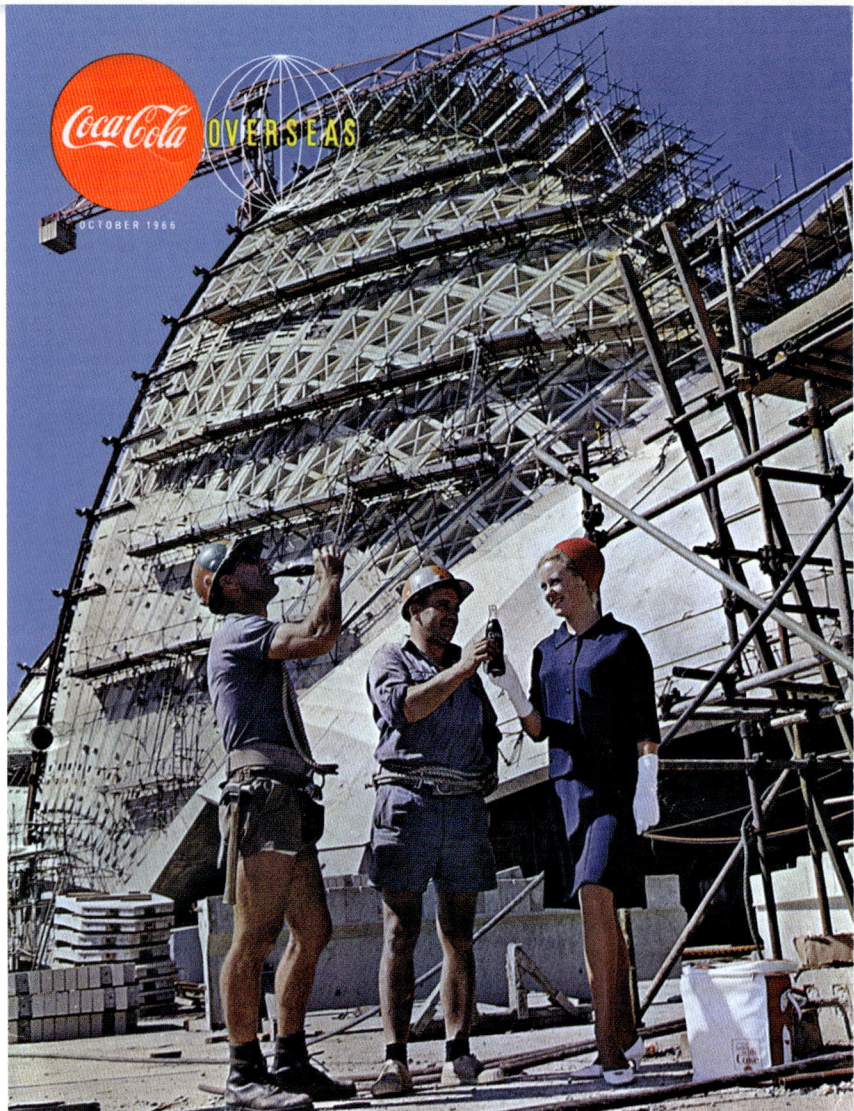

SPAM SPAM SPAM, WONDERFUL SPAM

Monty Python fans the world over treasure the comedy troupe's tribute to Spam—a tinned, pre-cooked meat product, which has been in production for more than 80 years. Launched onto the American market in 1937, it famously powered the Allied forces through the Second World War, when it was jokingly referred to as 'ham that didn't pass its physical'. But the troops and ration-starved families across Europe were pleased to have it. By the time Monty Python put together its famous skit and accompanying song in 1970, two billion cans had been produced. The total passed eight billion in 2012.

None of which goes to explain why it's featured in *Recipes with Wine!*, one of a series of at least twenty cookbooks published around the 1970s to raise funds for what was then known as the St George School for Crippled Children in Sydney. Along with a prominent advertisement for Spam, the book includes several 'modern' recipes, including Braised spam with tomato and garlic sauce, Sauteed escalopes of spam with marsala sauce and, the pièce de résistance, Spam à la King.

It's not the only oddity about some of the St George books. Recipe book No. 20, *The European Adventure*, features recipes from India and Mexico, and *Ways with … Cheese*, a bargain at 30 cents, includes more than one recipe without cheese, and a full-page advertisement for margarine.

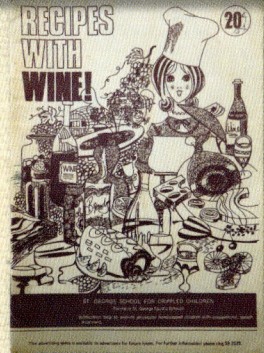

Above: *Recipes with Wine!*, c. 1970s (State Library of NSW). Below: A Spam label from 1969 (courtesy Hormel Foods Corporation).

RECIPES

from the

FAMOUS

A *Royal* MYSTERY

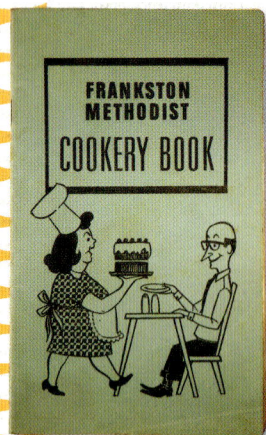

One of the more mysterious recipes that pops up frequently in community cookbooks produced during the 1960s is the Queen's Cake, also sometimes labelled the Queen Mother's Cake.

It was usually published alongside brief text explaining that the recipe was a favourite of either Queen Elizabeth II, or her mother, depending on the version, and the only cake the Queen ever made herself. It always came with a warning: 'It must not be passed on—but sold only for Charity'.

The trouble is that it's doubtful the recipe has anything to do with the Royal Family. Trying to solve the mystery more than twenty years ago, two highly acclaimed food writers from Canada, where a similar version remains popular, went to the trouble of contacting Buckingham Palace. According to *A Century of Canadian Home Cooking*, Carol Ferguson and Margaret Fraser were told by the Queen Mother's Lady-in-Waiting: 'I fear I have to tell you that, although we have known about this recipe for many years, it did not originate from either Buckingham Palace or Clarence House [the late Queen Mother's London home]'.

Even if it did, it would be untrue that the recipe was the only cake the Queen has ever made, if Australian newspaper reports in the 1930s are anything to go by. As she approached her teenage years, a series of stories applauded her efforts in the kitchen. Explaining that the young princess had inherited her mother's cooking skills, one report in 1939 noted that Princess Elizabeth spent several hours a week practising in the kitchens at Buckingham Palace under expert instruction from the palace chefs.

More interested in traditional baking than 'fancy' cooking, she had learned how to make 'homely cakes and scones of the kind which are baked daily in Scottish farmhouses'. She even baked cakes for family afternoon teas and, the year before, had made Christmas puddings as gifts, which were delivered to several friends by royal messenger.

The Queen's Cake

The recipe published in Australian community cookbooks is a simple cake made using dates and walnuts, topped with a hot glaze made with brown sugar and cream. In Canadian versions the boiled icing has morphed into a 'broiled' topping, with the cake being returned to the oven once it is iced, and coconut replacing the walnuts. I much prefer the Australian version, which is a sort of cake rendition of sticky date pudding. This recipe comes from the Frankston Methodist Cookery Book, published in about 1960, to raise money for a building fund.

Above: Princess Anne, the Princess Royal, and Sophie, Countess of Wessex, look on as Queen Elizabeth II cuts a cake at the Centenary Annual Meeting of the National Federation of Women's Institutes at the Royal Albert Hall in London on 4 June 2015. This event celebrated 100 years of the Women's Institute in Britain (image by Chris Jackson, WPA Pool/ Getty Images). Opposite: *Frankston Methodist Cookery Book*, c. 1960 (State Library of Victoria).

INGREDIENTS

160 g (1 cup) pitted dates, roughly chopped

250 ml (1 cup) boiling water

1 teaspoon bicarbonate of soda

220 g (1 cup) caster sugar

125 g butter, softened

1 egg

1 teaspoon natural vanilla extract

225 g (1½ cups) plain flour

1 teaspoon baking powder

½ teaspoon salt

30 g (¼ cup) chopped or crumbed walnuts, plus 2 tablespoons extra for decorating

Icing:

3 tablespoons dark brown sugar

2 tablespoons cream

20 g butter

METHOD

Preheat the oven to moderate (180°C). Grease and line the bottom of a shallow 20 cm square cake pan.

Put the dates in a small bowl, add the boiling water and stir in the bicarbonate of soda.

In a separate large bowl, cream the sugar and butter until light and fluffy. Add the egg and vanilla and beat until combined.

Sift in together the flour, baking powder and salt. Add the date mixture and the walnuts and stir until thoroughly combined. Pour the batter into the cake pan and bake for 40 minutes, until a thin skewer comes away clean when inserted into the middle of the cake.

To make the icing, put the sugar, cream and butter in a small saucepan. Set over low heat and stir until the sugar is melted. Bring gently to the boil and simmer for about 2 minutes, until thick and glossy.

While the icing is simmering, remove the hot cake from the pan and set it on a wire rack. When the icing is ready, spread it over the top of the cake, and scatter with the extra chopped walnuts.

LIZ' TIPS

- Don't leave out the salt — it is needed to balance the sweetness of the sugar and dried fruit.
- Start making the icing a few minutes before the cake is ready to take from the oven.
- Let the topping trickle down the side of the cake. Place the wire rack over a tray or a sheet of baking paper to catch the drips.
- This cake makes an ideal dessert, while still warm, served with cream.

Right: Back cover illustration from the *Frankston Methodist Cookery Book*, c. 1960. Opposite: *Star Spangled Cooking*, 1962.

COOKING *with the* WHITE HOUSE

When an American women's club based in Sydney put together its second cookbook in 1968, they pulled out all the stops. *More Star Spangled Cooking* features recipes from a United States president, and not one, not two, not even three, but four past, present and future First Ladies—Jackie Kennedy, Lady Bird Johnson, Pat Nixon and Nancy Reagan.

The fascinating cookbook was assembled in 1968 by the American Women's Club of Sydney. The club was established in September 1946 to welcome American women who had recently moved to Sydney and help link them up with other expats. It also set out to enhance relationships between Australia and the United States.

The organisation's roots lay in the First World War, when a group of American women formed what was known as the American Australian League of Help, to contribute to the war effort. Members met every day and held stalls where they sold handicrafts and American-style candies and cakes, often raising as much as £500 through a single stall.

There was a brief pause after the war because of the Spanish flu pandemic that killed about 12,500 Australians, with government authorities discouraging public gatherings to limit the contagion. When it was over, the group changed its name to the American Women's Circle and refocused its fundraising efforts to support charities, such as the Crown Street and St Margaret's women's hospitals, a hostel for the deaf and dumb, and a vaccination program immunising children in need against diphtheria. The women met monthly, getting to know new arrivals while they stitched baby clothes.

The group's efforts shifted once again to supporting the war effort when the United States entered the Second World War, after the Japanese attacked Pearl Harbor in December 1941. Australia became the base of operations for the south-west Pacific, and thousands of American servicemen and women poured into the country.

To provide them with a taste of home while on leave, an American Centre was established in Sydney in March 1942. It offered accommodation, entertainment, and food reminiscent of home, cooked by members of the Women's Circle as well as other volunteer workers. By the end of the war in October 1945, they had dished out more than a million meals.

With yet another war over, the women started thinking about forming a more permanent club for American women living in Australia. Their numbers were increasing, with more American companies sending over representatives to set up businesses. Such a club would help their wives to settle in and feel less lonely. The club met over tea on the first Wednesday of every month, at the Pickwick Club, until the venue became too small to cope. The gatherings later switched to formal luncheons with guest speakers, held at venues such as the Mark Foy's department store dining room and the Menzies Hotel.

Realising that more casual occasions would provide greater opportunity for women to get to know each other, in 1957 the club started holding informal luncheons once a month in members' homes. People brought their own sandwiches, then shared coffee and luscious cakes. These events not only created lasting friendships, but inevitably led to the women exchanging recipes.

The experience triggered the idea of creating a cookbook of favourites to raise money for Sydney charities. Published in 1962, *Star Spangled Cooking* was edited by Ann Williams Clark. A high-profile society hostess in Sydney, Ann was a former US Army nurse from Pennsylvania, who spent three years as a prisoner of the Japanese after being captured in the Philippines during the Second World War. She came to Australia in the late 1950s with her then husband, Rush, when he was appointed as the Australian director of Pan American Airways and stayed after they divorced some years later. Respected for her passionate love of gardening, she became well known for her contribution to the Garden Clubs of Australia, which still present a medallion for outstanding service in her honour.

Under Ann's guidance, the cookbook was so successful that a second followed six years later, under the auspices of The American Society, which leveraged its extensive contacts in political, diplomatic and business circles to gather up contributions with impressive credentials.

Current First Lady, Lady Bird Johnson, reflected her Texan roots by providing Mexican-influenced recipes for her favourite chilli and an hors d'oeuvre featuring tortilla (corn) chips and jalapeño peppers. Pat Nixon, whose husband would begin his notorious presidency the following year, gave a delicious double-layered chocolate cake recipe, and Nancy Reagan, wife of the future 40th president, proposed an elegant chocolate souffle. Five-star general and 34th president, Dwight D. Eisenhower, was no doubt drawing on his military life when he submitted an old-fashioned beef stew recipe, designed to feed 60 people.

Outside the political sphere, there were also recipes from American author Pearl S. Buck, famous crooner Bing Crosby and Broadway star Mary Martin. Some famous Australians were asked to contribute too, including the wives of two prime ministers, Dame Zara Holt and Dame Pattie Menzies.

Edited by Jo Rothenberger, whose husband was a chemical engineer with the Hercules Powder Company, *More Star Spangled Cooking* also provided handy tips explaining American ingredients and terms to Australian cooks. However, one of its most striking features is a series of black-and-white illustrations created by famous Sydney children's book author and illustrator Pixie O'Harris, who donated her time and talent to design the cover and striking section title pages.

Above: Children's book author and illustrator Pixie O'Harris, 1954 (Australian News and Information Services, National Archives of Australia A1200:L17297). Left: An illustration from *More Star Spangled Cooking*, 1968.

New England fish chowder

INGREDIENTS

1 kg haddock (or other firm, white-fleshed fish)

500 ml (2 cups) water

100 g speck or thick-cut bacon, diced

2 onions, thinly sliced

4 large potatoes, cut into about 1 cm dice

140 g (1 cup) finely chopped celery

1 dried bay leaf, crumbled

1 teaspoon salt

freshly ground black pepper

250 ml (1 cup) boiling water (approximately)

500 ml (2 cups) full-cream milk

30 g butter

This soup recipe was submitted by perhaps the most famous First Lady of all, Jacqueline Kennedy. It was said to be a favourite of her husband, President John F. Kennedy, who was assassinated five years before the cookbook was published. JFK was born in Massachusetts, which is part of the New England region on the eastern coast of the United States, where this is a signature dish, reflecting the importance of the local fishing industry.

According to a story published years later in The Boston Globe, *the recipe was sent to a disabled girl, who wrote to the president asking him what he liked to eat. White House staff put it before him with a memo saying, 'Please reply to her. She will be extremely happy. Do not mention anything in the letter about her handicap please!'*

METHOD

Put the haddock in a large saucepan with the water and simmer gently, covered, for 15 minutes. Drain the fish, making sure to reserve the liquid. Remove any bones, cut the fish into 5 cm pieces and set aside.

Sauté the speck in the same saucepan until crisp. Remove the speck from the pan with a slotted spoon and set aside.

Add the onions to the pan, cooking them in the speck fat until they are golden brown. Add the potatoes, celery and bay leaf, and season with salt and pepper.

Measure the fish broth and pour it into the saucepan with enough boiling water to make 750 ml (3 cups). Simmer for 20 minutes, or until the potato is tender. Add the fish, milk and butter and simmer for another 5 minutes.

Serve the chowder sprinkled with the diced speck.

LIZ'S TIPS

- If you can't find any haddock, try ling or snapper.
- The original recipe called for salt pork — I've adapted it to something more recognisable in Australia, and I've also increased the quantity to add more flavour. Avoid trimming away all the fat, as it's essential to the method and flavour of this dish.

- I've changed the original method to add the fish later in the cooking process, so there are some recognisable bite-sized pieces to enjoy.

- The original recipe used twice as much milk. If you prefer a thinner chowder, add more. If you want a thicker, creamier chowder than this version, substitute 250 ml (1 cup) of milk for pure cream. Avoid thickened cream products that contain extra ingredients.

- I prefer this chowder with generous amounts of cracked black pepper, and a small amount of thyme leaves complements the recipe beautifully, or try finely chopped flat-leaf parsley.

Clockwise from top left: United States President John F. Kennedy and Mrs Kennedy arriving in Dallas, Texas, on 22 November 1963, the day he was assassinated (image by Cecil Stoughton); President Kennedy aboard the yacht *Manitou* in Narragansett Bay, Newport, Rhode Island, August 1962 (image by Robert L. Knudsen); President Kennedy with (from left) his brother-in-law, Steve Smith, his niece, Maria Shriver, and his daughter, Caroline, aboard the presidential yacht, *Honey Fitz*, during a cruise near Hyannis Port, Massachusetts, July 1963 (image by Cecil Stoughton). (All images from the White House Photographs collection, John F. Kennedy Presidential Library and Museum, Boston).

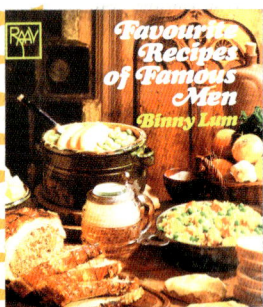

BINNY *and the* FAMOUS MEN

Few community cookbooks have the star power of a retro gem that more than lives up to its name. *Favourite Recipes of Famous Men* features contributions from Hollywood legends, such as Rock Hudson, Roger Moore and Bob Hope, British comedic royalty in the form of Derek Nimmo and Sid James, and musical masters Dave Brubeck, James Last and Val Doonican.

This extraordinary cluster of international talent was made possible because of the book's well-connected author and compiler, Binny Lum. The pioneering broadcaster and television personality, who died in 2012 at the age of 97, hosted the first daytime television program on Channel Nine in Melbourne, and enjoyed a radio career that spanned 50 years. Loved for her relaxed style and open friendly manner, no matter who she was interviewing, Binny managed to secure interviews with a host of famous people, including elusive stars such as Barbra Streisand and Vivien Leigh.

But her greatest coup without question, was an interview with The Beatles during a visit to London in April 1964, ahead of their groundbreaking tour of Australia two months later. 'I don't expect anyone to believe this, but I am actually with The Beatles,' she said at the beginning of the chaotic session, which was broadcast across Australia.

Originally from Adelaide, where she was born in 1915, Binny was the daughter of a respected doctor of traditional Chinese medicine, Lum Yow, and Eleanora Laker. As a child she loved music and dancing, and she flourished at school, winning prizes for poetry and music. She won a scholarship to study at Melbourne's Conservatorium of Music, but her father died so she put her studies aside to find paying work and support the family.

After acting with a suburban theatre company, Binny was offered a part in a drama broadcast by 3XY, beginning her long association with radio. Her career took off in the 1950s when she became co-host of the *Children's Session* on 3KZ, with Norman Swain. In 1957, a year after the first public Australian television broadcast, she took on hosting *Thursday at One* on Channel Nine.

Her main opportunity to interview famous figures came with an afternoon program on 3XY, which had a magazine format that allowed time for chatty conversations. Using a reel-to-reel tape recorder, she pre-recorded interviews with celebrities visiting Melbourne, including American entertainer

Fred Astaire, when he was in town in 1959 to film *On the Beach*, Russian ballet dancer Rudolf Nureyev, and American jazz musician Dave Brubeck, who she came to know quite well, even having him home for dinner.

Over a period of several years in the 1970s, Binny Lum harnessed her access to the stars to compile a cookbook for the Rheumatism and Arthritis Association of Victoria. *Favourite Recipes of Famous Men* features 104 food and drink recipes donated by both international and Australian identities, accompanied by brief biographies and explanations of how Binny sourced the recipes. In an obituary written for *The Age* after she died in November 2012, daughter Sharon Terry recalled Binny telling the family: 'Listen for the phone while I'm out—it could be Rock Hudson or Roger Moore'.

Binny was particularly impressed with American comedian and actor Bob Hope, who sent back his favourite lemon meringue pie recipe immediately after receiving a letter asking for a contribution. His reply was accompanied by a personal note thanking Binny for thinking of him, and wishing the book well. Given the star's status, she found the response refreshing.

Welsh singer and member of The Goons, Harry Secombe, chose Welsh cakes because he wanted people to enjoy something from his beloved homeland. American cookbook author and restaurant critic Robert Carrier contributed a specially devised chocolate ice cream recipe. South Australian premier and noted cook, Don Dunstan, gave a sophisticated paté recipe, which Binny thought reflected his up-to-date fashion image.

Left: Binny Lum with The Beatles, minus Paul McCartney, in London, April 1964 (courtesy Sharon Terry). Opposite: *Favourite Recipes of Famous Men*, 1975. (© MOVE muscle, bone & joint health).

Hot on the heels of the success of *The Adventures of Barry McKenzie*, producer and now well-known broadcaster and commentator, Phillip Adams, supplied a humorous recipe for Bazza beef, which involved cooking slabs of rump steak over an open fire, on a shovel, smothered in a sauce made with a generous amount of Foster's lager. Cricketing legend Sir Donald Bradman favoured devilled steak, while popular sports commentator and Collingwood premiership captain, Lou Richards, cheekily provided a recipe for Chicken à la Magpie.

The contribution from Barossa Valley winemaker Cyril Henschke was more a hint than a recipe: 'Next time you plan a dinner party and are featuring soup, put a teaspoon of whatever wine you are serving in each bowl. It enhances the flavour and gets the conversation away to a good start.'

A chilled tomato soup from British actor and comedian Derek Nimmo, came with a funny story explaining how he had made it on live television for the BBC, with the head chef from the Savoy Hotel standing over him. 'Everything went wrong as I was so thrown by his horribly beady eye [that] I was flustered, and told the viewers that it was one teaspoon of sugar and one tablespoon of salt instead of the other way round. My wife, who was watching, rang up the studio to correct me and I had to suffer, in front of 12 million people, the humiliation of the studio manager handing me a note with the correction upon it.'

Favourite Recipes of Famous Men was launched in 1975 at the Southern Cross Hotel, an icon of American style, which cost more than £5 million to build. Promoted as the largest hotel in the Southern Hemisphere and Australia's first international hotel when it opened in the early 1960s, it was the accommodation of choice for many celebrities, including Binny's new friends, The Beatles. Doing the honours at the book launch were Lou Richards, and his well-known sparring partner for many years, on and off the field, Jack Dyer, who also contributed a recipe.

'Binny was indeed a very good cook, but a self-taught one, a case of "have-to" as her mother became ill and her younger brother and sister were still at school,' Sharon recalls. 'She was a great believer in healthy eating, so her meals were always balanced and nutritious.'

Barbecued bourbon steak

SERVES 4

I'm shamelessly choosing to feature this recipe because, as a teenager, I had a huge crush on Rock Hudson, who was enjoying a second career on television as the star of McMillian & Wife. *During a hectic 24-hour visit to Melbourne to present at the 1972 Logie Awards, Hudson not only agreed to share a recipe, but put some effort into coming up with something he thought Australians would enjoy. The very simple recipe combines bourbon and barbecuing. What's not to like?*

INGREDIENTS

4 steaks, quality cut

4 tablespoons soy sauce

2 tablespoons bourbon

2 garlic cloves, crushed

METHOD

Place the meat in a large shallow dish.

Combine the soy sauce, bourbon and garlic and pour over the steaks. Cover with plastic wrap and place in the fridge for at least 2 hours.

Barbecue the steaks to your liking.

LIZ'S TIPS

- Rock Hudson left the quantity of garlic up to individual preference. Two cloves in this amount of marinade produces a relatively mild flavour, so you might like to add more.

- You do not need to season the steaks with salt — there is enough in the soy sauce. But you might like to add some freshly ground black pepper.

Above: An autographed image of Hollywood actor Rock Hudson from *Favourite Recipes of Famous Men*. Left: Illustration from *The Esk Valley Cookery Book*, 13th edition.

"Crisp and sweet, that's NICE!"

There's a simple elegance about Nice that sets them apart as very special biscuits for you. Crunchy, semi-shortbread... sprinkled with sparkling sugar...just right with tea or coffee!

Arnott's FAMOUS Biscuits

There is no Substitute for Quality

VARIETY *with* HEART

It is a bit hard to imagine two people less alike. One was a knocka-bout bloke who had worked as a rigger, most often seen in shorts, steel-capped boots and cut-off shirts. The other was closely related to British royalty; a man who had served as the last viceroy of India and held the highest rank in the British navy, usually resplendent in full regalia at formal occasions.

Australian comedian Paul Hogan and Lord Louis Mountbatten came together one memorable night in 1975 to help raise money for the newly estab-lished Australian chapter of the Variety Club. As inaugural chairman, Hogan was master of ceremonies for the evening, and the late Mountbatten was guest of honour. The two men traded repartee throughout the dinner at the Sebel Townhouse in Sydney, delighting a large gathering of the rich and famous, who responded by donating more than $100,000 to the cause.

Known today as Variety—the Children's Charity, the organisation had a fairytale beginning. On Christmas Eve in 1928, a month-old baby girl was left on a theatre seat in Pittsburgh, Pennsylvania. Pinned to her clothing was a note that read: 'Please take care of my baby. Her name is Catherine. I can no longer take care of her. I have eight others. My husband is out of work. She was born on Thanksgiving Day. I have always heard of the goodness of show business people and pray to God that you will look out for her.'

The plea was heard by a group of eleven men affiliated with the entertain-ment industry, who were members of a social club called Variety, because its members came from the world of variety theatre and its many different kinds of performing acts. The men agreed to pay for the child's support and edu-cation. Their good deed hit the front pages of newspapers across the United States, and they were soon being contacted by people who wanted to join the club and help. Taking to heart the mother's faith in their goodness, they spread their efforts to support other underprivileged children.

The concept came to Australia in 1975 after television producer, Reg Watson, and his friend and business associate, Royce Smeal, attended a Variety Club of Great Britain luncheon in London. Back in Australia they con-tacted celebrities they knew to help set up a local version of the children's charity. Recognising that his friend Paul Hogan would be able to attract the

Left: Australian comedian Paul
Hogan, who was Variety's first
Chief Barker in Australia (courtesy
Variety—the Children's Charity).
Opposite: *Variety Club Entertainers'
Cookbook*, 1983.

necessary publicity and goodwill to get the idea off the ground, Reg approached and asked him to be Chief Barker, the Variety term for chairman. It turned out to be a magic mix, with the comedian proving extremely popular with the children the charity supported, as well as the media and the general public.

Today Variety helps thousands of children across Australia who are sick, disadvantaged or have special needs and can't access government assistance. In 2016, almost $10 million was given out in grants, directly benefiting more than 100,000 children. The money was raised through private and corporate donations, and high-profile events such as car rallies, or bashes, gala dinners and lunches, cycle rides and fun runs.

In 1983, the sugar company CSR came to the party when it produced the *Variety Club Entertainers' Cookbook*. To acquire the small cookbook, people had to buy CSR products and send in vouchers found on the packets. It not only raised awareness, but CSR gave a percentage of the takings from its sales to the charity's Add a Little Variety fundraising program.

The book features contributions from some of Australia's best-known entertainment, media and sports personalities of the day, such as vivacious daytime television star Jeanne Little; television show hosts Tony Barber,

Daryl Somers, Ernie Sigley and Mike Walsh; singers Col Joye and Kamahl; actors John Meillon, Tony Bonner, Lorraine Bayly and Paul Cronin; cricketers Rod Marsh and Dennis Lillee, long-distance runner Cliff Young and his counterpart in the water, Des Renford.

Melbourne radio host Derryn Hinch cheekily suggested chicken souffle because 'you've got to get a rise out of something', and television legend Bert Newton put forward a chilled pumpkin soup 'ideal for lazy summer weekends'. Future Sydney Festival artistic director Leo Schofield opted for Mushrooms Florentine as the perfect after-theatre supper, and singer and comedic actor Barry Crocker submitted a curried chicken dish, with a note explaining that he felt it was his duty to eat as much curry as possible because his friend Kamahl, a singer born in Malaysia, didn't like it. *Bandstand* host and news presenter, Brian Henderson, proposed a raisin ice cream made with rum, suggesting people just drink the rum if it proved too difficult.

Below: Barry Crocker's curried chicken recipe as it appears in the cookbook. Opposite: Stuart Wagstaff's personal endorsement of his fish recipe, and the actor test-driving a car during a visit to Motorama car yard, Perth, 1972 (State Library of WA, 347439PD).

24

Barry Crocker's Curried Chicken

1½ kg chicken pieces
¾ cup honey
1 tablespoon curry powder
2 cm piece fresh ginger, grated
1 clove garlic, crushed
Salt, pepper
2 teaspoons dry mustard
2 tablespoons cooking oil
6 shallots, sliced diagonally for garnish

1. Combine the honey, curry powder, ginger, seasonings and oil. 2. Pour over the chicken pieces placed in 1 layer in a shallow casserole dish. 3. Cover and bake in a moderate oven until cooked, 45-60 minutes, turning once. Add the shallots. 4. Leave the cover off for the last 5 minutes so that chicken gets nicely glazed. Serve with mango chutney and rice.

Serves 4

As a boy one of my favourite films was 'GUNGA DIN' — need I say more - Also I feel it is my duty to eat as much 'CURRIED CHICKEN' as possible - cause I found out that KAMAHL doesn't like curries; one night when we dined together, I had to eat his as well. We often dine together, and I always order — CURRIED CHICKEN

BARRY

Fish with ginger sauce

SERVES 4

Several recipes in the book come from Variety stalwart Stuart Wagstaff. The ever-charming English-born stage actor came to Australia in the 1950s and built a career in theatre and television. In 1998, Wagstaff was made a Member of the Order of Australia for his service to the community, including his phil-anthropic work with Variety. He died in 2015, aged 90.

INGREDIENTS

4 whole fish (snapper, bream or other white-fleshed fish), weighing about 500 g each

250 ml (1 cup) water

salt

freshly ground black pepper

2 tablespoons oil

6 cm piece of fresh ginger, grated

10 spring onions, thinly sliced diagonally

2 tablespoons soy sauce

METHOD

Preheat the oven to moderate (180°C). Lightly oil a baking dish large enough to contain all the fish in one layer, without overlapping.

Place the fish in the baking dish and pour in the water. Season to taste with salt and pepper. Cover tightly with foil and bake for about 25 minutes, until tender.

When the fish is almost cooked, put the oil in a small saucepan over medium heat. Add the ginger and spring onions, stirring for a few minutes, then stir in the soy sauce.

Remove the fish from the oven, drain and place on a serving plate. Pour over the sauce and serve immediately.

LIZ'S TIPS

- Be careful not to overcook the fish. Remember that once out of the oven, the fish will continue to cook for another minute or two. When cooked, it should be firm but not flaking.
- Serve with a light Asian-style salad.

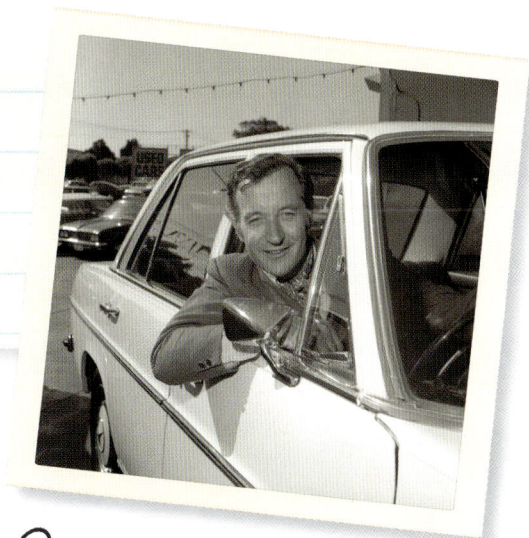

A beautiful tasty, but not heavy, dish

Stuart Wagstaff

IN AID OF THE
HOBART FREE KINDERGARTEN
ASSOCIATION

RECIPES *for the* UNDER-PRIVILEGED

The GREAT CREAM PUFF DILEMMA

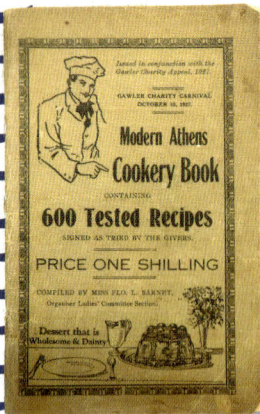

Florence Barnet and her brother William must have wondered what they had gotten themselves into, when they agreed to collaborate on producing a cookbook for Gawler's annual charity carnival in 1927.

William managed the printing section of the South Australian town's curiously named *Bunyip* newspaper, which the family owned for 140 years, and his sister was very active in the community as a charity worker. As head of the ladies committee, Florence oversaw the book's compilation with assistance from another volunteer, Miss Laura Farrelly, and the *Bunyip* offered to print it free of charge. People who contributed recipes were asked to commit to purchasing a copy for a shilling, with another 1000 copies to be made available to the general public at the same price.

Within a few weeks of the call going out, Florence and Laura were inundated. The intention was to publish 500 recipes but, well before submissions were due to close, they had received almost one thousand. Among them were no fewer than 26 versions for cream puffs. A story in the *Bunyip* explained that the task had assumed a stage of such magnitude that the 'harassed' printer could not cope with the scale of production required to print every submission.

Things did not get any easier. The *Bunyip* was flooded with orders from far-flung corners of the state, even before the book was printed, with 600 recipes squeezed into 64 pages. A special stall run by Laura at the carnival quickly ran out of stock, selling more than 500 copies in just a few hours.

William offered to print a second edition, but it wasn't enough. Within days the presses were running again to produce a third, which the over-stretched *Bunyip* warned would be the last. It wasn't—a fourth edition appeared in 1935.

Footnote: In an editorial decision that today's readers might find highly misleading, the publication was named the *Modern Athens Cookery Book*. There was not a single Greek recipe to be found inside the covers. The title was inspired by a soubriquet given to Gawler in the 1800s because of the town's 'civic vigour' and 'high intellectual standing', reflecting the reputation of ancient Athens.

Opposite: *Modern Athens Cookery Book*, 1927 (State Library of SA). Clockwise from top: Decorated vehicles parade along Murray Street in Gawler, c. 1925; advertisement from the *Modern Athens Cookery Book*; an illustration of the *Bunyip* office, and Florence Barnet (courtesy Gawler Now & Then); another advertisement from the cookbook.

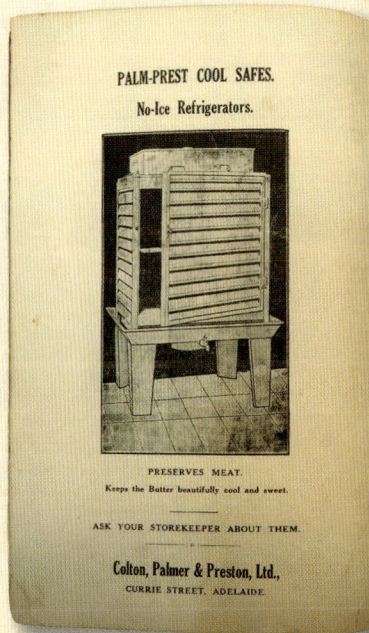

PALM-PREST COOL SAFES.

No-Ice Refrigerators.

PRESERVES MEAT.

Keeps the Butter beautifully cool and sweet.

ASK YOUR STOREKEEPER ABOUT THEM.

Colton, Palmer & Preston, Ltd.,
CURRIE STREET, ADELAIDE.

"The Bunyip"

Newspaper and Job Printing Works, Murray St Gawler. (Established 1857.)

IF YOU
Want a Cow
Want a Horse
Want a Situation
Want a Servant Man
Want to Sell a Piano
Want to Let a House
Want to Buy a Motor Car
Want to Buy or Sell a Farm
Want to Sell Farm Implements
Want to Sell House Property
Want to Sell Groceries or Drugs
Want to Sell Household Furniture
Want the Auction Sale well attended
Want to find Customers for Anything

ADVERTISE IN "THE BUNYIP."

A well-known Medium in South Aus.
Advertising Gains New Customers
Advertising Keeps Old Customers
Advertising Makes Success Easy
Advertising Begets Confidence
Advertising Liberally Will Pay
Advertising Shows Energy
Advertising Shows Pluck
Advertising Never Fails
Advertise At Once
Advertise It LONG
Advertise It WELL
Advertise
—NOW—

Wm. Barnet, Proprietor.

Whatever may be your requirements in Printing, see Us first.

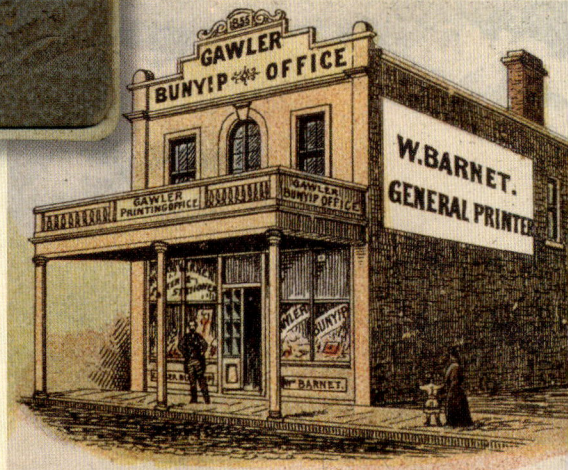

GAWLER
BUNYIP OFFICE

W. BARNET.
GENERAL PRINTER

GAWLER
PRINTING OFFICE

Cream puffs

In the end, Florence and Laura chose to publish just three cream puff recipes. This one came from Miss Sylvia Harris, the adopted daughter of Henry Harris, a well-known local store owner who was the son of Gawler pioneer, James Harris. Sylvia had only recently returned from an extended holiday in Europe with her parents, when she answered the call.

INGREDIENTS

120 g butter, chopped

250 ml (1 cup) water

150 g (1 cup) self-raising flour

4 eggs

250 ml (1 cup) cream

2 heaped tablespoons icing sugar, plus extra for dusting

½ teaspoon natural vanilla extract

METHOD

Preheat the oven to hot (220°C). Line a baking tray with baking paper.

Put the butter and water in a large saucepan and bring to the boil over high heat. Remove the saucepan from the heat and sift in the flour, stirring to form a smooth paste.

Allow the mixture to cool, then pour into a bowl and add the eggs, one at a time. Beat the mixture for 5 minutes, using an electric mixer on medium speed.

Place rounded dessertspoonfuls of mixture on the prepared tray, allowing about 5 cm between them. Bake for 25–30 minutes, until crisp to the touch and deep golden brown.

Set aside on a wire rack to cool.

Just before serving, cut the puffs in half. Whip together the cream, icing sugar and vanilla until thick. Spoon or pipe the mixture onto the bottom half of each puff. Replace the top, dust with icing sugar and serve.

LIZ'S TIPS

- Check the oven during cooking, and turn the tray after about 20 minutes to make sure the puffs cook evenly. Don't be tempted to open the oven door before this, because if the puffs are still soft in the middle they might collapse.

- It is easy to undercook these puffs. To double-check they are ready, tap the bottom — they should sound hollow. Then cut a small slit in one side to check if they are completely dry inside. If not, turn the oven off, wedge open the door and leave them for another few minutes and check again.

- Unfilled cream puffs store well in an airtight container. Before serving, just put them back in the oven for a few minutes to crisp up again.

Opposite: Recipe image by Kay Long.

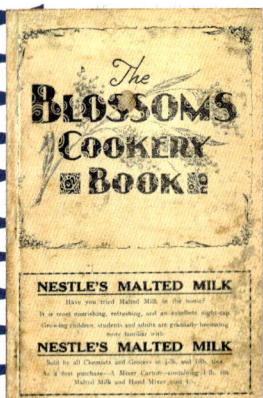

FEEDING *the* POOR *in the* LAND *of* SUNSHINE

Wilfred Magor was no stranger to the everyday life and struggles of the working class. The grandson of a Cornish miner, he grew up in the South Australian copper-mining town of Moonta, where he started his first job underground when he was only twelve.

Sometimes he worked standing in freezing water, and sometimes in stifling and dangerous conditions, more than 600 metres below the earth's surface, stripped to the waist and covered in grime. As a young man he moved to Broken Hill in New South Wales, where it was so hot in the mines that the per-spiration 'bubbled out through the lace holes of the men's boots'.

But Wilfred was happy enough and he enjoyed the camaraderie. He worked from choice, was paid a wage and was well fed, he told a South Australian news-paper. By comparison, never had he seen poverty so distressful as he was now witnessing in the industrial suburbs and slums of Adelaide's inner west. The interview was given in March 1929, seven months before the Wall Street stock-market crash that triggered the Depression and made conditions even worse.

By then Wilfred had hung up his mining boots and become a pastor in the Congregational church at Hindmarsh, where the standard of living for many roused his deep compassion. In a first for the church in Australia, he convinced its leaders to establish a non-denominational mission with a soup kitchen.

Whitefield's Institute opened in 1928 under his supervision. Within eleven weeks, it had served 8000 hot, three-course meals to children identified as being in need by the district's teachers. Within a year, the tally had reached more than 39,000 meals. Clothing, blankets, food parcels and tonnes of fire-wood had also been distributed.

The work was supported by women from across the city, often of high social standing, who volunteered their time to help in the kitchen and to raise funds. Among them was the governor's wife, Zara Hore-Ruthven. Later known as Lady Gowrie, she became famous for her work promoting child welfare, leading to childcare centres being established across Australia, named in her honour. When Whitefield created *The Blossoms Cookery Book* to raise money, Lady Gowrie provided the heartfelt introduction. 'The idea that there are hungry children in the vicinity of Adelaide, or anywhere in this beautiful land of Australia, is tragic in the extreme. Do buy this book and help them!' she urged.

Opposite: *The Blossoms Cookery Book,*
1931. Clockwise from top right: Children
drinking cocoa and eating sandwiches
at Whitefield's Congregational Institute,
1940 (State Library of SA B7798/125);
Lady Gowrie's introduction to the
cookbook; an image from the cookbook
of Wilfred Magor with the children at
Whitefield's; the cookbook's back cover
and an advertisement from the cookbook.

135

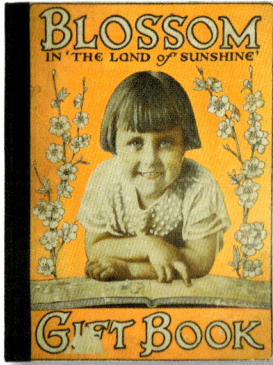

The cookbook was released in 1931, in conjunction with a unique publication for children with the optimistic-sounding title, *Blossom in 'The Land of Sunshine' Gift Book*. Featuring stories and illustrations by writers and artists with Adelaide connections, including landscape painter Hans Heysen and children's author May Gibbs, this beautiful little book was produced in limited numbers and remains a collector's item.

However, the cookbook appears to have quietly and quickly sunk into obscurity. Maybe it was something to do with the surprisingly modern attitudes to food and healthy eating revealed by the compiler, Mrs A.A. Drummond. A regular volunteer in the soup kitchen, she forecast the doom of suet pudding, the increasing popularity of wholemeal over white bread, and encouraged a varied diet of both cooked and fresh food, with plenty of fruit and vegetables.

BOOK

Published by
WHITEFIELD'S INSTITUTE
HINDMARSH
June, 1930
COPYRIGHT REGISTERED

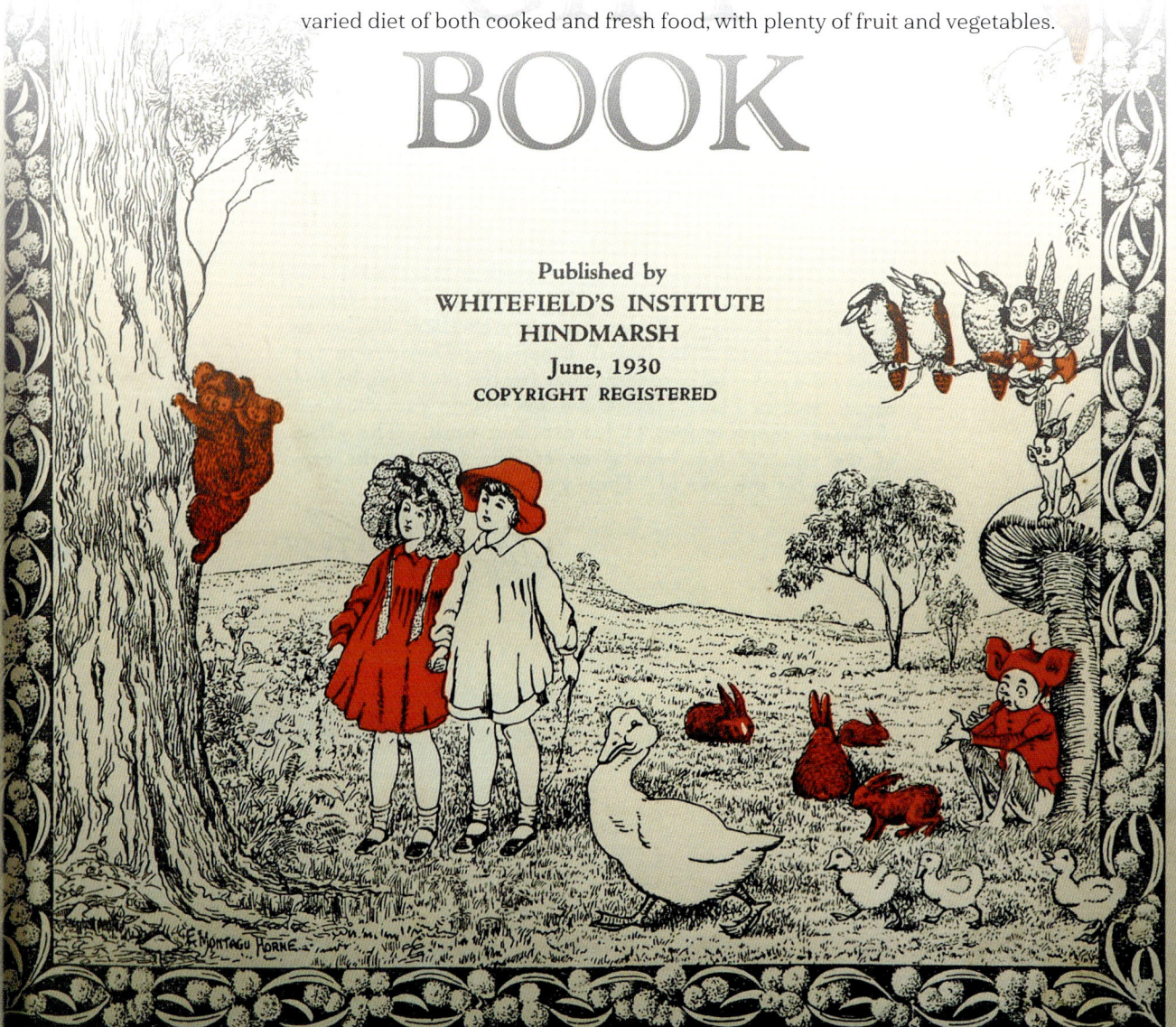

F. MONTAGU HORNE.

Economical soup

This soup recipe reflects very nicely Mrs Drummond's keenness for vegetables, and was most likely among the dishes served to Hindmarsh's malnourished children. Made without meat to make it more affordable, it's a simple, old-fashioned soup featuring vegetables that were popular at the time, and packed with nutritional goodness. The author also saw other benefits. 'It is generally agreed that soup is a stimulant rather than a food. The sight and smell of soup will make the mouth water and a free flow of saliva is very necessary to digestion,' she wrote.

INGREDIENTS

1 onion, diced

1 turnip, diced

1 swede, diced

1 carrot, diced

1 parsnip, diced

1 potato, diced

½ tablespoon olive oil

500 ml (2 cups) vegetable stock

500 ml (2 cups) water (approximately)

1 potato, diced

2 tablespoons pearl barley or split peas

handful of silverbeet or spinach, chopped

salt

ground white pepper

METHOD

Put the onion, turnip, swede, carrot, parsnip and potato in a large saucepan with the olive oil, and cook over medium heat for about 5 minutes, or until the onion is soft.

Add the stock, and then enough water to cover the vegetables. Bring to the boil.

Stir in the potato and pearl barley. Cover and simmer for about 30 minutes, until the barley is soft. Stir in the silverbeet and cook, uncovered, for a few more minutes, until tender.

Season to taste with salt and white pepper and serve.

LIZ'S TIPS

- Sweating the vegetables before adding the water brings out the natural flavours and reduces the amount of salt you need to add later.
- Make sure you cut the root vegetables the same size, so they cook evenly and produce a more attractive end result.
- Mrs Drummond recommended adding chopped parsley to soups just before they are served, for added flavour and colour.

Opposite: *The Blossom in 'The Land of Sunshine' Gift Book*, 1931, and its title page (State Library of SA).

LAND *of* APPLES NONSENSE

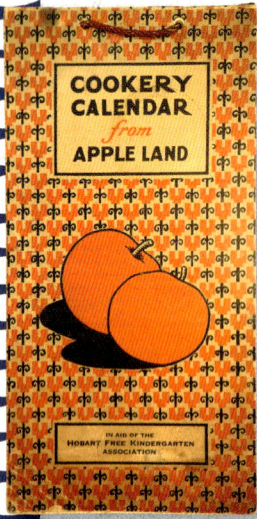

Emily Dobson was a formidable woman who liked to speak her mind. Even the last German emperor, Kaiser Wilhelm II, did not escape rebuke when she met him at a glittering social occasion in Europe. 'No woman had ever dared to object to anything he said until Granny,' recalled her granddaughter, Gladys. 'I do not know what subject he raised, but his opinion did not agree with Granny's ideas, and she had no hesitation in telling him so!'

The youngest of eleven children, Emily was born at Port Arthur in 1842, while her father was serving as a government official in the department responsible for provisioning Tasmania's penal settlements. In her mid-twenties she married Henry Dobson, a wealthy lawyer who later entered politics and became premier. Both were genuine philanthropists, keenly interested in social reform, with Emily campaigning fiercely on women's welfare issues well beyond the island state's shores until not long before she died in 1934. In an era when travel was far from easy, she made 33 trips overseas to attend gatherings of the International Council of Women, serving as president of the Australian delegation for fifteen years.

Although she was famous for her feisty qualities, there were many other sides to Emily's character. Gladys described her as devoted, loving and compassionate. A talented amateur actress and singer, she struggled not to laugh while performing comedy scenes and, in her spare time, loved playing chess and painting. She was also a keen cook, who charmed recipes from well-known European chefs and taught them to the household cooks she employed.

In her home state, Emily worked tirelessly with Henry to form community organisations and improve social welfare for the underprivileged. 'It was a family joke that she was the President of nearly everything!' Gladys recollected. Among the causes the couple championed together was establishing the Hobart Free Kindergarten Association in 1910, to run free preschools for children of the poor.

Towards the end of the Depression in 1933, the association published a cookbook to help fund the building of a new kindergarten, as well as its ongoing work training teachers and educating more than 260 children. The *Cookery Calendar from Apple Land* paid tribute to Tasmania's reputation as a leading apple producer. Designed to hang on the wall, it featured a striking cover, and a recipe for each day of the year. Not surprisingly, during the month of April, the height of the apple-picking season, every recipe showcased the popular fruit.

Above: Emily Dobson (*Tasmanian Mail*, 29 Sept 1900, p. 18, Tasmanian Archive and Heritage Office). Opposite top: *Cookery Calendar from Apple Land*, 1933 (State Library of NSW). Opposite bottom: Saying grace before eating at the Hobart Free Kindergarten, Watchorn Street (Tasmanian Archive and Heritage Office, AOT PH30/1/1136E).

Apple schmarren

SERVES 1– 2

Thought to originate from Austria, this delicious and extremely easy apple pancake was the recipe for 26 April in the calendar. It is an ideal option for a weekend snack or breakfast with a difference. Used informally in German, the word schmarren *means rubbish, or nonsense. It applies to this pancake because, in more traditional plain versions, you push the batter around as it cooks to create a messy or broken pancake, a little like the technique used to scramble eggs. However, in this version the pancake is allowed to sit and cook in one piece, although you shouldn't stress about it breaking up when you turn it.*

INGREDIENTS

1 heaped tablespoon self-raising flour

pinch of salt

1 egg, lightly beaten

2 tablespoons milk

1 large apple

15 g butter

2 teaspoons icing sugar

METHOD

Put the flour, salt and egg in a medium bowl and whisk together until smooth. Whisk in the milk.

Peel and core the apple, cut it into quarters and slice thinly. Stir the apple into the batter.

Melt the butter in a small, non-stick frying pan over medium heat. When the butter starts to foam, pour all the batter into the pan. Cook slowly over low heat until golden brown underneath, and the batter is set on top. Flip carefully and cook on the other side. Serve warm, dusted with icing sugar.

LIZ'S TIPS

- Use a generous heaped tablespoon of flour. The batter will still be very runny, but don't worry — it sets beautifully.

- Ideally, you need a non-stick frying pan of about 20 cm for this recipe.

- If the bottom of the pancake is becoming too brown and the top is still not setting, place a lid over the top of the frying pan for a few minutes.

- Use a large flexible spatula to flip the pancake over.

- For variation, try adding a little lemon zest or sprinkling the schmarren with cinnamon.

The BERRY STREET GIRLS

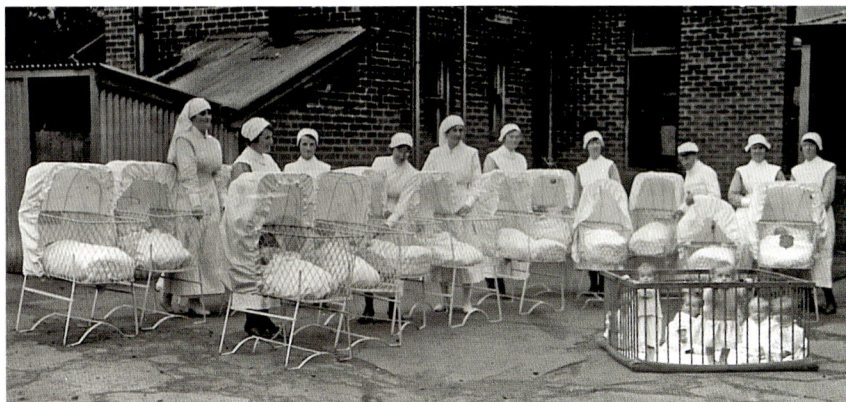

Dispensing advice to young mothers on caring for their newborn babies was an important part of life at the Berry Street Foundling Hospital and Infants' Home. Still operating after more than 140 years and known simply as Berry Street, the organisation has become Victoria's largest independent provider of child and family services.

The original institution was set up in 1877 with funds raised by a group of Melbourne women, concerned about the desperate plight of pregnant, unmarried girls, and the high mortality rates of their babies. Shunned by society, often with no money and no prospects, many resorted to infanticide or selling their children in a practice known as 'baby farming'.

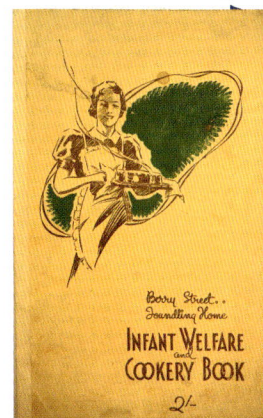

The home initially focused on providing accommodation, and maternity and adoption services but, in the early 1900s, it also became one of the state's most significant training centres for mothercraft nurses. Known as the Berry Street Girls and well liked by the local community, the blue-clad nurses became a familiar site in the area. In the 1930s they helped run pre- and post-natal clinics under the watchful eye of Matron Hilda McGain.

When the home decided to produce a cookery book to raise funds, it gave Matron McGain the ideal opportunity to share wisdom with a wider audience. The 1937 publication set out the best current thinking on everything from how a mother should look after her own health during pregnancy, to practical aspects of bathing and clothing babies, diet and dental care.

Should all else fail, the *Berry Street Foundling Home Infant Welfare and Cookery Book* also contained three full pages of cocktail recipes, such as the Depression Eliminator—a heady, well-shaken mix of gin, brandy liqueur, orange juice and egg white.

~~~~~~

Oatmeal hermits

MAKES ABOUT 30 BUNS

This is now one of my favourite baking recipes, and I'd never heard of it before discovering this cookbook. In a similar tradition to rock buns, oatmeal hermits contain a very comforting and tasty mix of rolled oats, dried fruit, walnuts and spices—best served with a strong cup of tea, not a cocktail!

INGREDIENTS

200 g (2 cups) rolled oats

170 g (1 cup) dried fruit (raisins or sultanas), chopped

60 g (½ cup) chopped walnuts

150 g (⅔ cup) caster sugar

300 g (2 cups) self-raising flour

1 teaspoon ground cinnamon

1 teaspoon ground nutmeg

2 eggs

220 g butter, melted

1 teaspoon bicarbonate of soda

125 ml (½ cup) milk

METHOD

Preheat the oven to moderate (180°C). Line a baking tray with baking paper.

Combine the oats, fruit, walnuts, sugar, flour, cinnamon and nutmeg in a large bowl.

Lightly beat the eggs in a separate bowl, then stir in the melted butter.

Dissolve the bicarbonate of soda in the milk, then stir into the egg mixture. Add the egg mixture to the dry ingredients and stir with a wooden spoon or fork until combined.

Drop heaped dessertspoonfuls onto the baking tray, allowing room for spreading. Bake for 15 minutes, or until golden brown.

Allow the buns to cool slightly on the trays, before moving them to a wire rack to cool completely.

Right: Advertisement from the *Berry Street Foundling Home Infant Welfare and Cookery Book.*

LIZ'S TIPS

- Raisins are my preference for these buns; their flavour works well with the spices.

- Don't be tempted to skimp on the nutmeg — it is important to the flavour, and well balanced with the other ingredients. A good-quality, shop-bought ground nutmeg seems to work better with this recipe than freshly grated.

- The buns should be quite rough on top, similar to a rock bun, so don't bother shaping them when you drop the mixture onto the tray.

- They keep well for several days, stored in an airtight container.

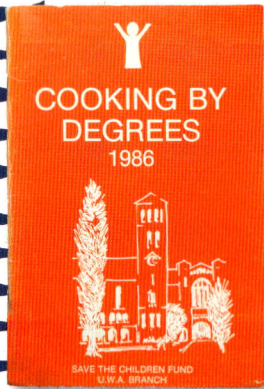

COOKING BY
DEGREES
1986

SAVE THE CHILDREN FUND
U.W.A. BRANCH

SAVING CHILDREN *one hundred thousand* BOOKS AT A TIME

This is a story about a librarian and a famous Australian writer, wrapped inside a story about a book, which is part of an even bigger story about many, many books.

Mary Alexander worked as a librarian at the University of Western Australia, in the Reid Library on the main campus in Perth. Her father, Professor Fred Alexander, was the founding head of the university's history department. An eminent historian who specialised in foreign affairs and policy, he also chaired the state library board for 30 years. Mary's mother, Gretha, was an Englishwoman, whom Fred met while studying at Oxford university in the 1920s.

In 1961, Gretha joined a newly established branch of what was then known as the Save the Children Fund. Comprising women staff members or wives of staff members, the university branch quickly set about raising funds for the Australian aid and development agency, which is dedicated to protecting children from harm and helping them to access quality education and health services.

Initial efforts included a cookbook proposed by the wife of the university's chief librarian. Elizabeth Jolley emigrated from England in 1959 with her husband, Leonard, their children and a trunk full of her unpublished writing, notebooks and diaries. By the time she died in 2007, Jolley was recognised as one of Australia's most acclaimed writers, the author of fifteen novels as well as works of non-fiction, and the recipient of multiple literary awards and honours.

By comparison, the cookbook she compiled was a modest affair. Numbering 40 pages, it included Jolley's own recipe for onion soup, as well as contributions from other branch members and university staff. Jolley wanted to call the collection *Greasy Joan*, which was taken from a song line in Shakespeare's play *Love's Labour's Lost*. But the branch decided on *Cooking by Degrees*, a clever play on words acknowledging the branch's setting and the academic qualifications of many contributors. The book raised £107 within twelve months of the branch being established in May 1961.

In 1964, members hit on the idea of holding a second-hand book sale. So they rounded up a small number of books and sold them for a total of £47. The branch still sells books to raise money, but the concept has ever expanded, ever so slightly.

Clockwise from top left: Author Elizabeth Jolley (image by Tony Miller, courtesy Monash University Archives); customers line up for the annual Save the Children book sale (courtesy The University of Western Australia); Mary Alexander presents a cheque for proceeds from the book sale to Save the Children's state secretary Reverend Gerald Coxon during her stint as treasurer (courtesy Jane Blanckensee); crowds searching for bargains at the annual book sale, 2017 (courtesy The University of Western Australia); *Cooking by Degrees*, 1st edition, c. 1961. Opposite: *Cooking by Degrees II*, 1986.

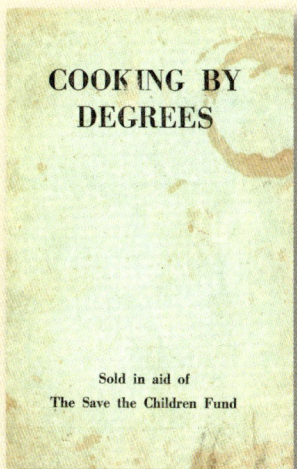

COOKING BY DEGREES

Sold in aid of
The Save the Children Fund

Today's event offers more than 100,000 books, and runs for six days. Takings have been known to pass the $45,000 mark within the first four hours. Some years the total exceeds $250,000. In fact the sale has become a Perth institution, with avid buyers queuing outside the venue hours before the doors open so they can secure first pick. One year, a particularly strategic buyer used binoculars to peer through the windows, pinpoint the location of key sections and devise a precise plan of action.

With the book sale generating so much money for Save the Children Australia, the university branch doesn't really need to worry too much about thinking up other fundraising activities. However, in 1986, members decided to compile a second cookbook, with different recipes. *Cooking by Degrees II* was dedicated to Mary, who died in 1985. The branch reckoned their past treasurer and champion fundraiser would strongly approve of the idea, with coordinator Joyce Billings commenting that 'we know for every one sold there would have been a smile of satisfaction on Mary's face at the thought of more help for impoverished children'.

Paying tribute to her in the book, Ruth Reid, long-standing branch member and wife of the then Governor of Western Australia, commented on Mary's industry, tenacity and untiring energy in fundraising for Save the Children. 'With her charm of manner she was an inspiration and a challenge to us all and is sadly missed.'

~~~~~~

Pickled cumquats and raisins   MAKES ABOUT 3 CUPS

INGREDIENTS

- 2 cups halved cumquats, seeds removed
- 1 teaspoon salt
- 500 ml (2 cups) cold water (approximately)
- 130 g (¾ cup) raisins
- 250 ml (1 cup) apple cider vinegar
- 285 g (1½ cups lightly packed) brown sugar
- 175 g (½ cup) dark honey
- 10 cloves
- ¼ teaspoon allspice
- 1 teaspoon ground cinnamon

One of Mary Alexander's favourites, this recipe was contributed to Cooking by Degrees II *by her sister, Anne Blanckensee. According to Anne's daughter, Jane, the women grew up in a house with a tree that produced 'a million cumquats', so they were always looking for suitable recipes. This chutney was not only enjoyed at home with curries or cold meats, but jars were sold to raise money for Save the Children. It takes a little time to remove the seeds from the cumquats, but the chutney is well worth making for its rich, dark flavour.*

METHOD

Place the cumquats in a large bowl. Dissolve the salt in the water and pour over the cumquats (they should be completely covered). Leave overnight at room temperature.

The next day, drain the cumquats and rinse well.

Put the cumquats in a large saucepan with the raisins and add just enough water to cover. Bring to the boil and cook for 20 minutes. Reduce the heat and simmer for another 30 minutes, uncovered, or until the fruit is tender.

Stir in the vinegar, sugar, honey, cloves, allspice and cinnamon and boil for another 5–10 minutes. Reduce the heat and simmer for another 30 minutes, uncovered, stirring occasionally to ensure the mixture doesn't stick.

Spoon into hot sterilised jars and seal while hot.

LIZ'S TIPS

- Internationally recognised citrus-growing guru and cumquat specialist, Ian Tolley, from the South Australian Riverland, recommends the Nagami variety of cumquat for this recipe, as it has more character.
- Cut the cumquats in half horizontally, not end to end, and use a knife with a sharp tip to remove the seeds.
- Light brown sugar works best for this recipe.

RECIPES

at

WAR

ANNIE CARRIES *on*

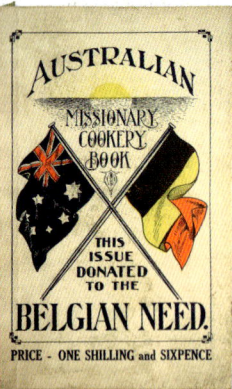

When the First World War broke out in August 1914, prize-winning Alstonville show cook, Annie King, was hard at work compiling a cookbook to raise funds for mission work.

Born in the inner-Sydney suburb of Redfern in 1858, Annie trained as a teacher and served at schools in Maitland and Albury before marrying in her mid-thirties. She and her husband, John, later settled down on a dairy farm in the Richmond River area of northern New South Wales, where they raised four sons.

While John devoted his energies to breeding prize-winning cattle, and the local agricultural society, Annie built a reputation for being a fine cook, winning numerous prizes at local shows for her baking and preserves, before progressing to become a judge. A keen churchwoman throughout most of her life, she also served as a deaconess in the Church of England, and showed a particular interest in mission work.

Deciding that harnessing her skills and knowledge in the kitchen was one of the best ways she could assist, Annie set about creating the *Australian Missionary Cookery Book*. The outbreak of war delayed her efforts, until she and a band of helpers became motivated by reports flooding Australian newspapers about atrocities carried out by the Germans as they stormed through 'poor little Belgium' on their way to invading France.

Australians threw themselves into providing relief aid to their Belgian allies through a national fund. Initial efforts culminated on 14 May 1915, which authorities declared as Belgian Day, encouraging communities to contribute by organising fundraising activities.

Annie and a band of supporters decided to knuckle down and produce a smaller version of her cookbook than originally intended, so it would be ready in time. The entire proceeds from the first issue of 5000 copies would be diverted to the 'Belgian need'. *The Evening News* urged all good housewives in Sydney to look out for the cookbook and its distinctive colour cover, featuring the crossed flags of Belgium and Australia. Within a short time the collection of simple, practical and up-to-date recipes raised more than £300.

War was still raging three years later when the modest, but very gratified, Annie finished work on a second edition, expanded to include about 180 more

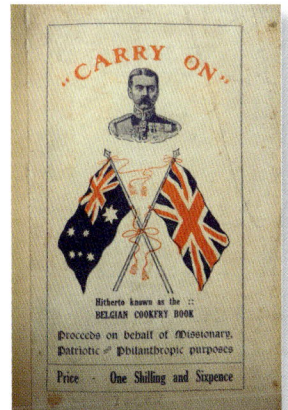

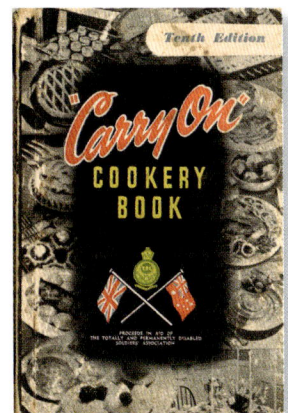

'tried and good' recipes. This time it was published as the *"Carry On" Cookery Book*, based around a catchphrase that aimed to reinvigorate flagging spirits after five long years of war.

It may well have had special meaning for Annie too. Her oldest son, James, had been invalided home in 1917 from France, where he served as a stretcher bearer, physically intact but suffering from shell shock. If the war continued much longer, her remaining sons would all have reached the age when they were eligible to serve too.

The cookbook went on to sell more than 30,000 copies before Annie's death in October 1950, at the age of 92. It was still in print five years later, when the thirteenth edition was produced by the Totally and Permanently Disabled Soldiers Association, to whom she had given copyright.

Mango chutney

INGREDIENTS

450 g ripe mangoes

½ quince

1 banana

1 large Granny Smith apple

2 tomatoes

230 g (1⅓ cups) sultanas

120 g (¾ cup) pitted dates

4 fresh chillies

½ teaspoon salt

½ teaspoon ground ginger

450 g dark brown sugar

1 litre (4 cups) white vinegar

Among items featured in the original Australian Missionary Cookery Book *are almost twenty jam, chutney and pickle recipes labelled as prize-winners, most likely from Annie's own repertoire of blue-ribbon efforts from her days entering show competitions. They include this rich, spicy recipe for mango chutney.*

METHOD

Peel and chop the mangoes, quince, banana and apple, and chop the tomatoes, then put them in a large, wide saucepan with a heavy base.

Chop the sultanas and dates and finely chop the chillies, then add them to the saucepan, along with the salt, ginger, brown sugar and vinegar. Stir over medium heat until the sugar has dissolved. Bring to the boil and simmer, uncovered, for about 90 minutes, stirring occasionally.

Spoon into hot sterilised jars and seal while hot.

LIZ'S TIPS

- If mangoes are not in season, use a 650 ml bottle of preserved mangoes, which should contain about the same weight of flesh as two fresh mangoes, once the skin and stones are removed.

- I love dates, so my preference is to double the quantity and halve the amount of sultanas.

- True to the preferences of show cooking, Annie's original instructions are to 'finely' chop the fruit, but you may not want to be so fussy if you are not intending to enter a competition. Don't make the quince or apple too large, though, if you are planning to use the chutney in sandwiches.

- This is a moderately spicy chutney. If you love chilli you may want to add a little more.

- Make sure you use lids that are plastic-coated inside, as metal may react with the acid in the chutney.

- Sterilise the jars by washing them in warm soapy water, rinsing and drying them thoroughly. Stand them on a baking tray, without touching, and place in a very slow (120°C) oven for about 30 minutes.

Opposite: *Advertisements from the* Carry On Cookery Book. *(courtesy Anne Fisher); and recipe image by Kay Long.*

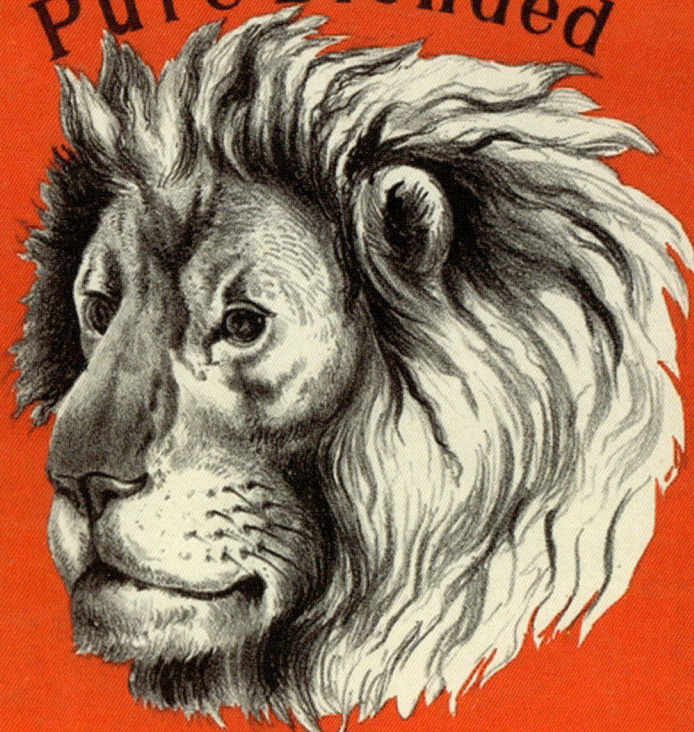

EMPIRE
COMPY'S
Pure Blended

TRADE MARK

Packet
TEA

The richest food source of the combined Vitamins B¹, B² and P.P.

(the anti-pellagric factor)

He's doing his bit for his Dad...

Young Peter loves Vegemite. . . and his mother loves giving it to him. . . but he's not getting so much these days, as his mother says: "It's nearly all going to Daddy, Peter." And she's right! The Vegemite is needed for our fighting men.

As you know, Vegemite is a concentrated extract of yeast, which contains three vital vitamins—B¹, B² and P.P. (the anti-pellagric factor). That is why Vegemite is so necessary to our fighting men at home and overseas.

B1—is the Nerve Vitamin. To have a strong, well stomach, and a normal, healthy intestinal tract, we need an ample supply of vitamin B1. Vegemite is one of the richest natural food sources of this vitamin.

B2—is the Growth Vitamin. When you get too little of the vitamin B2 it means poor growth and under-nourishment. Vegemite is rich in this vitamin B2. It helps proper growth and all-round development of the body.

P.P.—(anti-pellagric factor). Vegemite keeps skin clear and healthy because it supplies the system with the right amount of the skin-clearing vitamin known as P.P. Yes! Vegemite is a concentrated food. Rich food and energy values are packed into Vegemite.

So if you notice less Vegemite in your local shop, just remember that until we have won this war a lot of it will be going to the troops! Vegemite — the concentrated extract of yeast — the richest food source of the combined vitamins B¹, B² and P.P. (anti-pellagric factor). The food that helps keep the troops fighting.

VEGEMITE *is with the Troops!*

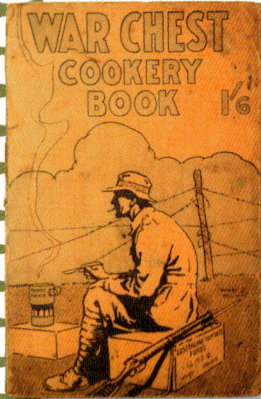

ALICE ANDERSON'S *astonishing* ANZACS

The *War Chest Cookery Book* holds a special place in Australian food history. Page 87 carries the first known recipe to be included in a printed cookbook under the name 'Anzac biscuits'. But there is considerable mystery around the tasty, jam-filled treats, given they bear very little resemblance to the biscuits baked today in tribute to diggers who fought in the First World War.

Released in 1917, the cookery book raised money for the Australian Comforts Fund to support its efforts supplying items such as food parcels, clothing and even sporting equipment to the troops. The book was published by the New South Wales arm of the organisation, known as the Citizens' War Chest Fund, which was set up within days of hostilities breaking out, by a group of Sydney-based business and professional men.

Apart from encouraging cash donations, the New South Wales fund established a depot in the heart of the city so that women unable to give money could contribute the 'work of their fingers'. In France, fund volunteers organised entertainments in the camps to help raise morale, and set up coffee stalls just behind the first-line trenches to serve hot drinks and soup, often at risk to their own lives. A War Chest Club was also established in London as a home away from home for men on leave or recuperating from injury and illness.

The heart of the operation was the depot in Sydney's Elizabeth Street, where women worked day in, day out to sort, label and pack items that flooded in from across the state. By early 1917, the depot had despatched a remarkable 75,000 kit bags, 70,000 pairs of socks, 47,500 handkerchiefs, more than 46,000 shirts, 33,200 balaclavas and caps, and 14,500 pairs of underpants, to men fighting in Gallipoli, Egypt and France, and to the Australian navy. Volunteers even prepared 44,000 bandages to help protect the legs of cavalry and artillery horses while they were being shipped overseas. Then there was the food—98,000 tins of lollies, 52,200 bottles of sauce, almost 38,000 jars of pickles, more than 120,000 tins of golden syrup and 2100 large tins of biscuits.

It's not certain that Alice Anderson was among the volunteers who helped at the depot, and it's highly unlikely that her version of Anzac biscuits was among those sent to the troops, because they would not have kept well enough. But she did step forward and supply at least four options for baked items when the fund put out a call for 'good tried recipes' for its proposed cookery book.

Like many women working for the organisation, Alice came from a middle-class background. Her mother, Isabella, was the daughter of Reverend Adam Thomson, a gentle Scot recognised for his wisdom and integrity, who was elected the first moderator of the Presbyterian Church of New South Wales when it was formed in 1865.

Her father, James, was Australasian general manager for the Alliance Assurance Company, and chairman of the North Shore Gas Light Company. Flags flew at half mast in the city when he died at a relatively young age in 1895, and his funeral service drew a large attendance at St Peter's Presbyterian Church, where he had led the choir for twenty years.

One of nine children and the fifth of seven daughters, Alice was in her mid-thirties, not yet married and living at home in North Sydney with her widowed mother when she contributed the recipes to the *War Chest Cookery Book*. By then, her younger brother James was serving in France in the Australian Army, and she no doubt tried to take comfort from the fact that she was doing what she could to make his life a little easier.

Above and left: Volunteers packing food for the War Chest Fund, and sorting clothing at the Sydney depot, c. 1915–18 (Mitchell Library, State Library of NSW). Opposite: *The War Chest Cookery Book*, 1917 (National Library of Australia).

Alice's 'Anzac' biscuits

MAKES ABOUT 30

INGREDIENTS

120 g butter, softened

120 g caster sugar

2 eggs, lightly beaten

150 g (1 cup) plain flour

1 teaspoon baking powder

1 teaspoon mixed spice

½ teaspoon ground
  cinnamon

160 g (1 cup) rice flour

raspberry jam

Icing:

125 g (1 cup) icing sugar
  mixture

small knob of butter

hot water

While Alice's version of Anzacs has long since been over-run by the officially approved biscuit, featuring rolled oats and made without eggs, her recipe is well worth reviving. It's easy to bake and produces a perfect accompaniment to tea or coffee.

METHOD

Preheat the oven to moderate (180°C). Line a baking tray with baking paper.

Cream the butter and sugar until the sugar is dissolved. Add the eggs and beat until combined. Sift in the plain flour, baking powder, mixed spice and cinnamon, then add the rice flour. Stir together with a knife to form a soft dough. Form the pastry into a ball, wrap in plastic wrap and refrigerate for 30–45 minutes.

Dust a board or work surface with plain flour, then roll out the dough until it is only a few millimetres thick. Use a plain round biscuit cutter, about 4 cm in diameter, to cut the pastry. Place the biscuits on the baking tray, and bake for 12–15 minutes, until golden. Allow the biscuits to cool on a wire rack.

When cold, join the biscuits with a thin smear of raspberry jam.

To make the icing, in a small bowl combine the icing sugar, butter and enough hot water to thin the icing, and mix it with a knife until smooth. Decorate the top of each biscuit with a thinly applied circle of icing.

LIZ'S TIPS

- Refrigerating the soft biscuit dough will make it easier to handle.
- Dip the cutter in flour so it doesn't stick to the dough.
- While baking, allow a few centimetres between the biscuits for spreading.
- The original recipe did not stipulate what kind of jam to use, but raspberry is my favourite. Plum jam also works well with this recipe.
- In case some of the biscuits have spread more than others, match up evenly — sized and shaped pairs of biscuits before you start filling them.

- For the icing, add the water to the icing sugar gradually to make sure the icing is not too runny. Substitute lemon juice if you would like a sharper flavour.
- Apply the icing sparingly, or leave it out altogether if you want to reduce the sweetness.
- The biscuits will keep for at least a week in a sealed container.
- The uncooked dough can be kept in the fridge, wrapped in plastic wrap, for at least a week before cooking. Allow to sit at room temperature for a few minutes before rolling.

THE BEST RECIPE
IN THE
BOOK
★
A BRIGHT
AND HAPPY
HOME
★
Always Look your best in a
"TANIWHA" APRON

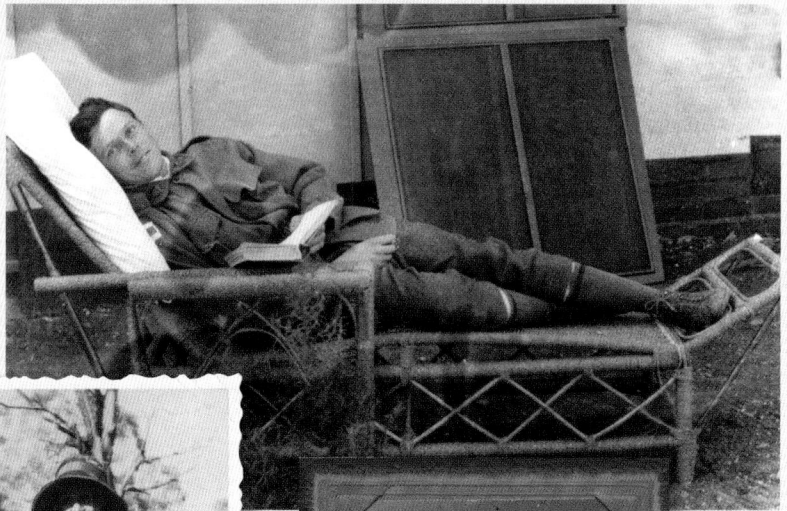

Clockwise from top left:
Advertisement from the cookbook;
a convalescent soldier at Bedford
Park, 1919 (State Library of SA,
B 49003); Miss K. Hammond of Co-
Op Stores and Miss M. Mulvihill of
Charles Moore & Co. selling badges
for the Tubercular Soldiers' Aid
Society, c. 1930 (State Library of SA,
B 71305); a view of Angorichina
Hostel, c. 1940 (State Library of SA,
PRG 1642 26 67); Matron Burns
and Ella Cleggett in the garden at
Angorichina, 1927 (State Library
of SA B 64383/25). Opposite:
The Angorichina Cookery Book,
1963 (State Library of SA).

AUNTIE CLEGGETT *and the* ANGORICHINA HOSTEL

Australian soldiers fighting in Europe during the First World War put their lives at risk from more than bullets and shellfire. Living in close proximity, often in extremely cold and wet conditions, they also faced the increased likelihood of contracting tuberculosis. By 1917, medical authorities were warning that caring for all the men being invalided from the front with the potentially deadly infectious disease would be a significant challenge.

In South Australia a dedicated Tubercular Soldiers' Aid Society lobbied politicians to help build a special camp so patients could recuperate in the warm, dry air of the Flinders Ranges. Leading the charge was a tall brunette known for her dedication and determination.

Ella Cleggett was almost 30 and teaching at a suburban school when hostilities broke out in 1914. Keen to support the war effort, the farmer's daughter from Mount Barker became actively involved in a school-based patriotic fund. Among the causes it supported was a sanatorium established in the Adelaide foothills for returned servicemen suffering from tuberculosis, also known as TB or consumption.

Ella visited the facility weekly, serving afternoon tea and organising entertainments to distract the men from their troubles. But it wasn't long before she realised that cake and concerts would not suffice. Many of the patients would never be fit enough to return to their previous jobs, leaving them and their families in desperate financial straits even if they did qualify for a pension. When the Aid Society was formed in 1921 to provide relief, Ella took up the position of honorary secretary. Four years later she resigned from teaching, and the society created a full-time paid position especially for her.

Ella's extraordinary contribution over the next 35 years earned her an MBE, as well as the undying appreciation of those she helped. Known affectionately as Cleg, or Auntie Cleggett, she treated tubercular soldiers like brothers, despite the stigma often attached to the disease, and took a personal interest in their welfare and the widows and orphans they left behind. Ella also worked tirelessly to generate funds for the society, which was still caring for 750 men in the mid-1950s.

By the time she died in 1960, at the age of 75, Ella had raised more than £250,000. A great deal of that money supported her favourite project—the

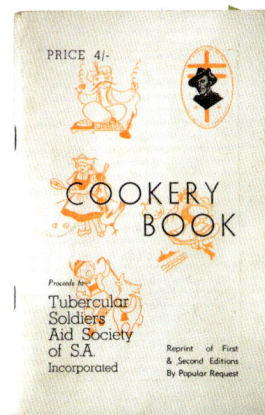

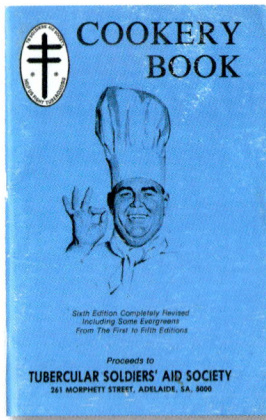

Angorichina Hostel. The sprawling outback complex of chalets and wards, with its own dispensary, was built between Blinman and Parachilna in the Flinders Ranges, on land donated by the owners of Angorichina station.

Officially opened by Governor Sir Tom Bridges in 1927, the hostel operated until 1973, providing winter respite to hundreds of tubercular sufferers and their families. Patients could sit in the sun or, if they were well enough, gradually rebuild their strength by doing light work in the hostel's vegetable garden, raising chickens, milking cows or making furniture from local red gum.

Among the fundraising activities that supported the hostel was *The Angorichina Cookery Book*. At least six editions were released, including one in 1963. The public was urged to spend four shillings to support the latest round of servicemen who picked up the disease during the Second World War, and help them keep 'that dreaded disease away from you'.

Apricot slice

Published in the 1963 edition, a version of this slice was a popular stand-by in our house. Mum made it very regularly for her children, grandchildren and then great-grandchildren. It was also her favourite way of using any jam that was left languishing in the pantry or a little bit past its best. Often it was plum jam because we had an enormous cherry plum tree in the backyard, and soon tired of the seemingly endless quantities on offer.

INGREDIENTS

225 g (1½ cups) self-raising
   flour
110 g (½ cup) caster sugar
115 g butter, chopped
1 egg, lightly beaten
225 g (⅔ cup) apricot jam

Topping:
75 g (⅓ cup) caster sugar
1 egg, lightly beaten
90 g (1 cup) desiccated
   coconut

METHOD

Preheat the oven to moderate (180°C). Line a slice pan (approximately 30 x 20 cm) with baking paper, leaving a few centimetres overhanging on the long sides.

Combine the flour and sugar in a large bowl. Rub in the butter using your fingertips. Make a well in the centre and add the egg, stirring with a knife, and then use your hand to form a soft dough. Press the dough into the slice pan using the back of a spoon, and spread with the apricot jam.

To make the topping, whisk together the sugar and egg, then stir in the coconut. Scatter the topping over the jam.

Bake for about 35 minutes, until golden. When cool, cut it into squares.

LIZ'S TIPS

- You can use any type of jam you prefer.

- The topping is quite wet. Just scatter it over, without worrying about filling every little space, as it will spread during cooking.

- Keep an eye on the slice after it has been baking for about 20 minutes. If the coconut is starting to burn, turn the oven down to moderately slow (160°C), and cover the top with foil.

- Served warm with custard or cream, the slice makes a lovely dessert.

- It keeps well in an airtight container. It also freezes well — once thawed, revive it by popping it in a slow oven (150°C) for 10 minutes.

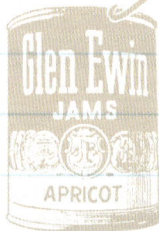

Just pure fruit and sugar...

GLEN EWIN
APRICOT JAM

True fruit flavour...

LONGREACH *goes all in*

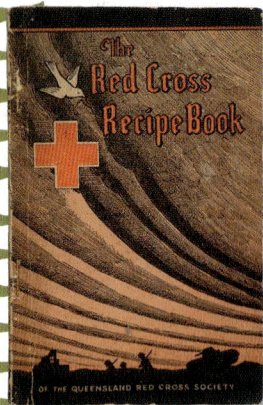

In 1942 the Australian Red Cross Society branch at Longreach made headlines for its contribution to the war effort. Within twelve months of being formed the previous July, the branch had signed up 400 members and raised £3000, despite the challenges of distance and petrol rationing.

This effort reflected not just the patriotism of the community, but genuine fears that, with war raging across the Pacific, Australia was in imminent danger of being invaded by Japan. That meant Queenslanders were living on the front-line. 'The enemy is at our entrance gates, and soon he will be coming up the main drive to the front gate,' the deputy chairman of Longreach Shire Council, Councillor A.A. Moffat, warned a public meeting in early February 1942. If anyone doubted the seriousness of the situation, that changed over the next few weeks as word spread that Singapore had fallen and the Japanese were dropping bombs on Darwin.

Heeding calls for an all-in effort, Red Cross members at Longreach banded together to run an intensive and sustained program of fundraising activities during the war years. Members met weekly to sew and do other work; every Monday they sold cakes and produce, and once a month they held a street day. They ran afternoon teas and dinners, sheep dog trials and gymkhanas, fetes, dances and raffles, baby and knitting competitions, and they were paid by the military to cook meals for servicemen passing through town. They also broadcast a weekly program on the local radio station to promote their activities and encourage support.

Guiding them through these endeavours was their capable president, Sheila Wallace, whose husband, Dr Thomas Wallace, was superintendent of the Longreach base hospital. Originally from Glasgow, Dr Wallace came to the town to work as a locum for six weeks in 1913, and stayed for 37 years. He and Sheila married in 1923 and had four children, including one son, Donald, who joined the RAAF the year he turned eighteen. The promising young scholarship winner, who had been captain of his boarding school at Toowoomba, excelled at sports and won a prize for leadership, was killed in action over New Guinea in August 1944.

The most enduring of the Red Cross branch's fundraising efforts was a cookbook, which proved so popular that it is still in demand. The first edition of *The Red Cross Recipe Book* was released in October 1943. The idea had been proposed almost a year before by Mrs D.M. Archer, Mrs W.J. McMaster and Miss H. White. The three women were country organisers for the branch, tasked with keeping in touch with members living on far-flung stations and encouraging their support. They were already busy collecting recipes in December 1942, when they received official encouragement from a committee meeting to push ahead.

Among the contributions they gathered up were recipes from 'our American Allies', most likely members of the United States Air Force squadrons, who flew bombers out of the Longreach airport between May and July that year. The Americans were billeted in the town's Civic Centre and Masonic Temple, and apparently adopted as 'surrogate sons' by local families.

Recipes also came in from Brisbane, after a brief notice appeared in the Brisbane *Courier Mail*, inviting people to submit recipes or household hints, which would be included for a fee of threepence each to help cover the printing costs.

One of Sheila's daughters later recalled that she would come home from school to find recipes spread out all over the kitchen table while her mother helped put the book together. Former branch member and keen local historian, Eva Tindall, understands that a local couple, Mr and Mrs George Avery, also contributed to the book by donating money towards the cost of printing the first edition. Businesses from Longreach, Barcaldine and Aramac, livestock studs and boarding schools also placed advertisements.

Above: United States Air Force personnel on parade at Longreach airport, 1942 (courtesy Qantas Founders Museum, Longreach). Opposite: *The Red Cross Recipe Book*, 1943 (State Library of NSW).

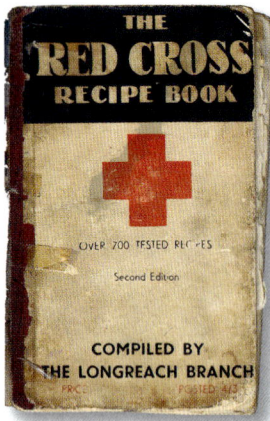

According to a note from Sheila at the front of the cookbook, wartime restrictions on paper supplies forced the compilers to squeeze the recipes into less space by removing the names of donors. However, she hoped the book would be 'of great help to our women-folk who, with faith and courage must ever "carry on" in their own homes; and trusting that, by purchasing this book, they will derive much pleasure from the knowledge that they have helped to give ease to the suffering, and comfort to many, in their darkest hour of need'.

The cookbook received high praise from rural weekly newspaper *Queensland Country Life*, which suggested it would make an ideal Christmas gift: 'The compilers' aim was to make available to busy, and often inexperienced, cooks who are working under great difficulties in the country, a comprehensive list of easy-to-follow, economical and healthful recipes. In this they have succeeded'.

Selling for three shillings and sixpence per copy, by June 1944 the cookbook had raised hundreds of pounds. A larger, revised edition, with a hard cover carrying a different design was published in 1946. Sales were still strong, so a third edition of 8000 copies followed in 1950. According to Eva, at some stage—most likely around the 1970s—divisional headquarters took over printing and distributing the book, with the branch experiencing difficulty securing advertisers and remaining commercial advertisements having to be dropped because of tax issues. The ninth and final edition appeared in 1993.

Two years later, headquarters offered the remaining stock of 1482 books back to the branch, which continued to sell them for five dollars a copy until supplies ran out in 2004. 'The Stockman's Hall of Fame at Longreach used to sell a heck of a lot too, and they still get inquiries,' Eva says. 'It's very reflective of the time and that's what people love about it.'

Above: *The Red Cross Recipe Book,* second edition, and an image from the back cover (courtesy Anne Fisher).

Johnny cakes

SERVES 9

Very popular in many parts of the United States, Johnny cakes, or Johnnycake, is a type of quickbread made with cornmeal, which was a staple part of the diet for native Americans long before European settlement. It is not to be confused with the Australian bush camp version made with wheaten flour.

Modern American recipes are often made without any type of leavening, like a pancake or flatbread, but this recipe uses both self-raising flour and baking powder to produce a light cornbread with a soft, fluffy interior and a crunchy golden crust. It is delicious served straight from the oven with butter, to accompany soup or a bowl of American-style chilli. Or try it with honey, as suggested in the five-page 'Contributions from our American Allies' section of The Red Cross Recipe Book.

METHOD

Preheat the oven to moderately hot (200°C). Oil a shallow 20 cm square cake pan.

Sift together the flour, baking powder and salt three times into a large bowl. Stir through the cornmeal and sugar, making sure the dry ingredients are thoroughly blended.

Put the eggs in a separate bowl and whisk together. Whisk in the milk, then the melted butter. Add the egg mixture to the dry ingredients, working quickly to stir the mixture until smooth.

Without losing time, spoon the mixture into the prepared pan. Bake for about 25 minutes, until golden and hard on top.

Remove from the oven, turn out onto a board or wire rack and cut into nine squares.

INGREDIENTS

150 g (1 cup) self-raising flour

2 teaspoons baking powder

¼ teaspoon salt

190 g (1 cup) cornmeal
  (or fine polenta)

2 teaspoons caster sugar

2 eggs

250 ml (1 cup) milk

50 g butter, melted

LIZ'S TIPS

- An old friend of mine from Atlanta, Georgia, told me that the trick to producing light golden cornbread was to pour it into a hot pan. Add ½ tablespoon olive oil, then put the pan in the oven as you start mixing.

- It is important to know that cornmeal and polenta are not always the same thing. The pre-cooked cornmeal Americans use for this recipe is more finely ground than most types of polenta, and can be made from white, yellow or even blue corn. If you can't get cornmeal, look for fine polenta.

- The mixture is meant to be reasonably stiff, but you may need to add a little more milk, depending on the brand of cornmeal or polenta that you use.

- The cornbread will cook quite quickly, so if your mixture is very stiff and you want a smooth-topped bread instead of a more rustic look, take a few seconds to run the back of a metal spoon over the mixture before it goes into the oven.

- The unnamed donor of this recipe suggested serving it with honey that has been warmed and made more liquid by adding a splash of hot water, so you can drizzle it easily over the top. Golden syrup is delicious too.

LADIES COMMITTEE

RECIPE BOOK

RECIPES

with a

SPORTING
EDGE

A *guilty* PLEASURE

It's the dish that family cooks from the 1970s are most embarrassed to talk about, but a favourite of the children who grew up eating it, even if they are now ashamed to admit it

Classic apricot chicken comprises just three ingredients—chicken, a packet of French onion soup mix and a tin of apricot nectar. In today's culinary-obsessed Australia, it fails on many levels. It uses pre-packaged flavourings laden with salt, and pre-cooked and pulverised fruit that comes out of a tin. There are no fresh herbs and exotic spices, no particular kitchen skills are required, and the maker cannot boast of spending long hours of virtuous labour producing it—which is exactly why the dish found its way into the *Wakehurst Golf Club's Selected Recipe Book*.

The home-produced cookbook was put together in the mid-1970s by Delia Geddes, who would rather spend her time out in the fresh air playing golf than in the kitchen. In fact, inspiration for the book struck one day while she was on the green. 'God, I have to go home and cook,' one of her playing partners said. 'I have the perfect recipe,' someone else replied. 'It takes five minutes. You just chuck it all in.'

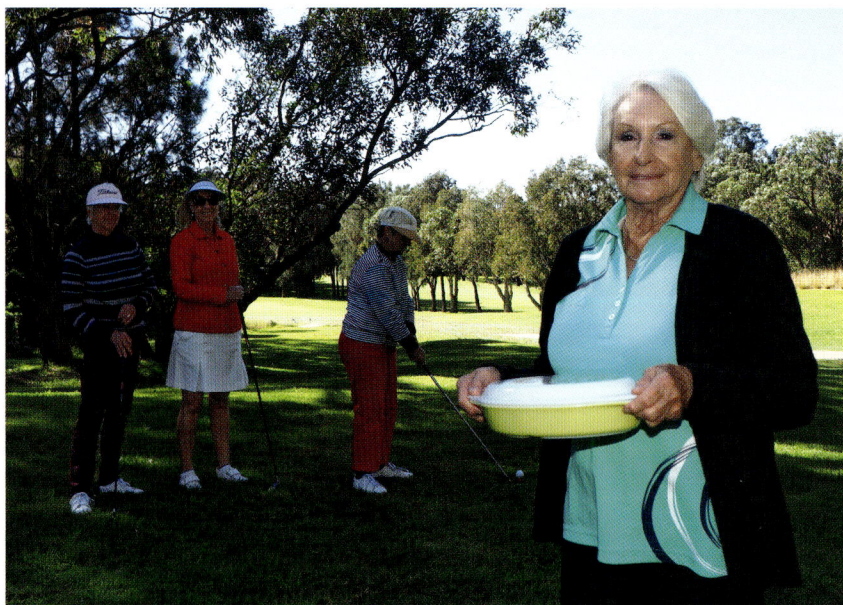

The conversation set Delia thinking. The ladies committee at Wakehurst had to raise funds to run its own competition at the club in northern Sydney. Why not put together a collection of recipes that could be prepared easily and quickly, leaving their members more time and energy to enjoy golf?

Delia put out a call for people's favourites, then produced the entire cookbook on her own. She typed up the recipes, used a roneo machine to print the pages, then stapled them together by hand. A keen amateur artist, she even drew the cover design. 'I don't remember exactly, but I think I only produced enough copies to cover how many ladies we had—probably about 50 or so,' Delia says.

Demand quickly outstripped the modest amount available, creating a significant problem. 'Without computers or photocopy machines in those days, there was no way to reproduce it unless I redid the whole thing.' So Delia did, adding some additional recipes because she doesn't 'like to do anything exactly the same way twice'.

Chicken in apricot nectar   SERVES 4

This apricot chicken recipe was contributed by Delia, who still makes it more than 40 years on. The imperative remains the same. She now spends as many as five days a week on the green, playing either golf or bowls for clubs at Mona Vale. These days she often dresses the classic dish up a bit by adding an extra ingredient or two, along with the paprika that she has always favoured.

METHOD

Preheat the oven to moderate (180°C).

Brown the chicken in a frying pan over medium–high heat in a little oil.

Place the chicken in an ovenproof dish. Sprinkle the chicken with the soup mix. Pour the apricot nectar over the chicken, covering all the pieces. Sprinkle with the paprika.

Cover the dish and cook for about 1 hour.

INGREDIENTS

1 chicken, cut into serving portions

oil

1 x 40 g packet French onion soup mix

400 ml apricot nectar

½ teaspoon sweet paprika

DELIA'S TIPS

- Use chicken marylands or drumsticks instead, and remove the skin if you prefer.
- You need a family-sized packet of dry soup mix for this recipe, not the single-serve variety made in a cup.
- If the sauce starts to dry out too much before the chicken is cooked, add a little extra water.
- Try garnishing the cooked dish with toasted flaked almonds for something a little different.
- Serve the chicken with steamed rice and a green salad.

DORIS *and* THE ROOSTERS

Doris Boyce used to joke that she drove an automatic car—the vehicle had been to the North Adelaide Football Club's home ground so many times that it could find its own way.

Doris was only five when her mother, Constance, a one-eyed Roosters fan, took her to see her first Aussie rules football match in 1922. Over the next 60 years, Doris missed just ten North Adelaide games, and then it was only because she was too ill to attend. As much an icon in the club as her favourite player, Barrie Robran, the avid fan and honorary life member left an indelible mark on both the club and her local community before she passed away in 1999, at the age of 82.

Doris grew up in Prospect, a northern Adelaide suburb in the heart of Rooster territory. An accomplished pianist who passed her music exams with honours, she was also a talented tennis player. Doris served on the Davis Cup Committee in 1956, and was president, life member and eventually patron of the Women's Midweek Grasscourts Tennis Association, which she helped establish in Adelaide. Then in 1963, she and her husband, Max, created the Boyce Medal for the state's most outstanding women tennis players.

Highly respected for her extraordinary commitment, Doris also served on the committees of several state sporting bodies, as well as charitable organisations such as the Asthma Foundation and the Crippled Children's Association. In 1982, she was awarded a British Empire Medal for community service and, in 1993, she capped off a lifetime of achievement, when she was presented with the keys to the City of Prospect.

Despite all these accolades, it was the Roosters who claimed much of her love and attention. Doris first volunteered as a fundraiser for the club in 1949, helping to bring in more than $1 million over the following seventeen years. In 1976, she beat five male rivals to become the first woman in South Australia to serve on a league football club management committee. The same year she was elected 'chairman' of the Ladies Committee, of which she was a founding member.

Doris led the Ladies Committee for more than thirteen years, and was the instigator of the *N.A.F.C. Ladies Committee Recipe Book*. Produced in 1977, the cookbook features favourite recipes from players of the day, such as Aussie

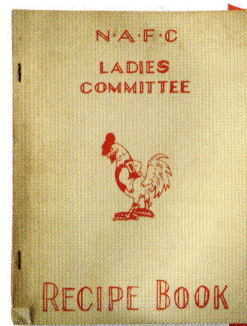

rules football legend Barrie Robran and his brother, Rodney; Tony Roach, who played more than 100 league games with the club before building a successful playing and coaching career in the South Australian Amateur Football League; and halfback flanks Bohdan Jaworskyj and John Riley, who were both listed in the Roosters Team of the Century.

'The idea at the time was that it would be a bestseller and a great fundraiser because members wanted to know what the players liked to eat,' recalls club stalwart Elaine Condon. 'If the real truth be told, Doris most likely went up to the boys during a training session and asked them what their favourite meal was, and then she would have found a recipe for it.'

Once Doris had rounded up the recipes, Elaine spent hours typing them up and then duplicating the pages. Volunteers then gathered around a long glass-topped table in the NAFC Committee room to compile several hundred copies by hand. 'There was a lot of love put into that book, and a lot of laughs too,' says Elaine.

'The women involved were certainly very good cooks. Every home game at Prospect Oval they had a cake stall, and people used to line up to get their favourite cakes from the ladies who made them. The committee had a fantastic band of helpers.'

Doris's culinary efforts didn't stop with the cookbook. For many years, every Tuesday night after training she would invite a few of the players around to her house for a three-course dinner. 'She would do anything to support her boys,' Elaine says.

That included standing up for Robran, a triple Magarey Medallist who was among the first players inducted into the Australian Football Hall of Fame and is widely regarded as South Australia's greatest ever player. Robran was in the prime of his career when he was injured in a collision with Hawthorn champion Leigh Matthews, known as 'Lethal Leigh' because of his physical style of play. Although Robran played again, the notorious incident virtually ended his career.

Recounting a story heard at Doris's funeral, veteran *Advertiser* journalist Greg Kelton explained that she 'was never afraid to speak her mind'. On meeting Matthews, Doris warned him that if she ever came across the Victorian player again, she would toss him into the River Torrens. 'With that, the burly footballer turned to jelly and fled,' mourners were told.

Above: Doris Boyce in her kitchen with NAFC players, from left, David Tiller and Stephen Riley, 1985 (Newspix). Left: Barrie Robran taking one of his famous marks for the Roosters (courtesy North Adelaide Football Club). Background: The autograph page from the cookbook, with signatures from the 1977 team.

Peppered steak

INGREDIENTS

4 thick eye fillet steaks

1 garlic clove

salt

2 tablespoons cracked black
  peppercorns

60 g butter

125 ml (½ cup) brandy, plus
  1 tablespoon extra

125 ml (½ cup) cream

This recipe appeared under Barrie Robran's name in the N.A.F.C. Ladies Committee Recipe Book. Although Barrie says he did not actually contribute it himself, it was his favourite dish at the time. Very popular in the 1970s when French cooking was influencing Australian palates, it combines brandy, cream and garlic, with generous amounts of cracked pepper.

METHOD

Trim the steaks if necessary, and shape them neatly. Cut the garlic clove in half and rub it over the steaks. Season with salt to taste.

Put the pepper on a plate and press the steak into it, so the steak is coated thinly and evenly on all sides.

Heat a large heavy-based frying pan and melt the butter. When the butter stops frothing, add the steaks and cook over medium–high heat for about 3–4 minutes per side. Remove the steaks from the heat, then pour over the brandy (125 ml) and carefully ignite the vapours, allowing the flame to burn out. Remove the steaks from the pan, cover with foil and place in a slow oven (150° C) to keep warm while you make the sauce.

Deglaze the pan with the extra brandy, then stir in the cream. Taste and adjust the seasoning if necessary. Reduce the heat and stir for 3–4 minutes until the residual juices have blended.

Put the steak on warm plates, pour over the sauce and serve.

LIZ'S TIPS

- If you can't buy cracked black pepper, crush some peppercorns coarsely, using a mortar and pestle or the back of a spoon.
- Shake the pan occasionally while the steaks are cooking to help keep the butter from burning.
- The timings suggested in the recipe aim for medium-rare, for a fillet that is about 4 cm thick.
- Make sure you don't have any flammable material near the pan when you flambé the steaks, and turn off any exhaust fan above the cooktop. If you have one, use a long-handled gas lighter to ignite the vapours.
- Serve the steak with home-made chunky-cut chips or crispy potatoes, and a green salad.

ICONIC CARTOONIST *has the* LAST LAUGH

Senior Constable Aaron Roche was a little impatient when an elderly man offered to help them catch the criminal who had just invaded his suburban Melbourne home and stolen his grandson's bicycle. The man wanted to sketch the offender, but time was wasting and the police officer didn't think a stick-figure drawing would help. Little did Roche realise that the 82-year-old crime victim was none other than celebrated cartoonist Bill Green.

Better known to his fans as WEG, Green only had moments to take in the burglar's face when he discovered the thief in his backyard one Sunday morning in January 2006. 'I heard this awful cursing and swearing. It was the foulest language I ever heard,' Green told *The Age* newspaper in a story that made headlines around the world. 'He tried to brush me aside, him being much bigger than me. I thought if I got into a fight, I'd lose my dressing gown and I'd end up starkers.'

Within seconds Green dashed off a likeness so accurate that the police recognised the perpetrator immediately when they picked him up fifteen minutes later for an unrelated crime. 'It was amazing,' Roche commented afterwards. 'After we had a look at this gentleman in the back of the divvy van, we just couldn't believe how much of a likeness it was to the picture that WEG had drawn. If anyone ever says "can I draw the offender", I'll be handing them a pencil pretty quickly.'

The burglar could not have chosen a worse backyard to run through. Green was famous for his humorous but accurate caricatures, which had been enjoyed by Aussie rules football followers and Melbourne newspaper readers for almost 60 years.

Above: Bill 'WEG' Green with his sketch of the offender, 2006 (image by Craig Abraham, Fairfax).

William Ellis Green was born in Melbourne in 1923. As a boy he collected Flash Gordon comic strips because he liked the style and strong lines of the drawings. Hovering between a career in architecture, or becoming a cartoonist, he heeded a warning from his mother that he would starve if he chose the latter option and enrolled in architecture at what is now the Royal Melbourne Institute of Technology.

His studies were interrupted when the Second World War broke out. As soon as he turned eighteen, Green joined the Australian Army and ended up in New Guinea, where he drew some cartoons, which were published in the *Army News*, and the Sydney-based *Man* magazine. The experience gave him enough confidence to take advantage of one of the retraining programs being offered to servicemen once the war was over, and study art at the National Gallery of Victoria Art School.

Green's efforts at painting did not impress instructor and esteemed war artist William Dargie, who advised him to 'go away and learn to draw'. Meanwhile, Green started submitting cartoons to *The Herald*. After filling in while another cartoonist was on holidays, his work found favour with editor-in-chief, John Williams, who offered him a permanent position in 1947. Green worked for the daily afternoon newspaper for almost 40 years, winning legions of fans for his humorous insights into issues of the day. But it was his iconic caricatures of Aussie rules football players, coaches and team mascots that truly won the hearts of many.

In 1954, Green drew the first in a long-running series of posters featuring premiership teams in the Victorian Football League, and later the AFL. The posters became so popular that *The Herald* sold as many as 100,000 copies every year, donating the proceeds to Melbourne's Royal Children's Hospital. The series continued even after the newspaper dismissed Green in 1986, claiming that his style of cartoon was 'no longer applicable'. By the time the artist died in 2008, the posters had raised more than $2 million, helping to earn him a Medal of the Order of Australia for his service to art and the community.

The series wasn't Green's only charitable endeavour. He was often asked to lend his skills to fundraising projects, such as *The Sportsman's Cook Book*, which was put together in the late 1970s to raise funds for the Epilepsy Social Welfare Foundation.

Green created the cover for the large-format book, which was published under the auspices of the Foundation's Brighton Auxiliary. The cookbook was suggested by *The Herald's* sporting editor, Jack Cannon, who also took on the task of collating material gathered from some of Australia's most famous sporting identities. They included legendary cricketer Sir Donald Bradman, Olympic gold medallist and runner Herb Elliott, world featherweight boxing champion Johnny Famechon, tennis champions Rod Laver and Neale Fraser, and world record–breaking long-distance runner Ron Clarke.

Fruity baked spare ribs

SERVES 4

Among the collection of recipes provided for The Sportsman's Cook Book, *was this tasty pork spare ribs dish from Roy Higgins. Nicknamed The Professor, the famous jockey won almost every major race on the Australian calendar during the late 1950s to the early 1980s, riding more than 2300 winners and claiming the Melbourne Jockey's Premiership eleven times.*

METHOD

Preheat the oven to hot (220°C).

Place the ribs in a large baking dish, in a single layer, and cook in the oven for 30–45 minutes, until brown, turning them once so they cook evenly. Remove the dish from the oven, and pour off as much fat as possible.

Mix together the garlic, undrained pineapple, brown sugar, allspice, vinegar, mustard, salt and orange juice. Season with pepper to taste.

Pour the mixture over the ribs, coating them thoroughly. Reduce the oven to moderate (180°C) and cook the ribs for another 45 minutes, basting and turning occasionally, until the meat is glazed and tender.

INGREDIENTS

1 kg pork spare ribs, cut into individual ribs

1 garlic clove, crushed

440 g tinned crushed pineapple in juice

2 tablespoons brown sugar

½ teaspoon ground allspice

1 tablespoon vinegar

1 teaspoon mustard powder

1 teaspoon salt

125 ml (½ cup) orange juice

freshly ground black pepper

LIZ'S TIPS

- The original recipe doesn't stipulate what type of vinegar to use, but my preference is brown vinegar.

- Roy warned not to let the ribs burn during the first phase of cooking. If you are baking them in a fan-forced oven, keep an eye on them after the first 20 minutes or so. If they are starting to dry out, cover them with foil for the remainder of cooking time.

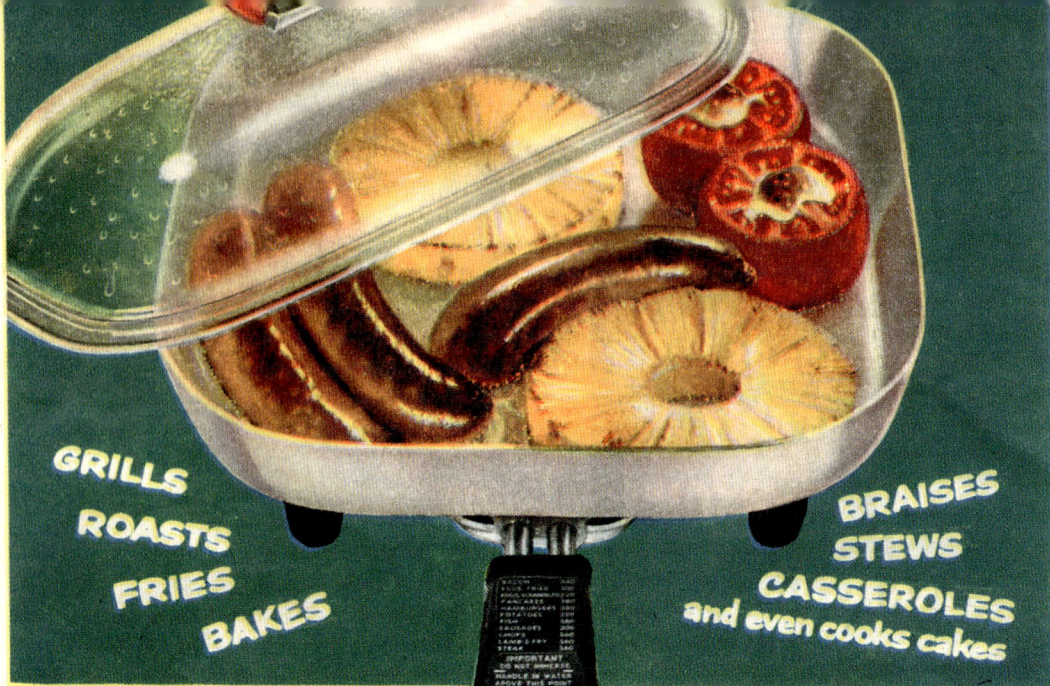  

NOSHIE *for* NEDDIE LOVERS

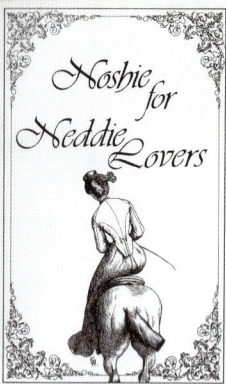

The late Eleanor Russell is known around the world for her best-selling books on dressage. To compile them, the Australian equestrian drew on her own extensive knowledge and the inspirational teachings of Portuguese master, Nuno Oliveira, a revered figure in the horse world, and her mentor. But of all the publications with Eleanor's name attached, it is a small spiral-bound book of recipes that best reflects her sense of fun and creativity.

Eleanor compiled *Noshie for Neddie Lovers* to help get the Australian dressage team to the world titles in Denmark in 1986. 'Dressage was still in its infancy here really and we were struggling to get horses qualified to compete at an international level,' explains her publishing partner, fellow horsewoman and friend, Joy Howley. 'She was a great ideas lady and she just wanted to do something to help.'

As a highly regarded horse breeder, coach, competitor and accredited judge, Eleanor had extensive networks in the horse sports community, so she wrote to everyone she knew asking for recipes. Joy's impression is that pretty well everyone agreed, resulting in a cookbook that was virtually a who's who of Australian equestrianism when it was put together in 1983. 'That is the level that Eleanor operated on. She was a great character and a little bit full on, but she had a heart of gold, and she really loved horses. She loved fun and having a bit of a laugh, and if there was a job to be done, she just did it, with very little fuss,' says Joy.

The two women set up a publishing business together in the 1980s to put out English-language editions of books originally written by Oliveira in Portuguese, as well as their own work, including *The Truth in the Teaching of Nino Oliveira* and *Gymnastic Exercises for Horses*, which were in turn translated into other languages. For a time, Eleanor and Joy lived only a few kilometres apart at Caramut, in western Victoria, where Joy still resides with her husband, Geoff, breeding stud Angus cattle.

Despite being a small farming community with a small population, the area has always had a stellar reputation for producing exceptional horses and riders. The local riding club is one of the oldest Equestrian Australia–affiliated clubs in the country, counting among its members numerous Olympic Games competitors, including the legendary Roycroft family.

Noshie for Neddie Lovers includes a boiled fruit cake recipe provided by the then head of the family, gold medallist Bill Roycroft, and his wife, Mavis, and recipes from the households of three of his sons, Barry, Wayne and Clarke, who were also Olympians.

Colin Kelly, who was president of the Equestrian Federation and competed in dressage events into his eighties, is in there with a chocolate cake recipe, which Joy still makes regularly. Triple gold medallist Andrew Hoy, who rode at seven Olympic Games, is in the book too, along with Bert Jacobs, the first Australian to win an international showjumping competition outside Australia, and Kitty Creber, winner of the very first prestigious Garryowen Perpetual Trophy at the Royal Melbourne Show in 1934.

Many of the recipes are for food that people took along to competitions or events, for picnic lunches sitting beside the horse float, or sharing between rides. Westernport Dressage Club patron and founding member, Gillian Handford, supplied detailed instructions for a traditional pork pie to feed at least twelve people, and there is a vegetable loaf 'guaranteed to fit the bill at lunch time at any Dressage Day', from Libby Anderson, a New South Wales competitor who later moved to the United States, where she set up a dressage training facility.

Above: Eleanor Russell (courtesy Emma Russell). Opposite top: *Noshie for Neddie Lovers*, 1983. Opposite bottom: An illustration from the cookbook.

The book also laughingly captures the challenges faced by the abandoned partners of 'horsey' women. Joy's favourite example comes from Eleanor's husband, James. Filling almost a page, it sets out a one-day menu for men left to hold the fort while their wives are away competing. It starts with a champagne breakfast, followed by soup from a tin 'jollied up' with herbs and a splash of white wine, or a pie and sauce with a good red, to give the diner strength to muck out horse boxes and feed the horses fortunate enough to be left behind. Then there are several options for a hearty dinner followed by four Drambuies to ensure a good night's rest and inspire dark thoughts about people who dream up unnecessary horse functions. 'He had a great sense of humour, and he understood strong women,' says Joy.

Joy is not too sure how many copies of *Noshie for Neddie Lovers* were printed, but she remembers Eleanor being very satisfied with the amount it raised. Reflecting on her friend's death in 2011, Joy says, 'I was very fond of her and I still go to tell her something, and then I remember she isn't there. I still miss her.'

Doc's double value roast chicken with tomatoes

INGREDIENTS

4 tablespoons lemon juice

2 tablespoons oil

1 teaspoon salt

2 large chickens

70 g butter

500 g fresh tomatoes, chopped

1 teaspoon freshly ground black pepper

4 teaspoons dried oregano

Known affectionately as Doc, because of his skill in treating sick and injured horses, the late Owen Matthews was chief riding master and horse instructor with the Victorian Mounted Police. From 1965 to 1975, he and his thoroughbred horse, Aintree Boy, mesmerised packed audiences at the Royal Melbourne Show every year with their spectacular routines of dressage movements performed under lights, to music, in the main arena.

When Eleanor asked him for a contribution for her cookbook, Doc provided his favourite recipe along with a cover note explaining why he liked it so much. Not only did its delicious taste and tantalising aromas rejuvenate drained riders, grooms, trainers and truck drivers after a long day, it satisfied hungry appetites the next day too, when there was pressure to grab a quick meal during lively competitions. The feat was achieved by roasting two chickens at the same time, then saving one to serve cold the next day. Of course, home cooks not facing a similar challenge can simply halve the recipe.

METHOD

Preheat the oven to moderate (180°C).

Mix together the lemon juice, oil and salt and brush it over the chickens—both inside and out. Place the chickens in a large baking pan and cook for 1 hour.

Melt the butter in a large saucepan over medium heat, and add the tomatoes with the pepper and oregano. Simmer, covered, for 10 minutes. Pour the mixture over the chickens and continue to roast for another 30 minutes, basting occasionally until the chickens are cooked.

Serve hot with roast vegetables and greens, then cold with a light salad.

LIZ AND DOC'S TIPS

- Doc suggested using tinned tomatoes instead of fresh. If you choose this option you only need to cook them with the butter and herbs for a few minutes.

- Keep an eye on the chickens after adding the tomatoes — if the topping starts to dry out too much, cover them with foil.

- Depending on the size of the chickens, you may need to adjust the cooking times. Allow 25 minutes per 500 g when cooking at a moderate temperature.

- When the chickens are cooked, remove them from the pan, pour off any fat, then deglaze the pan with verjuice or white wine to make a sauce.

- Doc recommended serving this dish with a good, crisp riesling.

RECIPES

for

WELLNESS

The GIFT THAT KEEPS ON GIVING

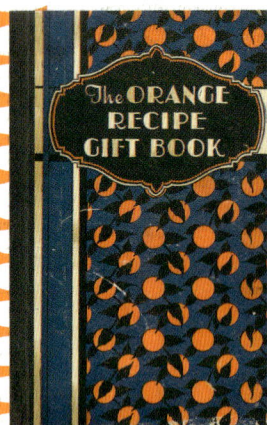

The Orange hospital auxiliary is a force to be reckoned with. Every year its band of volunteers raise a staggering $300,000 to $400,000 through a cafe they run in the hospital foyer.

Their contribution is so important to the quality of care offered at the regional public hospital, that the Orange Health Service quickly dismissed a proposal to replace them with a private contractor when the facility moved onto a new site in 2011. 'They soon realised they couldn't do without the funds,' says Tracy Wilkinson, who was auxiliary president at the time. 'The health department doesn't upgrade equipment fast enough so the hospital relies heavily on the auxiliary, and we buy extra medical equipment which helps attract the best surgeons and specialists.'

The 90 or so men and women who achieve such astounding results follow a long tradition, which began when 25 women gathered at what was then known as the Orange District Hospital, in December 1924. According to local author and historian Liz Edwards, the meeting was part of a wider movement that emerged in the 1920s to harness the considerable experience women gained in fundraising and organising during the First World War.

The new auxiliary immediately took charge of looking after the hospital linen, relieving pressure on the matron and nurses who had been spending most of their spare time sewing. They set to repairing sheets, making pyjamas and mosquito nets, and collecting or stitching dozens of towels and pillowslips. Within twelve months they had made 630 new items. Meanwhile, a special sub-committee raised nearly £40 hiring out crockery and cutlery.

The women soon expanded their efforts to catering at the local show, collecting and selling flowers and eggs, and holding card parties. They impressed the hospital secretary, William Bouffler, so much that in 1927 he urged nearby Wagga Wagga to set up a similar organisation. 'No hospital should be without a women's auxiliary. It is an immense help, and does a lot of good work,' he said.

As the Depression began to bite, the auxiliary stepped up its efforts under the leadership of the accomplished Aimee Lane. An obituary published after her death in June 1939, described Aimee as someone 'gifted with extraordinary organising ability, a charming manner and artistic attainments', which she harnessed for the good of others.

Originally from Dandenong in Victoria, Aimee was a widow with a young son when she moved to Orange in about 1915. She had owned a florist business in Melbourne and worked as a fashion buyer for two Orange stores, before causing great excitement among local women by opening her own elegant fashion shop and beauty parlour in 1919. Aimee sold the business after becoming engaged the following year to Tracy Lane, a high-profile grazier, who was also a single parent, with four children. He owned Narrambla, where famous Australian poet Banjo Paterson was born, and went on to serve as president of the local shire council and show society.

Aimee was president of the hospital auxiliary from 1929 until 1937. During that time she oversaw the production of a fundraiser that is still earning money for the hospital almost 90 years later.

The Orange Recipe Gift Book is a collection of about 600 recipes covering everything from breakfast to supper dishes, baking and preserving. It begins with a very brief introduction by Aimee, urging people to support the venture, with an unattributed quote that could well be the motto for the auxiliary: 'Each can do but little; but, if each will do that little all will be done'.

The first edition was published in 1930, during a period when the hospital's finances were in a particularly bad state, with money owed to local tradespeople as well as the bank. Every penny counted to keep the hospital operating during these difficult years, and sales of the cookbook brought in hundreds of pounds. By May 1932 a second edition had almost sold out. A third edition of 10,000 copies followed, with at least three more subsequent editions over the next 30 years or so.

By the time Aimee stepped down as president in 1937, the auxiliary had raised more than £9000 for the hospital through a series of innovative and energetic enterprises. Among them was establishing a refreshment kiosk in the brand new base hospital built in Orange in 1933. The kiosk began trading in January 1934. Within weeks it was hosting functions for visiting dignitaries, including Enid Lyons, wife of then Prime Minister Joseph Lyons, who came to town to speak at the first ever regional conference of hospital auxiliaries, which Aimee convened.

The auxiliary has operated a kiosk, or cafe, ever since. Today's version sits in the foyer of the main hospital building, which is part of a larger health campus situated about four kilometres from the city centre and ten minutes

Mrs Tracy Lane.
President of the Orange Hospital Auxiliary, 1928-37
A Loving Tribute from the
Ladies' Hospital Auxiliary.

Above: Aimee Lane (reproduced from *In Sickness and in Health: how medicine helped shape Orange's history,* courtesy Orange City Council). Opposite: *The Orange Recipe Gift Book,* c. 1930s (courtesy Special Collections, Deakin University Library).

Clockwise from top: Betty Hocking
sitting outside the auxiliary's
cafe knitting for the cause, 2013
(courtesy *Central Western Daily*);
the official opening of the Orange
Base Hospital, 1933, and a
photograph of the hospital
(courtesy Orange Health Service);
advertisement from the third
edition, 1939.

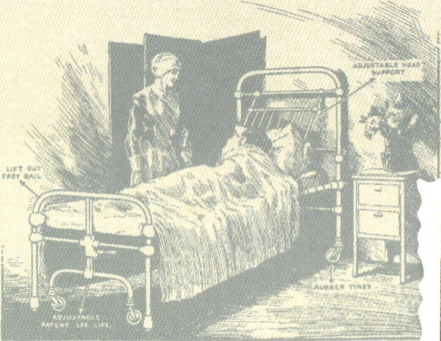

*Acme Bedsteads
for Elegance and Utility*

from the nearest commercial coffee shop. Now the largest rural hospital in the state, it has hundreds of beds, a large staff and a host of visiting medical practitioners; all of which means the auxiliary is busier than ever.

The cafe opens every day of the week, for as long as twelve hours a day, with trading times reduced at weekends because there are not enough volunteers to go round. It takes an average of fourteen people per day to operate the business. They butter their way through 40 loaves of bread to make sandwiches, churn out hundreds of cups of coffee and tea, and dish up hot and cold baked goods from a bakery at Blayney. 'We used to make all our own cakes and things, but the turnover is too high now, so we have to buy them in,' explains Tracy Wilkinson.

Volunteers are rostered on for four- and six-hour shifts. Some help out once a month, many once a week, and there are others who work as much as 24 hours a week. In 2017, the longest-serving member was Betty Hocking who, at 85 years of age, was still catching the community bus every Wednesday to sit in the cafe and sell raffle tickets. Betty joined the auxiliary in 1972.

After she went home, the next shift on most Wednesday nights was taken up by three generations of the Miller family. Nakita started coming with her

Below: Members of the United Hospital Auxiliary Orange branch (from left), Leonie Horspool, Tracy Wilkinson, Bob Selwood, Dorothy Collins, Lyn Selwood, Barbara Horan, Gail Woods and Brian Brooks, 2011 (image by Steve Gosch, courtesy *Central Western Daily*).

mother and grandmother, and her twin sister, Aliera, when she was eight years old. Aliera has since moved to Adelaide but, 26 years on, the others are there every week on the same night. 'It really is extraordinary when you think about it,' admits Tracy. 'In total the volunteers contribute something like 19,000 hours a year, without being paid.'

Regional coordinator of twelve United Hospital Auxiliaries in the Central West, Tracy is particularly proud of the Orange group, which is just one of 129 across the state. The government gives head office $186,000 a year to coordinate them, and in return they raise $6 million profit, a spectacular return on investment. Orange sits at the top of the ranking for regional auxiliaries when it comes to fundraising, alongside their Newcastle peers.

Contributing a small sum towards keeping them at the top of the leaderboard is *The Orange Recipe Gift Book*. The auxiliary rediscovered it in 2014 and started selling reprints at the cafe. 'They have been selling like hotcakes,' Tracy says.

Blue Ribbon Championship sponge

INGREDIENTS

3 eggs

150 g (⅔ cup) caster sugar

150 g (1 cup) self-raising flour

30 g butter, chopped

3 tablespoons milk

This recipe was contributed by Mrs A. Thornton of Hurlstone Park in Sydney. It won her a large silver cup in a special competition held in September 1930 to raise money for the Deaf Dumb and Blind Institute at Darlington. To qualify for the lucrative championship prize, cooks had to win at one of a series of fortnightly parties. The overall champion was chosen during a Blue Ribbon Cabaret held at David Jones department store. Competitors danced and listened to a musical program while the judge toiled away in a small adjacent room. It is a lovely recipe, and a good place to start for cooks who may not have made a sponge before.

METHOD

Preheat the oven to moderate (180°C). Grease two 20 cm sandwich (round) pans, and line the base with baking paper.

Put the eggs in a large clean bowl and beat with an electric mixer for 5 minutes, until thick. Gradually add the sugar and beat until it is completely dissolved.

Sift in the flour and gently fold it into the mixture with a large metal spoon, working in figure-eight motions.

Put the butter and milk in a small saucepan and bring to the boil. Pour the hot milk into the sponge mixture, stirring lightly and quickly to make sure it is thoroughly incorporated.

Divide the mixture between the two sandwich pans and bake for 15–18 minutes, until golden and springy to the touch. Turn the sponges out onto a wire rack, covered with a clean tea towel.

LIZ'S TIPS

- Use eggs that are at room temperature.
- Once you have added the hot milk, you need to work quickly to get the mixture into the oven.
- If you want to make sure the sponge layers are even in height, weigh the pans before you put them in the oven. If you want them to appear exactly the same once the sponge is constructed, put one more spoonful of mixture in one pan than the other, then place the slightly larger mixture on the bottom. It will compensate for the compression that happens when you add the filling and top layer.
- Unfilled, the sponge will keep for a week in an airtight container in the fridge.
- Serve one half topped with cream and strawberries and keep the other for the Trifle recipe on page 32.

"I've never had a failure! because I always use

GOLDEN CRUST Self-Raising FLOUR

Left: Advertisement from *The Leader Spare Corner Book*, c. 1930. Opposite: Advertisement from *The Orange Recipe Gift Book*, third edition, 1939.

COOKING *with* SOCIETY'S ELITE

'It is a generally accepted fact that a recipe for which a successful hostess is famous can't be found in an ordinary recipe book. Nor can you coax it from her. It is always a closely guarded secret.' So begins the book jacket blurb for a sophisticated volume of recipes put together in 1958 to support an ambitious campaign raising money for cancer research.

We Cook at Home is not your everyday community cookbook. Featuring recipes from Melbourne's social elite and priced at one guinea, it was clearly aimed at the upper echelons, or those aspiring to join them. The hardcover book even carried photographs of table settings created by the wives of some of Melbourne's leading figures, so readers could replicate them at home. Among the contributors were the governor's wife, Lady Brooks, and Merlyn Myer, the widow of Sidney Myer who founded the famous Myer retail company.

Noted for her charity work, Mrs Myer chaired the Cancer Campaign Appeal's Women's Committee, which produced the book. The committee was part of a massive effort that set out to raise £500,000 to help find the cause of, and a cure for, cancer. Driven by the Anti-Cancer Council of Victoria, it changed fundraising in Australia forever when it became the first appeal to employ door-knocking. More than 40,000 volunteers gathered up more than £300,000 through the door-knock, with 95 out of every 100 homes in Melbourne making a donation.

Combined with money from sponsors and schemes, which saw thousands willingly agree to have donations deducted from their weekly pay, the final tally was almost three times the original target.

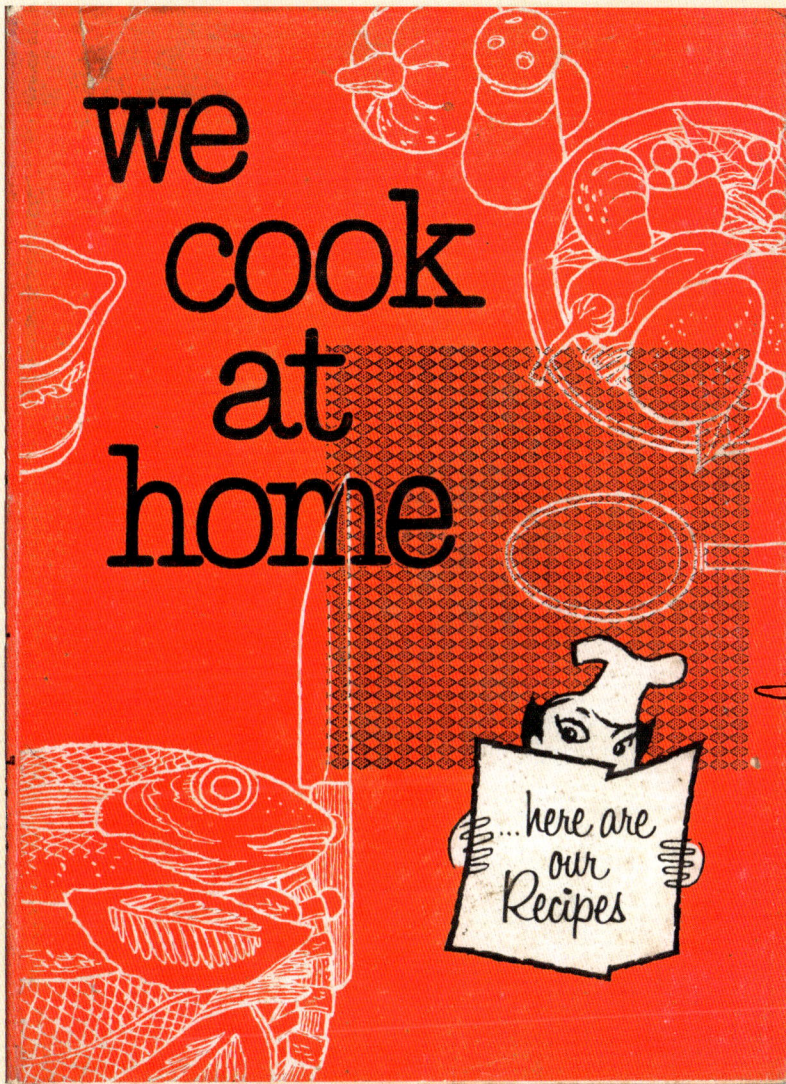

Left: *We Cook at Home*, 1958. Below and opposite: illustrations from the cookbook. Bottom, from left: Featured dining settings— Harold and Zara Holt's table for a 'do it yourself' dinner at their Toorak home, featuring Siamese silk mats in green, khaki and dark brown, and Italian glassware; an official table for a dinner dance hosted by Mrs Sidney Baillieu Myer, with

Brussels lace tablecloth and silver candelabra; a striking luncheon table setting from the home of award-winning modernist architect Roy Ground, who went on to design the National Gallery of Victoria; a Regency setting by Mrs Baillieu Myer.

Rum and coffee pavlova

SERVES 8

INGREDIENTS

4 egg whites

220 g (1 cup) caster sugar

1 teaspoon unsweetened
coffee essence, plus
¼ teaspoon extra

1 teaspoon dry sherry

250 ml (1 cup) cream

1 tablespoon rum

100 g (½ cup) black cherries,
pitted

30 g (¼ cup) crumbed
walnuts

This recipe was contributed by Mrs T.F. McMullen, whose husband managed the Union Bank of Australia branch in Collins Street, until he retired in 1950 and took up positions on the boards of several leading companies. It's a classy twist on the classic pavlova, and indicative of the stylish, French or continental-style dishes in the book, which includes a special chapter featuring international recipes from the households of various consuls, vice consuls and commercial attachés based in Melbourne.

METHOD

Preheat the oven to very slow (120°C). Line a baking tray with baking paper.

Put the egg whites in a large, clean, dry bowl and beat until soft peaks form. Gradually add the sugar, beating continuously between additions. Continue beating for about 5 minutes, until the sugar is completely dissolved and the meringue is thick and glossy.

Fold in the coffee essence (1 teaspoon) and the sherry.

Spread the mixture on the baking tray to form a circle about 23 cm in diameter. Bake for 1–1½ hours, until dry to the touch. Cool in the oven with the door slightly ajar.

To make the topping, whip the cream until thick. Beat in the rum and the extra ¼ teaspoon coffee essence.

Just before serving, spread the filling over the cold pavlova shell, and decorate with the cherries and crumbed walnuts.

LIZ'S TIPS

- The eggs should be at room temperature.
- Coffee essence has a very strong flavour so don't overdo it in the cream.
- Pitted morello cherries work beautifully with the coffee and rum.
- Use crumbed or broken walnuts as they look nicer than chopped.

CARING *at* KANIVA

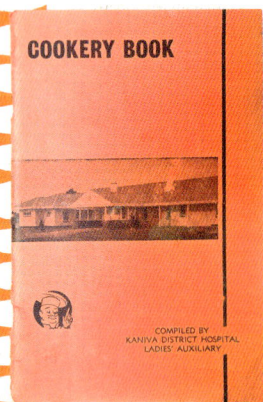

COOKERY BOOK

COMPILED BY
KANIVA DISTRICT HOSPITAL
LADIES' AUXILIARY

At the height of the Depression in 1931, Flora Champness made headlines with an act of generosity that brightened Christmas Day for swagmen wandering the Victorian Wimmera. She prepared a sumptuous three-course meal for seven unemployed men, who were camping in Kaniva while they walked the roads looking for whatever work they could find

Flora was a well-known member of the community. Her husband, Roy, served as shire president for a number of years and was highly regarded for his farming abilities, while Flora was appreciated for her splendid efforts supporting the Kaniva hospital. When an auxiliary was formed in 1924 to raise money for the facility, Flora was elected as the first president. She held the position for 22 years.

The auxiliary was still going strong in the early 1960s, when the next generation of the Champness family stepped up. Flora's daughter-in-law, Elva, served as treasurer for about six years. Roy's nephew, Harry, another capable farmer who also served on the shire council, spent about 25 years on the hospital board, while his wife, Jean, was auxiliary secretary for nine years.

'They really worked hard to get the hospital going and keep it going,' says daughter Shirley Ashfield, who is payroll manager for West Wimmera Health Services, which now runs the hospital. 'Mum had German measles when she was pregnant with one of my sisters, and she was born with an eye problem. They had to get lots of help for her, and I think from that they realised we didn't have much in the way of health care in Kaniva. In the background of it all, they were just community minded people.'

With four daughters born less than four years apart, Jean didn't have a lot of spare time, but she often harnessed her cooking skills to support worthy causes, struggling to keep the children's fingers out of the baking mixtures while she whipped up sponges, cakes and puddings.

Shirley remembers Jean and her mother, Mary Hall, baking hundreds of pasties and sausage rolls to sell at a 'farm shop' trading table in Kaniva once a week and, for many years, she was part of a Methodist church catering committee, which served up meals for just about every type of private and public occasion, from weddings to governor's visits.

'What she cooked, she cooked really well—the sort of things that men really liked when they had afternoon tea. Mum had a good name for scones. She used to make a really nice date slice, and she would take her plum puddings everywhere and anywhere. She was also into sponges and little pinkies,' says Shirley, using the family name for jelly cakes. 'They were to die for!'

Similar traditional but delicious recipes are a feature of the Kaniva District Hospital Ladies' Auxiliary *Cookery Book*, which Jean played a key role in compiling sometime around 1960. Shirley says the women involved used their knowledge of who cooked the best version of something to select what appeared in the book if more than one recipe came in for the same thing. 'The recipes are all very simple, and you know they are going to work. There is no mucking around,' she says.

No-one is exactly sure how many copies have been sold over the years but, by 2017, the cookbook was in its fifteenth edition and still raising money for the hospital auxiliary. Filling more than 70 pages with diverse recipes, from soups to sandwich fillings, baking, preserving, confectionery and drinks, the contents haven't changed, although the latest edition is spiral-bound. 'It's just been so popular,' says auxiliary president Lorraine Vivian.

Above: Harry and Jean Champness, c. 1940s (courtesy Valerie Goldsworthy). Opposite top: The Kaniva hospital auxiliary *Cookery Book*, fifth edition (Special Collections, Deakin University Library). Opposite bottom: The old Kaniva hospital (courtesy Kaniva and District History).

The recipe book was already a hit when Lorraine married a local farmer and moved from Nhill in 1962. Encouraged by a neighbour, she joined the auxiliary in the late 1990s after shifting into Kaniva to live, and was elected president in 2008.

There are only about a dozen members now, both men and women, who get together once every two months to discuss what the hospital needs and to plan the Melbourne Cup week lunch and Christmas raffle, which are their main fundraisers. The well-equipped hospital has six acute-care beds, a low-care hostel with ten places, and aged-care accommodation for up to eleven frail residents. The auxiliary purchases mainly small items, such as cushions, electric blankets, armchairs, heaters and televisions to help make life a little more comfortable for the patients.

A keen cook like Jean, Lorraine followed in her footsteps too by joining the church catering committee, which became part of the Uniting Church. She was in charge of the group for 25 years, priding herself on never getting flustered, no matter what went wrong or how big the crowd that had to be fed. Everything was home-made, and sit-down meals often involved preparing three courses.

'I had four children and the youngest was nine when I took it on, and of course being on a farm you've also got cows and chooks and pigs and everything else. I would never want to own a catering business but it's something

Below: Dean and Peter Wallis, standing outside the Kaniva hospital, c. late 1950s (courtesy Peg Wallis).

that I loved doing. We catered for six weddings one year, all over 100 guests, and we had a Lions Club convention dinner here with over 300 people. It was in our sporting complex, and we used the high school kitchen, which meant we had to carry things across a road, but I had a lovely lot of help,' Lorraine says.

The Lions delegates feasted on home-made soups, cold meat and salads, pavlovas and apple crumble for just twenty dollars, with about 30 volunteers helping to prepare and serve the food, and then do all the dishes. 'The next morning I had to hand in the bill, and the one in charge shook my hand and he nearly shook it off, they were that pleased with everything,' Lorraine says, smiling at the memory.

These days Lorraine mostly confines herself to cooking for her family, the CWA or the Kaniva show, where she has been known to win more than a few prizes for her cakes, often with recipes taken from the hospital auxiliary cookbook.

Golden syrup dumplings

INGREDIENTS

225 g (1½ cups) self-raising
   flour

30 g butter

1 egg

80 ml (⅓ cup) milk
   (approximately)

Syrup:

500 ml (2 cups) water

110 g (½ cup firmly packed)
   brown sugar

30 g butter

2 tablespoons golden syrup

Proving it was extremely popular, this recipe was contributed by Jean Champness, along with three other women—Mrs G. Heinrich, Mrs Gwen Eastwood and Mrs A. Hobbs. It remains one of Shirley's favourites, and mine too. Economical and quick to make with ingredients once kept in every farm-house pantry, it brings back family memories of the perfect comfort food, after coming inside from milking the cows on a cold winter's night.

Some recipes include golden syrup in the dumplings but this version is lighter, and there is enough sweetness in the syrup. Even though it wasn't included in the Cookery Book *version, Shirley says the preferred family approach is to bake the dumplings in the oven, rather than cook them on the stove top. 'It makes a nice crispy top that is golden brown and always looks inviting, and we used to eat them with fresh cream, which we separated ourselves, from milk taken from our own cows,' she says.*

METHOD

Preheat the oven to moderately hot (190°C).

To make the dumplings, put the flour in a large bowl, then rub in the butter until the mixture looks like fine breadcrumbs.

Break the egg into a 125 ml (½ cup) measure and lightly beat it with a fork. Top the cup up with milk, then beat again with the fork. Pour the egg mixture into the flour mixture, then stir it with a knife to form a stiff dough. Roll dessert-spoonfuls of the dough into balls.

To make the syrup, put the water in a large saucepan with the sugar, butter and golden syrup. Stir over medium heat until the sugar has dissolved, then bring gently to the boil.

Pour the boiling syrup into a baking dish (approximately 24 x 18 cm), and then immediately add the dumplings. Spoon a little syrup over each one, and bake them, uncovered, in the oven for about 20 minutes, until golden brown and crispy on top and a skewer comes out clean.

Serve with cream or ice cream.

LIZ AND SHIRLEY'S TIPS

- If the dumpling mixture is too dry, add a little extra milk to bring it together into a stiff, slightly sticky dough.

- You should get eight dumplings from this mixture — make sure they are the same size so they cook evenly.

- The syrup needs to be straight off the boil when you put it in the baking dish.

- Jean preferred to use a metal baking dish, rather than ceramic because it doesn't cool the syrup down as much when you pour it in, and it seems to cook the dumplings faster and produce a better result.

- Leave plenty of room between the dumplings, rather than packing them in tight, so they have room to expand.

- Stand the dish on a tray, in case it overflows.

TRIPPING DOWN MEMORY LANE
with PINEAPPLE ROYALTY

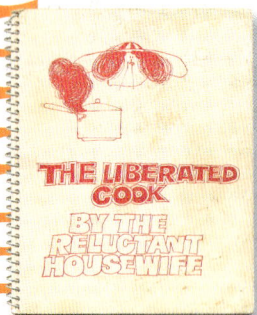

They're known as the Pineapple Princesses—two women who share a passion for the versatile fruit that Australian cooks seemed to put in everything they made in the 1960s.

Dungog community artist and photographer, Anne Fisher, and former home economics teacher, Ann Rocca, from Queanbeyan, got to know each other when they taught together in Canberra in the 1980s. One day in 2012, Ann found an old recipe book at an op shop, written by Queensland home economist Ruby Borrowdale. After chuckling over the retro wonders it contained, the two women became curious about Ruby and decided to do a little research.

They discovered that, apart from *The Golden Circle Tropical Recipe Book*, she had written cookery articles for regional newspapers in the 1950s. Under the nom de plume Patricia Dale, she had a weekly cooking column in the Brisbane *Telegraph*, and she made appearances on television and radio. For many years in the 1940s and '50s she was in charge of the test kitchen for Brisbane-based flour millers Simpson Bros. She later established her own test kitchen at Fortitude Valley, testing products and writing cookbooks for various companies, including Golden Circle, which began as a growers' cooperative in the 1940s, producing around 40,000 tonnes of tinned pineapple per year.

Anne and Ann were captivated by Ruby's tropical cookbook and its colourful images of artfully arranged pineapple rings, boiled eggs and beetroot slices, which evoked memories of their childhoods. 'I jokingly suggested that we cook our way through the book, a little like Julie Powell cooking through Julia Child's *Mastering the Art of French Cooking*,' says Anne.

Ann immediately saw the potential to record their triumphs and disasters via a blog. *Pineapple Princesses* was launched in July 2012, with a quick succession of seventeen posts about Ruby and her recipes for things like Sunny sausages—a breakfast recipe featuring sausages, sliced pineapple, eggs, tomatoes and parsley—and a Banana boat dessert, with mashed banana, chopped walnuts, pineapple pieces and cream mixed together and stuffed into banana skins, then garnished with maraschino cherries.

The blog was an instant success. Within six months it attracted around 30,000 hits, which staggered the authors, given they were complete unknowns. Soon people were sending them pineapple recipes from their own childhoods, or recipes that they had discovered, found astounding and wanted to share. Then, in 2014, the blog won a pineapple recipe competition run by ABC Radio National and its *Bush Telegraph* program in conjunction with the Queensland Gallery of Modern Art, which was holding an exhibition celebrating food in art. Anne and Ann were flown to Brisbane, put up in a plush hotel and wined and dined for the weekend.

While many of their posts, and the images that went with them, generated howls of laughter and a lot of head-shaking, for both women there is a serious side to the project. For Anne, it provides a platform to take the mickey out of the food-worship culture that has emerged in western societies in recent years and, for Ann, it's a way of acknowledging the hidden contributions of women like Ruby.

'It is too easy to dismiss Ruby's book as quaintly old fashioned, when in fact it contains good recipes that can be quite delicious. She was obviously trying to improve the limited culinary offerings from Australian home kitchens while working for the pineapple processors, not just to improve the company's bottom line,' Ann wrote. 'Many food manufacturers at the time employed home economists to develop recipes and promote their products, but today these talented women are invisible if they exist at all.'

Below, from top: Anne Fisher (image by Les Fisher); the banana boat dessert from the *Golden Circle Tropical Recipe Book* (image by Anne Fisher) one of the cookbooks that has featured in the blog; Ann Rocca. Opposite, from top: *The Liberated Cook by the Reluctant Housewife*, 1975 (courtesy Anne Fisher); and the Pineapple Princesses' recreation of a pineapple cartwheel salad from the *Golden Circle Tropical Recipe Book* (image by Anne Fisher).

EXCITING AS A TROPIC

Golden Circle BRAND
TROPICAL FRUIT SALAD

It's a tropical treasure of golden fruit flavour and Vitamin C. Sunny chunks of pineapple and papaw and creamy banana, basking in the juice of sweet oranges and deep purple passionfruit. Tastes just like you'd make yourself——yet it's ready to serve in a One · Two · Three !

Scenes from the Great Barrier Reef North Queensland

your easiest ! your quickest ! the most popular sweet of all !

HOLIDAY !

Golden Circle TROPICAL

FRUIT SALAD

THE C.O.D. CANNERY, NORTHGATE, BRISBANE, Q.

Pineapple fruit cake

INGREDIENTS

440 g tinned crushed
   pineapple

500 g mixed fruit, chopped

220 g (1 cup) white sugar

1 teaspoon bicarbonate
   of soda

1 teaspoon mixed spice

125 g butter, chopped

150 g (1 cup) plain flour

150 g (1 cup) self-raising flour

2 eggs, well beaten

This moist, boiled fruit cake is one of Ann's favourite pineapple recipes. She bakes it every Christmas to include in a basket of seasonal goodies for her family. The recipe comes from a book produced in 1975 to raise money for the Muscular Dystrophy Association of New South Wales. Titled The Liberated Cook by the Reluctant Housewife, *it was compiled by Valerie Bursill, who unashamedly admits in the introduction that she dislikes cooking. 'There are so many more interesting things for me to do than spend hours in the kitchen preparing food,' she wrote. In line with this reluctance, the cake is quick and easy to make. Hopefully, Ruby would have approved.*

METHOD

Preheat the oven to moderate (180°C). Grease and line a deep, 20 cm square cake pan.

Place the undrained pineapple, mixed fruit, sugar, bicarbonate of soda, mixed spice and butter in a large saucepan. Bring to the boil over medium heat, stirring until the sugar dissolves. Boil for 3 minutes, then remove the pan from the heat and set aside to cool.

Sift the flours together, then stir them into the cold fruit mixture along with the eggs and beat until thoroughly combined.

Spoon the mixture into the prepared pan and bake in the oven for 1½–2 hours, or until a skewer inserted into the middle of the cake comes out clean. Cool the cake in the pan.

LIZ AND ANN'S TIPS

- The fruit mixture needs to be cool enough so that it doesn't start cooking the eggs when you add them.
- Line the pan with two double thicknesses of paper, laid across each other to form a cross pattern, so there are four layers covering the bottom, and two up each side. This will help to prevent the cake burning on the outside before the centre is cooked through.
- Cooks baking fruit cakes for competition prefer to use old-fashioned greaseproof paper instead of baking paper, which can make the sides of cakes dark and unnaturally shiny. Make sure it's proper greaseproof paper — not the shiny white version sometimes sold.

- Old hands also swear by an added layer of brown paper, placed between the pan and the greaseproof paper, to provide extra protection against the cake browning too quickly.

- To fill the cake pan, start by spooning in the mixture to a depth of about 2 cm, then working it well down to eliminate air pockets. When all the mixture is in the pan, drop the pan on the bench to settle it further.

- If the top of the cake is becoming too brown during cooking, cover the top — make a lid that you can use again by covering a piece of thick cardboard with foil.

- Ann likes to drizzle a tablespoon or two of dark rum over the cake when it comes out of the oven, to enhance the pineapple flavour and help it stay moist and keep longer.

From BAKING WITH BISCUITS to BOYUP BROOK

When Rhonda Parker was four years old, her grandfather crafted her a miniature stove made out of wood. Fashioned in the style of the latest electric models, it was painted yellow, with black hobs and little dials at the back. 'It was the bee's knees,' says Rhonda.

The eldest of four children, Rhonda grew up in the southern Sydney suburb of Jannali. She loved cooking even before receiving the wondrous gift, although she is not too sure how that passion started. It certainly didn't come from her mother, Joan Mason. 'Mum cooked so we had something to eat. She didn't enjoy cooking, and she didn't like entertaining. It freaked her out even when relations were coming for a meal. She thought it was fancy if she made coleslaw!' Rhonda recalls.

However, when it came to old-fashioned cornflake cookies, Joan was a master. 'If you asked each of the four of us what she made best, we would all say cornflake cookies. We had them at her funeral. She would probably make them every week, and if she had to cook something for a fete that is what she would make.'

Although it was a happy childhood, money was tight. Rhonda's father, Bob, had a decent job with the Sydney County Council as an electrician but, having lived through a depression and a war, the Masons did not like to see anything wasted. 'When I was cooking in Mum's kitchen I had to be very frugal. I wasn't allowed to waste anything, or burn anything, and you certainly wouldn't just go to the fridge or the cupboard and help yourselves to food. We would get back home from school and there were four little piles of afternoon tea set out on the table, and that was our share.'

By the age of ten, Rhonda was attending local community cooking classes and dreaming of becoming a home economics teacher, so she could teach others to cook. She gave up on the idea of tackling a full teacher's degree, in part because of the expense it was likely to involve, and also because she was convinced her grades might not be good enough. Instead, Rhonda completed two years of home economic studies at the East Sydney Technical College and then, at the age of about eighteen, found work in the test kitchen at the Arnott's biscuit factory at Homebush.

The position involved developing recipes using Arnott's biscuits, then travelling all over New South Wales to demonstrate them. The demonstrators would start by telling their audience the history of the iconic brand, from the early struggles of its founder, William Arnott, a Scottish baker who arrived in Australian in 1848, to building the Homebush facility, which became the largest biscuit factory in the Southern Hemisphere, employing 2500 people during the 1930s, making more than 10,250 tonnes of biscuits a year.

After two years, Rhonda returned to the East Sydney Technical college to complete a catering management course, which she loved. In the mid-1970s the additional qualifications earned her the position of catering manager at the Bank of New South Wales in Martin Place. The bank had its own cafeteria for employees, capable of dishing up 500 meals a day, including fish on Fridays, roasts every day, casseroles, salads and sweets.

'We did morning tea, lunch and afternoon tea every day, and in the evening we quite often had functions,' she says. Ironically, the biscuits served alongside cuppas delivered by office tea ladies, were from Arnotts.

During this period, Rhonda married her first husband and, in 1976, they headed overseas to work and travel for two years. The marriage ended while they were living in Libya and Rhonda returned home without her husband,

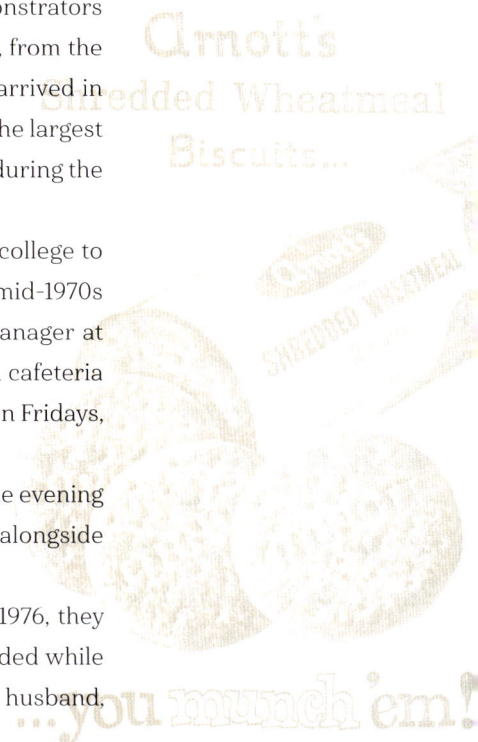

a single mother with a six-month-old baby. She was divorced and living back in Sydney when a friend convinced her to attend the official opening of the 50th Anniversary Convention of Apex Clubs in Australia, at Geelong in April 1981. Prince Charles was doing the honours and she thought Rhonda might enjoy it.

During the event, Rhonda started talking to a group of people from Western Australia. One of them, Neville Parker, was a sheep and wheat farmer from Boyup Brook, in the south-west of the state. She married him seven months later.

'When I went home and told my parents that I had met someone from WA, and he lived on a farm, Mum and Dad thought I had gone stark raving mad,' Rhonda says with a laugh. 'I was a city girl, but now I don't think I could live in the city. I'm not saying everything has been a bed of roses. When I first moved here it was a real learning curve, but I was embraced by the local community and it's been an excellent life.'

Rhonda has certainly thrown herself into local activities. She was named a national finalist in the 2010 Australian of the Year Awards Local Hero category for her dynamic contribution as a volunteer to a multitude of community organisations over a period of 28 years, including ten years as music director of the Boyup Brook Country Music Club, which hosts the state's largest country music festival.

On more than a few occasions, Rhonda's input has involved harnessing her skills in cooking and organising catering, like the year parents in her son's primary school class took on just about every catering job in town to raise money so the students could visit Canberra for a week. 'I've still got the books I kept, with all the menus. We did something every three weeks, whether it was a cake stall at the hockey or a golf club dinner. All the parents contributed in one way or another and the students, who were barely twelve years old, did all the serving. We raised something like $18,000, and my son and the people he went to school with still talk about the trip.'

Rhonda is also a member of the CWA, and stewards the cookery section at the Upper Blackwood show every November. When she first moved to the district she used to enter, but she gave that up in the mid-1990s after becoming a judge.

Among Rhonda's large collection of cookbooks is *Country Cooking*. It was put together in the early 1980s as a fundraiser for the hospital auxiliary at Bruce Rock, a small town in the eastern wheatbelt of Western Australia, more than 300 kilometres from Boyup Brook. The now-battered book was given to her many years ago by one of the contributors, Margaret Teasdale, who she met through Apex.

The auxiliary is still going, although its membership has declined to about a dozen women. They meet monthly and run a series of fundraisers every year to purchase items that will make life easier for staff and more comfortable for patients in the small district hospital, which provides mainly aged care and hospice services. These days the main avenues for raising money are a Mother's Day raffle and two annual beetle days, when about 30 people gather at a local hall to play the game of beetle and share afternoon tea. 'We've been doing that for years, and it's pretty popular,' says president Edna Vaughan. 'It's a lovely afternoon out and we raise about $1000 between the two events.'

Below: Rhonda Parker making Worcestershire sauce, and (inset) preparing the ingredients (images by Sue Haynes).

Worcestershire sauce

MAKES ABOUT 1 LITRE (4 CUPS)

INGREDIENTS

750 g green apples, roughly
  chopped

2 garlic cloves, chopped

2 teaspoons white pepper

¼ teaspoon cayenne pepper

330 g (1½ cups) white sugar

1½ teaspoons chopped
  red chilli

1 teaspoon whole cloves

30 g fresh ginger, chopped

1 teaspoon whole black
  peppercorns

2½ tablespoons salt

2 litres (8 cups) malt vinegar

115 g (⅓ cup) treacle

One of the recipes from Country Cooking, *which Rhonda swears by, is this home-made version of a famous spicy sauce that was first sold in England almost 200 years ago. In the past it could be found on the competition schedules of more than a few country shows, and many women made their own versions to accompany steak, and flavour gravies and casseroles. The recipe is not attributed in the cookbook, but Rhonda understands that it came from a Mrs Schilling. Over years of making this recipe for her own family, Rhonda has modified the spices from the original version. The sauce is easy to make, full of flavour and keeps for many months, if not years!*

METHOD

Place all the ingredients, except the treacle, in a large, wide, heavy-based saucepan. Stir together over medium heat until the sugar has dissolved. Boil for 2 hours, uncovered and stirring occasionally, until reduced by about half.

Strain the mixture through a colander or coarse sieve, then strain it again through a finer sieve. Return the sauce to the pan and allow to cool.

Reheat the sauce, then stir in the treacle. Bring to the boil and simmer for a few minutes.

Allow to cool slightly, then pour into hot sterilised bottles and seal while hot. Store in a cool, dark place for about 2 weeks before using.

Right: Recipe image by Sue Haynes.

RHONDA'S TIPS

- There is no need to peel or core the apples. Just chop them roughly.
- The sauce strains better when it's hot.
- It will take at least 2 weeks to develop its true flavour — 3 is even better.
- Worcestershire sauce is delicious served with barbecued meats, or use a dash of it in your favourite beef stew or meat pie filling.

GIBLET SNACK ANYONE?

These days most Australians eat their evening meal sitting in front of the television. Yet, in the 1970s the concept was still rare enough for members of the Mental Health Auxiliaries of Victoria branches at Malvern and Caulfield to decide that it warranted a separate section in their Grub Stakes cookbook. However, their idea of what people might fancy while watching *Hey Hey It's Saturday* or *The Sullivans* was a little peculiar.

Among the treasures featured under the heading TV snacks, is Fried chicken giblets. Yes, that's right. The odd dark bits and pieces you find hidden away inside the cavity of a chicken, and usually throw away or feed to the cat, including the gizzard, heart, liver and kidneys.

The recipe uses a whole pound, or about 500 g, of them, which accounts for a lot of chickens. In case you feel tempted, it recommends that you toss them in a little plain flour and fry them in oil. Then you fry a tin of mushrooms, a sliced onion, 200 g French beans and about the same weight in bean sprouts. When they are brown, put everything in a casserole dish and toss it with soy sauce (amount not specified), then put it in the oven until tender.

Alternatively, you could whip up some Kidneys and bacon, Mock duck crumpets or Black pudding and apples. It may just be enough to drive people back to eating at the table!

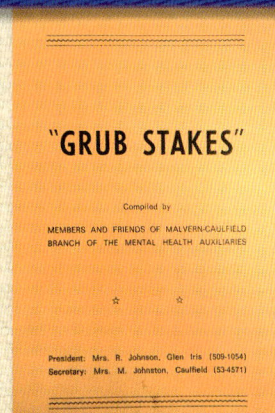

"GRUB STAKES"

Compiled by
MEMBERS AND FRIENDS OF MALVERN-CAULFIELD
BRANCH OF THE MENTAL HEALTH AUXILIARIES

☆   ☆

President: Mrs. R. Johnson, Glen Iris (509-1054)
Secretary: Mrs. M. Johnston, Caulfield (53-4571)

Above: *Grub Stakes*, c. 1970
(State Library of Victoria).

RECIPES
from the
OUTBACK

ALICE *and* THE WANGI CLUB

When Alice Dulhunty became engaged, the social pages of Brisbane's *Sunday Mail* described her romantic alliance as the coming together of city and country.

Alice was a 'society lass' whose activities had been reported regularly since her schooldays at Southport on the Gold Coast. Newspapers noted her excellent performances in Shakespearean and Greek plays staged by St Hilda's school for girls, where she won a special prize for dramatic art. They followed her into adulthood, describing the elegant dresses she donned for various parties and balls. And they recorded her wartime wedding one spring afternoon in 1944, at the imposing Gothic-style Anglican church of St Andrew's, where she walked down the aisle wearing her mother's brussels-lace veil.

Waiting for Alice in front of the altar, resplendent in his army uniform, was Lieutenant James 'Jim' Crombie, the son of a well-known outback family from central western Queensland. His grandfather, another James, took up several pastoral leases near Muttaburra, serving on various high-profile boards and in the Queensland parliament. His father, also James, managed Beryl station, near Longreach, where he and his wife, Gladys, raised nine children.

Alice met her future husband through a schoolfriend, whose brother was attending boarding school with Jim. It was not a case of love at first sight. According to their eldest daughter, Margaret Brown, they didn't really click straight away. Alice's response to her new home in the bush was a little similar.

The newlyweds moved to Marita Downs, a family property north of Longreach, not far from where Jim grew up. The shortest route to town was a 140 kilometre track, mostly on a black dirt road, which was impassable when wet. 'And there were eleven gates, so you only did it if you had a passenger,' Margaret explains.

While Jim looked after the sheep, Alice's domain was the house—a two-room corrugated iron shed, which expanded as three daughters came along. 'By the time we left out there in the 1960s, Dad had made us a lovely comfortable home. Mum loved to garden and she created an oasis, but the isolation was extraordinary,' says Margaret.

The loneliness became even more untenable once all the children went away to boarding school in the early 1960s. To cope, Alice spent hours talking to other women via the party line, a free, shared phone service connecting neighbouring properties. Among them was Judith Henderson, a 'breath of fresh air' from tropical far northern Queensland, who moved to Mahrigong station as a new bride in 1958.

The daughter of a Mossman sugar-cane grower, Judith met her husband, David, in Brisbane during the week of social activities for country families that coincides with the Royal Queensland Show. David's family lived in Brisbane, but they had owned Mahrigong for generations and he visited every chance he could. 'He had this great passion to live there,' says Judith.

Like Alice, the gregarious Judith soon discovered that opportunities to meet and spend time with other women were limited. 'We were in the middle of nowhere. I was the third bride that went to Mahrigong and the others left in disgust,' Judith says. 'We had our own picnic race meeting, we had a local branch of the graziers association and the Country Party, and we had a gun club but everything was really for the boys.'

The social scene improved in 1962 when the Muttaburra sheep show started up, with women soon getting on board to organise a cocktail party and displays reflecting their interests. However, the event was only held once a year and Alice wasn't interested in the other more frequent alternative— joining the CWA. 'She supported the Queen but didn't like the idea of the CWA pledge said at every meeting, or anything like that. She had a rebellious streak really,' admits Margaret.

Alice's solution was to create the Wangi Club, where women could 'meet regularly for our own interest and satisfaction, and to raise money with our various functions for chosen charities'. The club was named after a local indigenous word that Judith believes means something like 'having a discussion'. Made up of no more than ten women from properties within about 80 kilometres of Marita, the club usually gathered at the Crombie homestead, where members would discuss everything from politics and health issues to the arts, while the children played outside.

In the first year, the club ran a fete at Marita, raising £500 to furnish the new wing of a disabled children's home in Townsville. Harking back to Alice's

Opposite, from top: *Once a Jolly Jumbuck*, 1967, and Alice Crombie with the cookbook at the time it was released (courtesy Margaret Brown). Above: Judith Henderson, c. 1960s (courtesy Judith Henderson).

enthusiasms at boarding school, the women even staged plays, and people passing through were invited as guest speakers. 'We had one man that ran a wine tasting, and we got so pissed it made Alice very cranky,' recalls Judith, still irrepressible in her eighties, with a warm, rich laugh.

The Wangi Club became even more essential to the women's wellbeing during a prolonged and terrible drought in the late 1960s and early '70s. The disaster drained the country of feed and water for livestock, and placed enormous strain on station families. Being part of the club helped the women to cope, in more ways than one.

With finances stretched to breaking point, stations carrying sheep relied even more than usual on home-killed mutton to supply their daily needs in terms of meat. Mutton, the meat from aged sheep, has long been an outback staple because it is readily to hand, plentiful and of the lowest value compared with lambs and hoggets, which are kept for sale or as breeding stock. Hard to come by in Australian butcher shops, mutton also has a stronger flavour, even when raised in the best conditions. 'In a drought, the protein in the animal breaks down and the meat smells of urine. It becomes very dark, and it's very unattractive,' Judith explains.

So the Wangi Club put together a cookbook of creative recipes using mutton, which might help improve its appeal, and bring some variety to station tables. 'We had no idea what we were doing,' confesses Judith, who played a key role in compiling the recipes, having established a reputation for being a capable and adventurous cook.

'They were all good cooks in Mossman. They were skitey cooks. They were smarty pants cooks. For every event they tried to outdo each other, and make the most amazing and wonderful things,' she explains. 'When I went to my first gun club thing at Muttaburra, someone brought a leg of mutton in a dish, with the fat still in it, then I started making smarty pants things from where I came from and it started to change.'

Every member of the club contributed recipes to the cookbook, including Bebe Seccombe from Kenya station, whose family settled in the area around the 1870s. 'Mum was an excellent cook,' recalls Bebe's daughter, Margie Webb. 'She wasn't flamboyant or adventurous like Judith, but her food was always tasty and nicely presented. She entertained all sorts of people including governors, but her simple everyday meals were equally delicious. People were always calling in, and most of them would tell you that you never had a bad meal at Kenya. Mum had an Aga stove and she would whip something up, like lamb brains in breadcrumbs.'

Ways to make use of every part of the sheep, including the brains, was an important part of the cookbook, which the women cleverly titled *Once a Jolly Jumbuck*. The 96-page publication included sections for offal, soups, sandwich fillings, chops, cutlets and roasts, boiling, stewing, minces and moulds, cold meat and pastries, and a 'luxury' section with more exotic fare, such as terrapin of lamb, French-style gigot, Finnish hot pot, Turkish pilaf, and shish kebabs.

Margaret Clark-Dickson, a talented artist from Culladar station, illustrated the cookbook with witty sketches and created a striking orange-and-cream cover design featuring the stylised outline of a sheep's head hovering over a frying pan. Jim Crombie penned some entertaining doggerel and, much to everyone's astonishment, celebrity chef Graham Kerr agreed to provide the foreword. 'It was right at the beginning of anyone taking any interest in food, and he used to do the most extraordinary things, like mix a salad in a cement mixer. So we wrote to him, fearlessly, and he was thrilled,' says Judith.

Printed in Brisbane, the first edition of *Once a Jolly Jumbuck* was released in November 1967, followed by a second edition in May 1968, and at least one more in 1981, long after the Wangi Club disbanded. Proceeds were directed to the Queensland Bush Children's Health Scheme, now known as BUSHkids, supporting its work providing medical and dental care to children from outback communities, while they enjoyed much-needed holidays in seaside homes set up close to the facilities.

Poring over a copy that her mother gave to her, complete with handwritten notes, Margie Webb considers the cookbook a remarkable achievement. 'It was a labour of love, and everybody was so proud of it,' she says.

The cookbook may have been successful, but the drought exacted a heavy toll, with many families leaving the district, never to return. The Clark-Dicksons headed to Brisbane in the late 1960s, followed by the Hendersons and their five children in 1971, and then the Crombies. 'We didn't know what was ahead of us, but what we considered to be our life forever changed, and we had to start all over again,' says Judith.

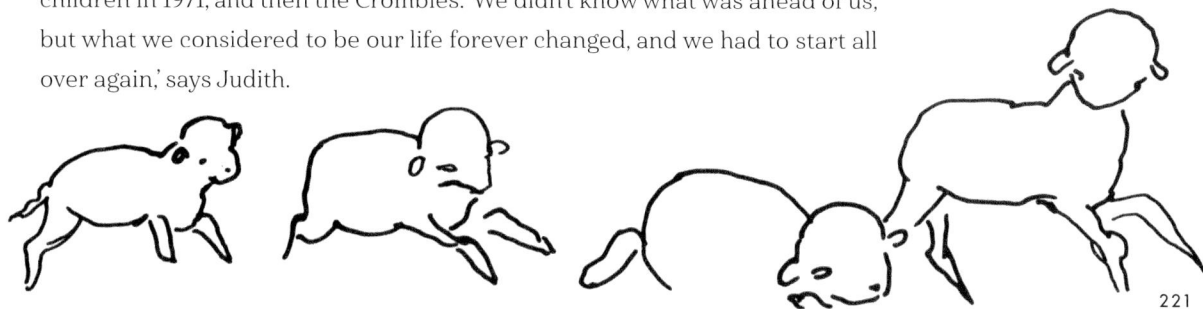

One of the last surviving Wangi Club members, Judith looks back with great fondness on her time at Mahrigong, and the women who became such close friends. 'I wouldn't have missed it for quids. It was so fantastic. I loved everything about it,' she says. 'It was very, very remote and yet we did all these wonderful things together. It was a remarkable neighbourhood.'

In later life, Judith completed a course at La Petite Cuisine School of Cooking in London, then taught others to cook from her own kitchen. She even went back out west to run some cooking classes. Meanwhile, Alice gathered her old friends and formed a new club in Brisbane, based on similar lines, called The Delvers. 'They were such extraordinary women,' says Judith.

Wangi casserole
SERVES 4–6

This delicious old-fashioned casserole is a meal in one dish, with a gravy that is quickly stirred together from ingredients found in most station stores. Margie Webb says that in her own copy of Once a Jolly Jumbuck, *her mother has written a note alongside claiming the recipe was hers, although she doesn't remember Bebe making it. 'Everyone contributed recipes but we decided to keep it anonymous,' says Judith.*

INGREDIENTS

1 kg shoulder mutton, cubed

2 tablespoons plain flour

2 medium onions, sliced

2 medium tomatoes, sliced

2 medium potatoes, sliced

3 or 4 lean bacon rashers,
    cut into large strips

2 tablespoons brown vinegar
    (optional)

2 tablespoons tomato sauce

1 tablespoon Worcestershire
    sauce

1 teaspoon mustard powder

1 teaspoon sugar

salt

freshly ground black pepper

250 ml (1 cup) water

METHOD

Preheat the oven to moderate (180°C). Oil a large casserole dish with a lid (minimum 2 litre/8 cup capacity).

Toss the meat in the flour, ensuring it is well coated. Put a layer of meat in the casserole dish. Cover with layers of onions, tomatoes and potatoes, then repeat, finishing with a layer of potatoes. Lay the bacon rashers across the top of the potatoes.

In a separate bowl, mix together the vinegar (if using), the tomato and Worcestershire sauces, the mustard powder, sugar and seasoning to taste, to form a smooth paste. Stir in the water. Pour the mixture over the casserole. Cover and cook for approximately 1½–2 hours, or until tender.

Remove the lid and cook for another 15 minutes, allowing the bacon and potato to brown.

- You can substitute the mutton for hogget, which is more readily available, or use diced lamb, although the flavour is not as strong.

- Depending on the size of the dish, two layers should be enough to use all the meat and vegetables, but you may need three.

- Keep an eye on the casserole during cooking and add a little more water if necessary.

- Experiment by adding different vegetables such as sweet corn and celery mixed in with the onion.

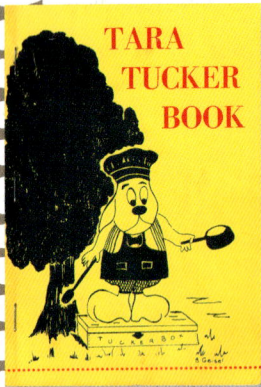

TUCKING IN *with* TARA

Truckies have a reputation for knowing where to find a good meal, but it seems they also know a good cookbook when they see it. Over the years, they have bought more than a few copies of the *Tara Tucker Book*, while passing along the Leichhardt Highway connecting Queensland to Melbourne. In fact, since the first edition was released in 1971, copies of the little cookbook from the western edge of the Darling Downs have ended up all over the world.

The cookbook was put together by the women's auxiliary associated with the Tara Show. The publication marked the tenth anniversary of the auxiliary, which was formed to support the annual event and raise funds for improvements at the local showground. At the helm of the project was Betty Gill, who edited seven editions, supported by a willing committee and her sister, Barbara Geisel, who illustrated it.

It wasn't the first time the sisters had harnessed their energy and talents in the name of a good cause. Betty and Barbara were encouraged to be actively involved in their local community from a young age. Born at Goondiwindi, they moved to the Tara district when their parents, Dick and Monica Travers, took over Kinnoull station in the early 1940s.

Keenly interested in wool, horses and breeding stud Poll Hereford cattle, Dick was president of the show society as well as chair of the local branch of the Queensland grazier's association and patron of the rodeo club. As soon as they were old enough, Betty and Barbara were roped in to help. They also joined organisations like the Red Cross and the CWA, organising balls and baking for street stalls, and raising money to build accommodation at Tara hospital for parents who came in from the bush with sick children.

Described as a 'quietly spoken dynamo', Betty continued volunteering after marrying local grazier, Arthur Gill, who was no slouch either. Among many other things, he served on the board of the Western Downs Co-Operative, and was a shire councillor for years, spending most of the week attending meetings of one sort or another.

Arthur's death in 1982 didn't slow Betty down, despite the fact that she and her son, Andrew, now had the farm to manage. In 1989, she was awarded a Medal of the Order of Australia for community service, and elected president of the Show Society. Impressed by how well she coped with the responsibility, people persuaded her to stand for election as chair of the shire council. Betty was attending a local government conference in Cairns in 1991, when she died suddenly, at the age of 64.

Meanwhile her sister, Barbara, carved an international reputation for her unique images of Australia, made out of wool, straight from the sheep's back. Always artistic, Barbara played the organ and piano, wrote songs and experimented with various forms of painting and craft. 'She would rather do that than housework,' recalls her son, Bill. 'She lived for music and her wool pictures. Right up until the day before she went into hospital with a brain tumour, she was working. She made over 3000 wool pictures in the long run.'

Bill isn't too sure why Barbara started, but he remembers friends with sheep bringing her wool, which she would wash and then colour using natural dyes from local sources, such as brigalow leaves. At first she entered her work in the Tara Show, then she spread her wings, winning blue ribbons at the Brisbane Ekka and the Royal Melbourne Show, where she was runner-up in the Florence Monod Memorial Award for the best craft exhibit. She was a finalist in the Dame Mary Durack Outback Craft Awards run by the Queensland Art Gallery, and exhibited work at national and state sheep shows, the Australian Stockman's Hall of Fame, and various Brisbane venues. 'People started knocking on the door to buy one,' Bill says.

Before long, Barbara's work was the gift of choice for international dignitaries visiting Australia. Pieces were presented to the Premier of China, world presidents of Rotary International, the Assistant Secretary-General of the United Nations, ambassadors and business leaders. The Commonwealth Trading Bank in New York commissioned a piece, and so did NASA astronaut Don Lind. Her work also hangs in private collections across Europe, as well as in Asia and Africa.

Back in Tara, Barbara regularly donated pictures to raise funds, and she was a tireless worker for the show, volunteering in one way or another for more than 60 years. 'She loved the show,' says Bill. 'She was still insisting on going to help, right up to not long before she died in 2013 at the age of 84.'

Below, from top: Launching the first edition (from left), Betty Gill, Monica Travers and Beryl Bougoure, 1971, and launching the latest revised edition at the 2016 Tara Show (from left), Kylie Fourie, Fiona Borchardt and Majella Hetherington. Opposite: *Tara Tucker Book*, 1981 edition. (courtesy Tara Women's Show Auxiliary).

When Betty came up with the idea for the cookbook, Barbara created the cover, inspired by the famous Australian yarn about a drover's dog sitting on a tuckerbox near Gundagai. She also provided a series of quirky sketches, which the auxiliary kept when it revised the cookbook—45 years, more than 10,000 copies, and another seven editions later.

President Fiona Borchardt says that even though it was a lot of work, it was nothing compared to what was involved in preparing and selling the early editions when there was no such thing as email. 'The letter writing involved was incredible,' she says. 'They had letters come from all over the state after a story appeared in *Queensland Country Life*, and they had to write a letter back explaining how much it was, and then another letter would come back with the money, then they would write again, posting the book.'

It took eighteen months to prepare the latest version, which was launched at the 2016 show and has already been reprinted to meet demand. The show's long-standing cookery steward, Beryl Bougoure, who helped with the very first edition, reviewed all the original recipes, keeping the most popular and cutting out anything that took too long to prepare.

Proud of local cooks and the standard of cookery exhibited every year at the Tara Show, Beryl says she doesn't have a favourite recipe in the cookbook because they are all good. 'You could open it at any one, and if you had a failure you can't cook, that is what it amounts to,' she says.

Strawberry cheesecake

SERVES 6–8

This recipe was contributed by Betty Gill. 'I'm not biased at all, but Mum was a good cook,' says Betty's son, Andrew. 'My grandmother always made sure there was plenty of food in the house, enough for the man on the road with his swag if he dropped in. That was the old Goondi way, and how Mum was brought up. At harvest time, she would be in and out with everything that was happening, but she would still come down the paddock with a fantastic smoko, then she would disappear and come back again with lunch.'

INGREDIENTS

Base:

150 g butter

250 g plain sweet biscuits, finely crushed

2 teaspoons ground cinnamon

Filling:

175 g (1 cup) chopped strawberries, plus extra strawberries for decorating

1 tablespoon rum

METHOD

To make the base, melt the butter in a large saucepan over medium heat. Add the crushed biscuits and cinnamon and mix well. Use the mixture to line the base and side of a 20 cm springform pan. Refrigerate while preparing the filling.

To make the filling, place the chopped strawberries in a small bowl with the rum, then set aside, stirring occasionally.

Soften the gelatine in 125 ml (½ cup) of the cold water and set aside. Place the cream cheese in a large bowl and set aside.

Put the egg yolks, sugar and remaining water in a double boiler, or a large metal bowl placed over a saucepan of boiling water. Stir the egg mixture over the boiling water for about 10 minutes, until it thickens slightly and has the consistency of a runny custard.

Add the gelatine mixture and keep stirring until it has thoroughly dissolved. While the combined mixture is still warm, strain it through a sieve into the large bowl of cream cheese. Beat until smooth and creamy. Beat in the lemon juice, zest and salt. Place in the fridge to chill.

Lightly whip the cream. In a separate bowl, beat the egg whites until stiff peaks form.

Remove the cream cheese mixture from the fridge (it should have just started to set). Fold in the whipped cream, then the egg whites in two batches. Gently fold in the chopped strawberries and rum.

Pour the mixture into the biscuit base, cover with plastic wrap and refrigerate for 6 hours, or overnight.

Before serving, decorate with the extra strawberries, glazed with the melted redcurrant jelly.

1 tablespoon powdered gelatine

250 ml (1 cup) cold water

500 g spreadable cream cheese

3 eggs, separated

110 g (½ cup) caster sugar

2 tablespoons lemon juice

2 heaped teaspoons grated lemon zest

¼ teaspoon salt

170 ml (⅔ cup) cream

4 tablespoons redcurrant jelly, melted

LIZ'S TIPS

- Use a metal spoon to press the biscuit base firmly into the bottom and side of the springform pan. The filling is a large mixture, so try to push the biscuit base as high up the side as possible.

- You will need at least 250 g strawberries for this recipe, depending on how densely you want to cover the top of the cheesecake. For the filling, depending on the size of the strawberries, quarter them or chop so they are about 1.5 cm square.

- The flavours are better if you refrigerate the cheesecake overnight.

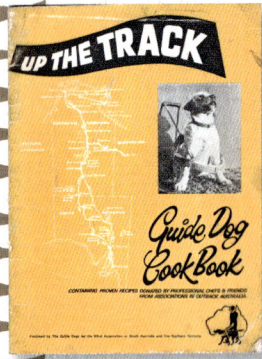

UP *the* TRACK

In 1974, Bevan and Paula Rutt left Adelaide on a seven-week 'whistle-stop' adventure, towing a very special caravan. The purpose-built mobile display unit was destined for Darwin to help raise money for the Guide Dogs for the Blind Association of South Australia and the Northern Territory, and to promote its services to the visually impaired.

As executive officer of the association, Bevan decided to deliver the caravan to the Top End himself, taking time to visit supporters along the way. So he and Paula set off by road to Port Augusta, where they loaded their vehicle and the van onto The Ghan for the long haul to Alice Springs.

From there the Rutts hit the road again, making a 900 kilometre round trip to Uluru, via Curtin Springs and Victory Downs stations. Then they headed north to attend the annual Barrow Creek races, which raised money for the association, before driving on to Tennant Creek via Warrego and Peko mines. Stretching their odyssey even further, Bevan and Paula then diverted east on a return trip along the Barkly Highway to Camooweal, just inside the Queensland border.

Eventually reaching Darwin, they handed over the caravan to the local auxiliary, led by Mike Gray. Then they flew 800 kilometres east to the mining community of Nhulunbuy on the Gove Peninsula, where they were greeted on the outskirts of town by a road sign declaring that 'Nhulunbuy supports Guide Dogs'. Living up to the promise, the local Lions Club presented the Rutts with a cheque for $1500, while the club's ladies auxiliary reported that it had managed to sell more than $2000 worth of Guide Dogs merchandise in the previous nine months.

Not done yet, the Rutts flew on to remote Groote Eylandt in the Gulf of Carpentaria. Then they returned to Darwin to collect their car and begin the 3000 kilometre journey home, with more fund-gathering stopovers along the way at places such as Kulgera, Coober Pedy, Kingoonya and Woomera. 'Mission accomplished above expectations in all respects,' Paul reported to an executive committee meeting within days of their return.

For Bevan, the trip was a return to his roots. His grandfather, Walter Rutt, was an engineer who assisted with surveying the first Western Australian railway and, in the 1870s, was second in charge of building the Overland Telegraph Line to Darwin. He ended his career as South Australia's Chief Engineer for Railways.

A qualified architect like his father before him, Bevan also worked for the railways. His first job after graduating in 1939 was with the Chief Engineer's Department of the South Australian Railways. Bevan went on to establish a successful architectural career in private practice, but it was his volunteer efforts with the Apex and Lions service clubs that led to his involvement with guide dogs.

Bevan was a member of Apex until he reached the membership age limit of 45, and served as president of the World Council of Young Men's Service Clubs in the early 1950s. In 1961, he was elected charter president of the first Lions Club in South Australia, the City of Adelaide.

When Apex decided to take on setting up a guide dogs for the blind association in South Australia, they invited Bevan along to a gathering called to discuss the idea. 'Bevan was the first person I spoke to, because he had been in Apex, and it was the best thing I have ever done,' says Frank Beauchamp who, at the age of 25, was given the task of leading the project. 'He was a hard worker and he knew everyone.'

Frank was elected president and Bevan honorary secretary treasurer at the first formal meeting in 1957, and the newly formed association hit the ground running. Within a few months the first guide dog was placed in South Australia. Later that year Bevan was appointed to the helm of a national appeal committee to raise funds for a national training centre and headquarters in Melbourne. He also became chief executive of the Adelaide-based association.

Working alongside him was his wife, Paula, who edited the association's *Faithfully Theirs* magazine, and helped raise money through activities such as appearing on *The Bobo Show*, a children's television program, which was the first program to screen on Channel 10 in Adelaide when it began broadcasting in 1965.

It was Paula who took on the responsibility of creating a fundraising cookbook for the association, based around the Rutts' northern adventures. As they travelled, she gathered up recipes from people encountered along the way, including cooks and professional chefs at places where they stayed or stopped for a meal, such as the Opal Motel at Coober Pedy and the Threeways Roadhouse at Tennant Creek.

To round out the collection, *Up the Track* also featured recipes supplied by Adelaide supporters, who were so delighted with the contributions of their colleagues 'up yonder', that they decided to pool their own favourites and send them back.

Above, from top: Bevan Rutt with his dog, Phreddrika, 1967, and Bevan presenting the keys to the mobile display unit to Darwin auxiliary president Mike Gray, 1974 (courtesy Guide Dogs SA/NT). Opposite: *Up the Track*, 1974.

Beer cake

INGREDIENTS

300 g (2 cups) self-raising
  flour
220 g (1 cup) caster sugar
2 eggs
60 g butter, melted
250 ml (1 cup) beer
85 g (½ cup) sultanas

Topping:

110 g (¾ cup) plain flour
1 teaspoon ground nutmeg
165 g (¾ cup) white sugar
60 g butter, melted

Below: Advertisement from the
cookbook.

This recipe is essentially a cheat's version of a German-style streusel cake, which can be put together in about ten minutes, using beer instead of yeast to create a similar flavour. The recipe was contributed to Up the Track *by Pat Morton from Victory Downs, a cattle station on the South Australian–Northern Territory border. You can bet it is a favourite with station cooks everywhere.*

METHOD

Preheat the oven to moderately hot (190°C). Grease and line a shallow slab cake pan (approximately 30 x 22 cm) with baking paper.

Put the flour in a large bowl and stir in half the sugar.

Put the eggs in a medium bowl with the remaining sugar and whisk until combined. Whisk in the melted butter, then the beer.

Add the beer mixture to the flour mixture and beat until it forms a stiff, smooth batter. Stir in the sultanas and pour into the prepared pan.

To make the topping, combine all the ingredients in a small bowl and mix thoroughly, using a fork, to form a crumbly texture. Sprinkle the topping evenly over the cake and bake for about 30 minutes, until a skewer comes away clean when you test the middle of the cake.

LIZ'S TIPS

- The top will be quite loose and crumbly after cooking, so when you are lining the pan let the baking paper overhang on opposing sides, so you can use it to lift the cake out.

- The beer can be fresh or flat. If it's fresh, pour it slowly into the measuring cup to avoid frothing.

- The original recipe called for just a 'handful' of sultanas. Half a cup is relatively sparse in such a large cake, so you might want to use more if you like sultanas.

- The cake is lovely eaten warm, or served the next day with butter. It also freezes well.

TAKING FLIGHT *at* KANANDAH

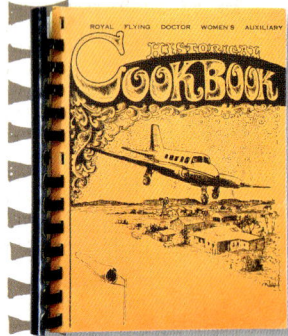

Ruth Swann was wrangling four children, including a baby, when she moved onto a brand new pastoral property with no amenities, in one of the world's most isolated places.

Her husband, Eric, was the first manager of Kanandah, a sheep station carved out of the flat Nullarbor Plain after the Western Australian government opened it up for settlement in the early 1960s. 'There was nothing there,' recalls the Swanns' eldest child, Jenny Kroonstuiver. 'Dad went out to start setting things up, and Mum and we four children were left in Adelaide but Mum got a bit jack of that so she sent a telegram to say that we were on the way.'

Although the station was about 350 kilometres east of Kalgoorlie, in the middle of nowhere, it did have the advantage of straddling the Trans-Australian Railway line, so Ruth loaded the family onto a train. There were no buildings on the property when they arrived. With limited options for temporary accommodation, Eric made an eight-hour round trip to Kalgoorlie in search of a caravan. The only one he could find was in such bad shape, that by the time he got it back to the station it was virtually falling apart. Happy to be reunited with her husband, Ruth made do.

Ruth grew up on a small farm near Kingaroy in Queensland, and trained in Brisbane as a mothercraft nurse. She met Eric after heading out west to work as a governess. He was originally from western New South Wales, where his father took up a soldier settler's block after the First World War. Always fascinated by stories about inland Australia, Eric found work as a jackeroo on the Barcoo River. After he and Ruth married in Brisbane in 1954, he took up a position as overseer on Mount Marlow, near Blackall, where Jenny was born, followed by David and Russell. Then, for a while Eric managed Tatala, near Charleville, in south-western Queensland, where their youngest child, Susan, came into the world.

Eric and Ruth had been married about eight years when the job at Kanandah came up. It was an exciting challenge for Eric, who was instructed by the South Australian company that owned it, to bring the new property into production as quickly as possible.

To make that happen, between twenty and thirty men were employed in the first few years, either as station hands, or as contractors to help build the

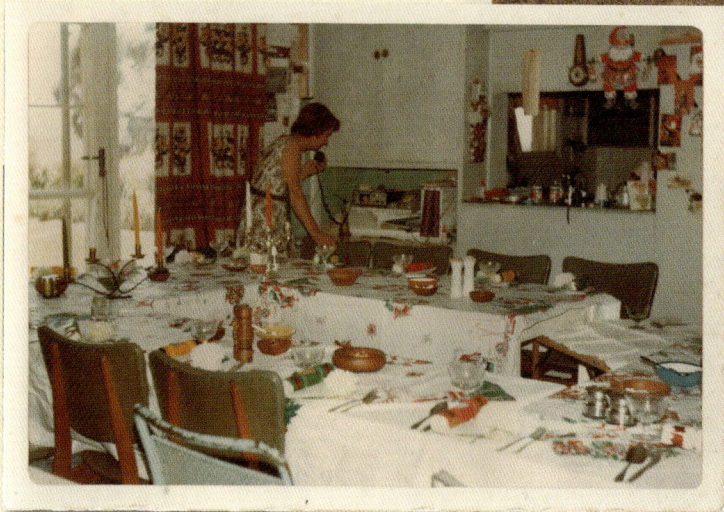

Clockwise from top: The Swann family's first home at Kanandah, c. 1962; Swann family Christmas photo taken on the lawn at Kanandah, c. 1970s; Ruth speaking on the Flying Doctor radio during preparations for Christmas dinner, when everyone living on the station joined the family; Eric and Ruth Swann, c. 1990s (courtesy Jenny Kroonstuiver). Opposite: *Historical Cookbook*, 1977 (State Library of WA).

infrastructure. Priority was given to the men's quarters, which the Swanns lived in while the manager's house was completed.

There were no doors or windows at first, but it seemed luxurious after eight months in the caravan. It also had a big range so, apart from feeding the family and teaching her children, Ruth took on the job of cooking for all the staff. Jenny can remember being roped in to peel an awful lot of potatoes, a task she has avoided ever since.

The nearest shop was in Kalgoorlie, but groceries were delivered by train to a siding about fifteen kilometres from the home paddock. 'In the early days we had quite a good service but it was gradually wound back and supplies came once a fortnight and the mail came once a week. Sometimes they would forget, so it could be spasmodic,' Jenny says.

That meant Ruth had to be inventive. Like most station women she learnt to be versatile and manage with very little. 'Mum was an incredible station cook. She was one of those people who could look at what was available and construct an amazing meal around it. She could make something out of nothing, and she would do it for 20 or 30 people.'

According to Jenny, Ruth was particularly well known for her slow-roasted mutton, cooked in a wood oven until the meat fell off the bone. She would use every part of a sheep by routinely making things many home cooks today would never dream of trying, like pressed tongue and brawn. And she was a pretty good cake cook too, which opened the door to raising funds for the Swann family's favourite cause.

Like most outback families, the Swanns relied on the Royal Flying Doctor Service (RFDS), not just for medical emergencies but for routine health care for them and the station's other employees. Eric had become aware of the importance of the service while he was jackerooing. He started about 25 years after the inaugural flight out of Cloncurry in 1928, and many of the people he met recalled vividly what life was like before. 'They had constant reminders of this period with the numerous graves at most homesteads—for a large extent, graves of women and children,' he wrote in a brief account of his life.

The importance struck Eric even more strongly when he decided to get married, and began having his own children. 'All our four children were born under the Flying Doctor's care. The one thing that became obvious to me at this time was that without the backup of the [RFDS] I would not have considered marrying, having a family and living in that environment. This was a country subject to floods which cut people off from the outside world for weeks at a time with roads which were then only dirt tracks.'

At Kanandah, the site for the new homestead was chosen carefully, so it was handy to a suitable stretch of ground for a decent airstrip. It was important for company personnel flying in and out, but it also allowed the RFDS to include the station on its monthly clinic runs. Jenny remembers the excitement of those visits. 'It was a really vital lifeline for us, especially with such a big staff,' she says.

The runway was used for emergency evacuations too, unfortunately not always with a happy outcome. In 1973, Eric and Ruth's son David had a horse-riding accident while he was mustering. David was transported to Perth by the RFDS, but he died in hospital a couple of days later. He was seventeen.

The terrible tragedy only reinforced the family's commitment to the RFDS. 'Because the RFDS played such a big part in that emotional chapters of our lives, [it] almost became a religion to Ruth and myself,' Eric wrote. 'It allowed us to live the life we loved with medical security for our family. It saw to our children's births, through any illnesses ... And last but not least, it gave our eldest son his one chance of being saved ... If I lived and worked to support the service till I was 100, I would still be in debt.'

Eric didn't manage his ton, but a few months before his death in 2015 at the age of 86, he was still collecting donation tins and attending meetings at Esperance, where he and Ruth retired in 1991, after Ruth was diagnosed with Parkinson's disease. Eric was inaugural president of the auxiliary, which he was asked to set up in the late 1990s.

In fact, Eric spent most of his adult life helping to raise money or serving the RFDS in various volunteer capacities. The year that David died, Eric was encouraged to nominate for the Eastern Goldfields Section council and give the pastoral community a voice. The monthly meetings in Kalgoorlie finished late at night but, with help from Ruth, he drove back to the station afterwards so they were home by daylight, ready to start work. He served on the council for twenty years, and was awarded life membership after resigning in 1992. Jenny then followed in his footsteps, accepting a nomination to join the council, and going on to become president.

Considering the new community at Kanandah and its isolation, in 1964 Eric and Ruth decided to organise a gymkhana, which would bring people together while also raising money for the RFDS. Within a few years, it became the biggest social event on the calendar, even drawing people from outside the district. The Kanandah Gymkhana Club ended up raising more than $35,000 for the RFDS over seventeen years, resulting in a new plane being named after it. The event continues to this day. Now known as the Nullarbor Muster, it's held at Rawlinna during the autumn school holidays.

Ruth had the challenging task of organising meals for the early gym-khanas, which centred around the station woolshed. In the meantime, she and Heather Crombie also started baking cakes to raise money for the RFDS. Heather came to live on the station with her first husband, David, when he was employed there as the overseer. Their son ended up marrying one of the Swann girls.

Both women were among the first members to join the Eastern Goldfields Auxiliary of the RFDS, when it was set up in June 1966 to raise money for a range of RFDS projects, equipment and maintenance; and to promote the service and assist patients brought into hospital by the Flying Doctor. Within a year, the auxiliary had 45 members and was relying primarily on cake stalls held in Kalgoorlie's main street to raise money. 'Because the station had a clinic once a month, Ruth and I would make fruit cakes and give them to the pilot and the doctor to take back,' Heather recalls.

When the auxiliary decided to put a cookbook together as a special project for 1977, Heather was part of the group that worked on it. 'I lived out in the bush and I knew the station people so it was my job to contact them and ask for recipes,' she says. 'We asked them for menus, things they might have for an ordinary evening station meal. People were also asked to send what information they could about the properties they were on.'

The resulting *Historical Cookbook* combines both menus and individual recipes, histories of the RFDS and various towns, prepared by local historian and author Norma King, as well as the information that people on the stations provided, and clever sketches by local artist Henry Giblin. A few members used their own money to cover the printing costs, receiving reimbursement once it started to sell.

They didn't have long to wait. The first edition of 2000 copies printed in November 1977 quickly sold out with a second following six months later, and a third before the end of 1978. A revised version with additional recipes remains one of the bestselling items at the RFDS visitor centre at the Kalgoorlie–Boulder airport.

Even though she now lives more than 700 kilometres away, on the coast at Australind, Heather is still a member of the Eastern Goldfields Auxiliary, which is going strong. One of the reasons she has stayed involved, is the support auxiliary members provided after her first husband died of cancer, leaving her a widow with three young children. They had moved into Kalgoorlie a few months earlier, and he encouraged her to go to the meetings.

'It was a very good outlet for me after I was widowed,' she said. 'I was very shy, and I was also very deaf and I found it very hard to get myself motivated. Because David knew what was going to happen, he said to me one day, "I don't want my children growing up hermits". He used to make me go to auxiliary meetings. He would drop me off at the rooms where we met and someone would bring me home afterwards. Those ladies were such a help to me, they took me under their wing.'

Heather is also deeply committed to the RFDS because it has saved the lives of nine members of her immediate family over the years, including two of her grandchildren. They came to the rescue when her eighteen-month-old grandson found some old sheep dip on a neighbour's property and tasted it, and they were there again when her two-year-old granddaughter was accidently run over. 'They are both healthy young adults now, but things would have been much different without the RFDS.'

Eggless steamed pudding   SERVES 6

This old-fashioned steamed pudding from the Historical Cookbook *was a 'never-fail' favourite with station men, according to a cover note from Ruth, and she made it regularly. Handy when the chooks stopped laying, it was also quick to mix and could sit bubbling away on the back of the wood-fuelled range while she got on with other things. The pudding relies on golden syrup and the fruit for sweetness. Although it takes a while to cook, it can be made in advance and reheated in a microwave, or steamed gently for another 30 minutes.*

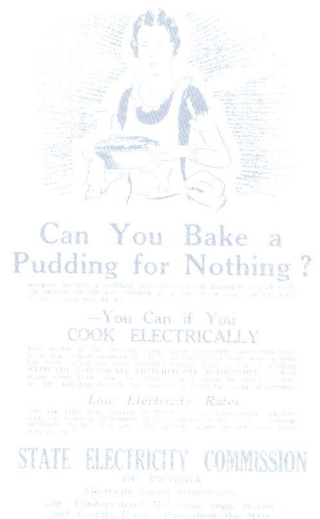

Can You Bake a Pudding for Nothing?

—You Can if You COOK ELECTRICALLY

Low Electricity Rates

STATE ELECTRICITY COMMISSION

INGREDIENTS

250 ml (1 cup) milk

2 tablespoons golden syrup

120 g butter, chopped

½ teaspoon bicarbonate
of soda

150 g (1 cup) self-raising flour

1 cup dried fruit

METHOD

Grease a 1 litre (4 cup) pudding basin.

Put the milk, golden syrup, butter and bicarbonate of soda in a large saucepan and bring to the boil. Cook for 5 minutes, then set aside to cool.

Sift in the flour, then stir in the dried fruit. Pour the mixture into the pudding basin and steam for 2 hours.

LIZ'S TIPS

- Ruth suggests honey as an alternative to golden syrup.
- You can use any dried fruit — I like sultanas for this recipe, but currants are nice too.
- Stand the pudding basin on an upturned saucer or small plate while it is steaming, to lift the basin off the direct heat.
- Serve the pudding with lemon custard for the perfect cold-weather treat.

The BUFFALO HUNTERS

As a teenager, Judy Anictomatis and her five sisters used to drive out into the bush several times a week to hunt wild water buffalo. Wielding .303 rifles, they would find a good-sized beast and most days bring it down with a single shot. Wielding extremely sharp knives, the sisters would then work together to skin it, remove the legs and as much meat from the carcase as they could, and take it home.

Judy was born a long way from buffalo country, on an irrigated sheep and wheat farm near Rochester, in northern Victoria. 'A drought came on and my father made the big drift into the centre in 1949, when I was only six or seven months old,' she says.

Burge Brown took up Murray Downs station, about 350 kilometres north of Alice Springs, where he set out to adapt small-scale farming methods to a cattle run covering more than 4000 square kilometres. Working in collaboration with the CSIRO and a neighbour, he trialled new pasture grasses and livestock management techniques, developing a reputation as a progressive pastoralist. Using overflow from bores on the station, he even pioneered growing fruit and vegetable crops, selling produce to nearby mining and Aboriginal communities.

Above, from top:
Buffalo Cook Book,
1981, and Judy
Anictomatis (image by
Helen Pereira).

His wife, Ida, a noted horsewoman, helped with the mustering and droving cattle to Alice Springs, in between raising eight children and two adopted Aboriginal boys. 'My mother had three children under the age of three, and then four months after arriving she had twins,' says Judy, who was the third born. 'She spent a lot of time in hospital at Alice Springs because she had a baby every year. She was very tolerant and very resilient, and she just learnt to live with the situation.'

One of Judy's earliest memories is begging to be allowed to operate the pedal-powered radio, while her older brother and sister sat in on sessions for School of the Air. 'I was only four, and I really wanted to do it,' she says. She also recalls her father resorting to cracking his stockwhip to get the attention of his large and noisy brood and all the other children who lived on the station, including a family with five girls.

'There were other families that worked on the station and we all ate together,' Judy says. 'The meals were cooked in the homestead kitchen, with the help of Aboriginal ladies. We killed all our own beef, and we had chickens and pigs but most of the meals were steak and chops. I can remember a lot of stews cooked in the oven, shepherd's pie and corned beef—lots of corned beef.'

After years of continuous drought, the family left the station when Judy was about eight, and moved to Banyan Farm near Batchelor, about 100 kilometres south of Darwin, where they grew pineapples and bananas. 'It was very different,' Judy says with considerable understatement. 'We went from the desert to the tropics, to green and water and rain.'

Then about four years later in 1962, they upped sticks again and moved to the other side of Rum Jungle in the Darwin River area, where Burge and Ida became caretakers of buildings left behind by the Royal Australian Air Force. There were hundreds of feral water buffalo grazing in the vicinity, so the Browns secured a permit and started shooting and processing them for pet food. Ida sold the meat in a pet shop they opened in Darwin, but other businesses were soon lining up too, with orders for about a tonne of meat every week.

'My oldest brother wasn't at home, and my other brother was too little, so it was mainly the girls' job to go and hunt and shoot and slaughter the buffalo,' says Judy, matter-of-factly. 'We started when I was about twelve and we did that for maybe eight or nine years. My mother and father taught us how to use a rifle at a young age, and we had a good eye. We would go to school, come home, do a bit of homework, jump in the Nissan Patrol and go out three times a week.'

Once they had brought down their quarry, the girls had to complete the gory and physically demanding task of slaughtering the animal and loading it into the vehicle. 'The more meat you could get off the beast, the less you had to shoot and the quicker you could go home,' Judy says. 'Buffalo hide is over half an inch thick. We would cut down the backbone, then go down the legs, skin that back and then take the whole leg off the carcase. We'd take all the meat off and then turn it over and do the other side. We were very good at our job.'

They were still hunting buffalo when Judy starting going out with her future husband, Ross. 'We used to take him out and he thought it was wonderful. He loved hunting buffalo,' Judy says.

The couple met one night in Darwin at the Hong Kong cafe, where Judy was eating out with friends. Ross was the youngest of three sons born into the well-known Anictomatis family. One of his older brothers, John, served as the Territory's administrator from 2000 to 2003.

Left: Buffalo hunting on the plains south of Darwin, 1952 (National Archives A1200, L14579). Opposite and over page: Illustrations by Jan Oldham from the *Buffalo Cook Book*.

Their father, Christos, became a leading light in Darwin's large Greek community after emigrating in the 1950s. He and his wife, Chrisoula, set up an eating place, which offered the first 'blackboard' menu in the city, featuring Chrisoula's home-made Greek dishes. The cafe also served as an unofficial centre for migrants to collect their mail and find work, with Christos constantly raising money for various causes, and becoming a prime mover behind having a Greek Orthodox church built. But there was no Greek Orthodox priest in town when Judy and Ross got married in 1966, so the ceremony was held at the city registry office.

Very early in their marriage Judy learnt to cook Greek food, becoming particularly fond of traditional Greek sweets. 'I have always cooked a lot. I am a keen cook,' she says. She also loved craft, which is what drew her into joining the CWA. A couple of members saw Judy keeping busy making things while she sat outside the kindergarten waiting for her children, and invited her to attend a meeting.

Judy can vaguely remember her mother being part of a CWA of the Air branch when they lived at the station, sitting in on sessions held over the radio.

Then when the family moved to Batchelor, Ida joined the Rum Jungle branch. Judy signed up with the branch in Darwin in the early 1980s, and has since served several terms as Territorial President, covering a total of twelve years.

She wasn't yet a member when the organisation brought out the first edition of the *Buffalo Cook Book* in 1981. Featuring more than 70 recipes using buffalo, the book was endorsed by the Territory's chief minister of the day, Paul Everingham, who congratulated them for showcasing ways to use a local product and potentially help increase demand. 'Since their introduction to the Territory by the early settlers . . . the Asian Water Buffalo has been synonymous with the Northern Territory, more particularly the Top End,' he wrote. 'I have eaten and enjoyed buffalo steak many times, but not as often as I would have liked, for the simple reason that it is not always available.'

That was never a problem for Judy. 'We ate buffalo, because we could,' she says. 'We would pick the best cuts, so mainly fillets and scotch fillets. Buffalo meat is much leaner than beef, and the texture is a bit different. I like the taste—it's not strong, although sometimes it can be a little bit gamey. It's very moist if you cook it on the barbecue, and the scotch fillet is always nice roasted.'

Berrimah steak sartee

SERVES 4

This is one of four sartee, or satay, recipes provided in the Buffalo Cook Book*— adapted versions of a dish that came to the Territory with Asian immigrants. It is very different from what many of us know as satay, which is usually served with a rich peanut and coconut cream sauce. As the recipe book points out, no matter what you call it, it's essentially grilled cubes of meat cooked on a stick! Most people will find it difficult to source the buffalo, so try it with beef instead.*

INGREDIENTS

1 kg buffalo fillet

2 tablespoons vindaloo curry paste

2 or 3 chillies, finely chopped

4 garlic cloves, crushed

2 tablespoons soy sauce

2 tablespoons brandy

1 tablespoon sugar

METHOD

Cut the meat into bite-sized cubes and place them in a large bowl. Mix the meat with the curry paste, ensuring every piece is coated.

Combine the chillies, garlic, soy sauce, brandy and sugar in another bowl. Pour the mixture over the meat and toss to combine. Cover with plastic wrap and leave in the fridge for 2–3 hours.

Thread the meat onto skewers and grill or barbecue until cooked.

LIZ'S TIPS

- If you can't buy vindaloo curry paste, you can substitute vindaloo simmer sauce, although the flavour will not be quite so intense.

- If you intend to use any left-over marinade as a sauce, then don't forget to cook it first, as it has been in contact with raw meat.

- Judy's family recipe is slightly different from the above version. She blends together two garlic cloves with $2^{1}/_{2}$ teaspoons soy sauce, a 3.5 cm piece of fresh ginger, 1 tablespoon curry powder, $1^{1}/_{2}$ tablespoons sugar and a dash of sherry, which is poured over the skewers of meat and left to marinate.

MAKING DO IN A HURRY

The Royal Flying Doctor Service *Cookery Book* prepared by the Alice Springs women's auxiliary air branch in 1962 contains dishes all about making do with what was readily to hand.

Among them is an Early birthday cake, made with an emu egg, provided by branch president Rose Chalmers from MacDonald Downs station, whose mother, Mrs Agars, was roped in to sort, arrange and type up the recipes.

Then there is a Plenty River curry, which requires twelve goat chops; and a Drover's curry from Doreen Braitling at Mount Doreen station, which she suggests is an ideal way to produce a tasty meal in a hurry with only a piece of cooked salt beef. Like most outback curry recipes of the day, it relies on the ubiquitous pre-mixed powder found in every station store, combined with an onion, powdered milk, a bit of flour and sugar, and a pint of water.

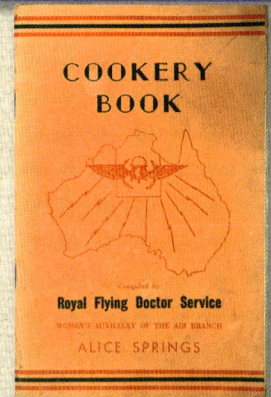

Above: The Royal Flying Doctor Service *Cookery Book*, 1962 (Special Collections, Deakin University Library).

RECIPES

for the

YOUNG

The INVISIBLE WOMAN

Annie Sharman should be a household name. And yet, even in the state where she has influenced generations of cooks through one of Australia's best-loved and longest-lived cookbooks, hardly anyone has heard of her.

Annie compiled the revered *Green and Gold Cookery Book*, which is still in print after more than 90 years, selling more than 500,000 copies. Officially designated a Heritage Icon in South Australia, it is so treasured that early editions are treated as family heirlooms.

The recipe book was created initially to raise money for King's College, a new private boys' school established by the Congregational and Baptist churches in the leafy Adelaide suburb of Kensington. Annie and her family were very active in the Congregational Church, so when the call went out in 1923 for churchwomen to get behind the venture, the attractive twenty-year-old, who preferred to be called Anne, stepped forward.

'Well, I haven't got any money to give, but I've got a few talents,' Anne told Emma Morris, who was president of a committee set up to organise a school fete. The two-day event in March 1924 was the focal point of fundraising efforts by the women of both churches, who worked together to plan and promote it, and stock the stalls with enticing items for sale. As her contribution, Anne proposed putting together a small cookery book.

Mrs Morris thought it was a splendid idea, and agreed to act as guarantor, advancing the capital required to produce it. Then she and her energetic committee secretary, Constance McRitchie, set about rounding up advertising to cover the costs. Meanwhile, a call was put out to Congregational and Baptist women across the state for tested recipes and household hints. To help make sure there was a good response, individual churches were encouraged to appoint a recipe collector.

Some 30 congregations took up the suggestion, and recipes began pouring in from both churches and individuals, mainly from South Australia but also as far away as New South Wales and Queensland. As editor, Anne then took primary responsibility for receiving, checking and sorting them. The end result was more than 200 pages of practical dishes, wrapped in a hard cloth-bound cover of dark green, embossed with gold letters, to match the new school's colours.

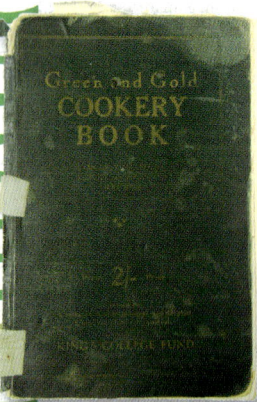

'Every housekeeper has some one thing which she cooks better than anybody else; this "Green and Gold Cookery Book" contains just those things,' Mrs Morris wrote in her preface to the first edition. 'It is a purely Australian book—the ingredients it calls for are those in daily use in every Australian house—and it should therefore commend itself to all Australian women. Our little book does not profess to compete with such complete manuals of the culinary art as Mrs Beeton's, for example; but I dare to say that with no other guide than this, the inexperienced housewife may prepare a breakfast, cook a dinner, and serve up a dainty tea that will rival, if not out-rival, "what mother used to make". Could any young bride desire more?'

The new cookbook was very well received, with the *Register* newspaper praising its practical and reliable methods, and complete, clear and satisfactory index. Priced at two shillings, the first edition of 5000 copies sold out within twelve months, raising £250. 'Praise has come from America, India, New Zealand, and all parts of Australia,' reported the Congregational church journal. 'One lady from the far north-west of Australia has put her other cookery books on the shelf, and uses only the Green and Gold.'

Both churches worked hard to drive sales after the fete. Mrs McRitchie called on 250 Congregational women to take on the challenge of selling ten copies each, and her Baptist counterpart on the committee, Florence Benskin, urged 250 Baptist women to follow their example. A second edition was printed in 1925, with women volunteers again taking responsibility for promotion, distribution and sales. Then, in 1927, the committee signed the responsibility over to a commercial publishing house, which paid the school royalties instead.

By 1960 there had been 31 editions, with Anne occasionally adding extra recipes and tips or a fresh preface. By 1974 the cookbook had generated more than $15,000 in royalties. That year, King's amalgamated with Girton Girls' School to form Pembroke School, and the cookbook continued. After more than 50 editions, it is still raising money for the school.

The *Green and Gold Cookery Book* did more than aid a worthy cause and help to make South Australians better cooks. It changed Anne Sharman's life.

The second-eldest of seven children raised by Thomas and Kate Sharman, Annie Louisa was born in June 1893 at Saddleworth in the Mid North, where her mother's family lived. Her father, Thomas, grew up in the Hindmarsh Valley on Fleurieu Peninsula, and trained as a butcher. Anne spent her early years living in the Mid North, where times were tough because of a serious economic depression, which saw many Australian banks collapse.

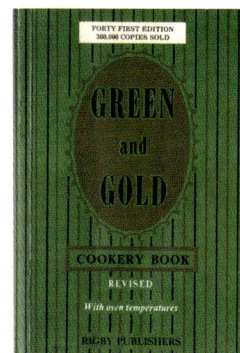

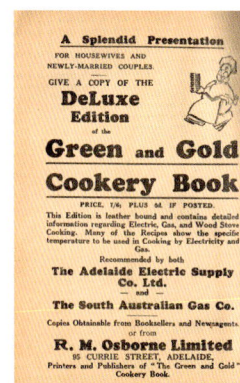

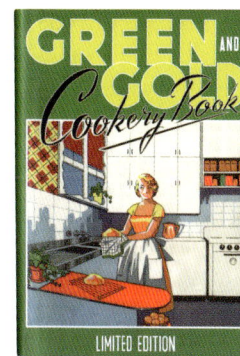

Above, from top: *Green and Gold Cookery Book*, revised edition reprint, 1987; advertisement for the cookbook from the twentieth edition, c. 1940s; the limited edition, 2013. Opposite: The first edition, 1924 (courtesy Pembroke School Archives).

In 1900 the Sharmans moved to Adelaide because they wanted their children to have a decent education. Thomas opened a butcher shop in Unley, and helped to establish the Adelaide and Suburban Master Butchers' Association. Anne did well at school, winning a bursary to attend the Methodist Ladies College. In fact all four sisters were bright scholars and given extraordinary opportunities to further their education. Anne's older sister Florence, and a younger sister Ethel, gained tertiary degrees at the University of Adelaide, at a time when very few women attended university. They later taught at the Presbyterian Girls College, and their youngest sister, Katherine, also became a teacher.

After finishing high school, Anne, a skilled needle-worker, stayed at home for a few years and took private lessons in dressmaking. Then, in about 1916, she started a two-year course training as a domestic science teacher at the Domestic Arts Centre in Norwood. Established in

Above: Annie Sharman, who preferred to be known as Anne, 1926 (courtesy Pembroke School Archives). Right: Believed to be Anne, giving a cookery demonstration in the Sagasco pavilion at the Royal Adelaide Show, 1937 (State Library of SA, BRG 350/34/11/32).

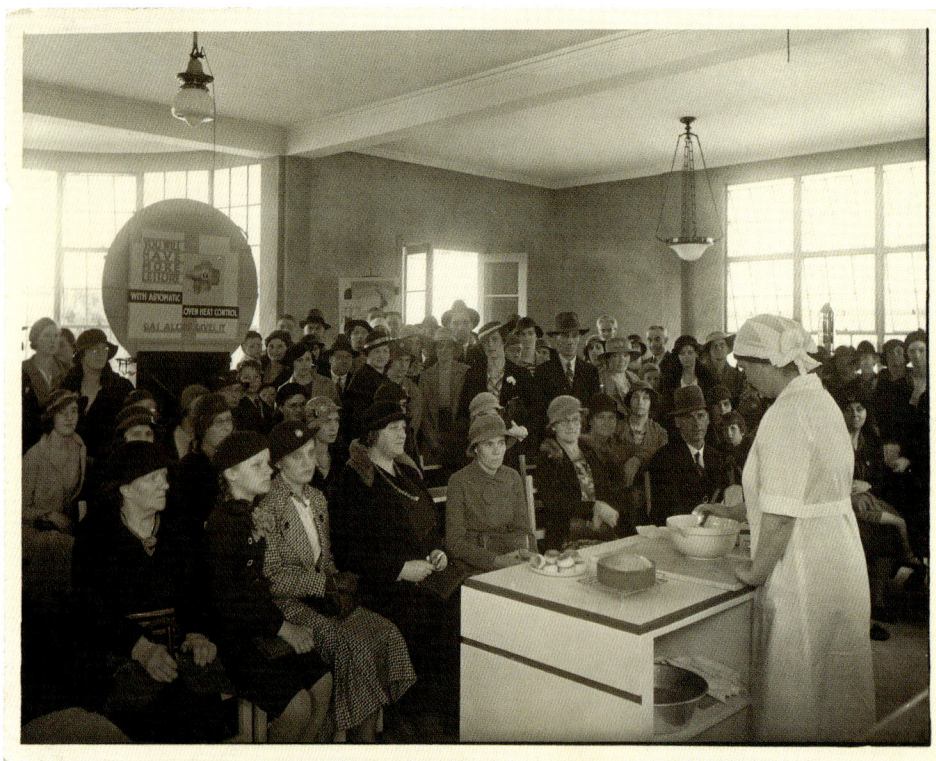

1911, it was the first education facility of its kind in the state, teaching young girls cookery, sewing, laundry work, housekeeping and childcare. After qualifying, Anne taught at Unley, Norwood and at Gawler, where she opened a new domestic arts centre for the Education Department.

Within months of the Green and Gold being released, Anne was offered a job as chief demonstrator with the South Australian Gas Company (Sagasco), which had noted the book's success. She stayed with the company for fourteen years, running adult cookery classes and giving cooking demonstrations at the company's showrooms in Waymouth Street, and at public venues and shows in Adelaide as well as regional centres. She also judged cookery at the Royal Adelaide Show for many years. In 1931, she added to her accomplishments by producing the *Sagasco Cookery Book*. By the 1940s, she had returned to teaching domestic science, this time at Woodlands girls' school at Glenelg, and in the 1950s she taught needlework for the Education Department. Anne died in May, 1985, at the age of 92.

Chocolate layer cake

This cake recipe was published during the 1940s, in the twentieth edition of the Green and Gold Cookery Book, *with a note that it was a favourite of Queen Mary, the grandmother of Queen Elizabeth II. Apparently, a housekeeper from Windsor Castle dropped into the Anne Page Cake Shop near the castle one day, and asked for the baked delight, which Queen Mary described as the nicest chocolate cake she had ever eaten.*

The story is not as unlikely as it might sound. It was originally told to an Adelaide newspaper by Mildred Sheard during a visit in 1938. Originally from Gawler, Miss Sheard was acting general secretary of the Young Christian Women's Association in Adelaide when she resigned in 1930 and sailed for England, intending to stay for only a few years. She ended up running the cake shop, with a friend who trained in domestic science in Scotland and did most of the baking.

The recipe was donated by Mrs E.H. (Octavia) Bakewell, the daughter of a Congregational minister and an ardent worker in the church. The recipe remained in future editions, but the covering note disappeared. The original version of this recipe had very little method, so hopefully my interpretation is close to what Mrs Bakewell intended, and Queen Mary enjoyed so much.

INGREDIENTS

90 g butter, softened

165 g (¾ cup) caster sugar

2 eggs, separated

185 g (1¼ cups) self-raising
   flour

55 g (½ cup) cocoa powder

½ teaspoon bicarbonate
   of soda

170 ml (⅔ cup) milk

Filling:

40 g butter, melted

60 g (½ cup) icing sugar
   mixture

½ teaspoon natural vanilla
   extract

Icing:

120 g (1 cup) icing sugar
   mixture

1 tablespoon cocoa powder

1 tablespoon boiling water

METHOD

Preheat the oven to moderate (180°C). Grease and line two 18 cm sandwich (round) pans.

Cream the butter and sugar until light and fluffy. Beat in the egg yolks, one at a time.

Sift together the flour, cocoa and bicarbonate of soda. Stir into the egg mixture in batches, alternating with the milk, beating until smooth after each addition.

Beat the egg whites until soft peaks form, then gently fold them into the cake mixture.

Gently spoon the mixture into the two pans and bake for 20 minutes, until springy to the touch. Remove the cakes from the pans and allow to cool on a wire rack.

To make the filling, combine the butter, sifted icing sugar and vanilla in a small bowl and stir until smooth.

To make the icing, sift the icing sugar and cocoa into a small bowl, then gradually add the water, mixing until smooth.

Once the cakes are cool, spread the filling thinly over the top of one cake, using a spatula or a knife. Sit the other cake on top, then apply the icing.

LIZ'S TIPS

- Sift the dry ingredients for the cake mixture together twice to make sure they are thoroughly combined.
- Add one-third of the beaten egg whites first, to loosen the mixture, then add the rest.
- You can decorate the cake with crumbed walnuts, or use white sprinkles for a contrast to the chocolate icing.

THERE *was* NEVER A DOUBT

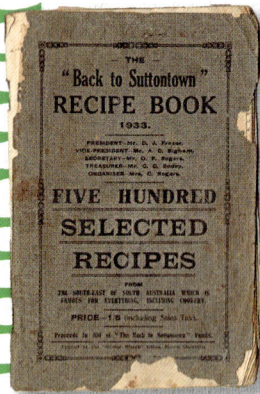

Jane Clezy never doubted that the love of her life would return home safely from the war, despite years of silence. Charles Gray was serving as a corporal in the Australian infantry forces, when he was captured by the Japanese during the Fall of Singapore in February 1942. He spent the next three and a half years in the notorious Changi and Kranji prisoner-of-war camps, surviving horrors that changed him forever.

The couple met in 1938, when Charles was sent to Mount Gambier as part of his training to become a minister in the Presbyterian Church. Jane grew up in the South Australian town where her father was an auctioneer, respected for his keen business sense and knowledge of livestock. Her mother, Elsy, was the daughter of a local bank manager, who moved to a fruit block at Coonawarra after his retirement.

The Clezys already had four sons and a daughter when the petite Elsy unexpectedly gave birth to twins in 1912. 'Mrs Clezy, I think there's another!' the midwife told her after helping to deliver Jane. Weighing a considerable nine pounds, she was quickly followed by six-pound Robert, known as Bob, who grew up to become a livestock agent like his father, and the local manager of Elders.

Meanwhile Jane studied at Umpherston College, a private girls school established by the town's Protestant churches, which paid her one pound per week to stay on as a student teacher. Her leisure time was crammed with church, sport and artistic endeavours, with Jane developing a reputation for her star turns at the local choral society and drama group. She also volunteered with the Junior Red Cross, and as inaugural secretary of a mothers and babies association.

In 1936, Jane persuaded her reluctant parents to let her go to Melbourne, where she boarded with an older brother and his wife, while training as a nurse at the Alfred Hospital. She was home for a visit, when Charles was invited to lunch one Sunday after the morning service. Apart from church, they had a great deal in common and apparently 'hit it off' immediately. Jane's parents were both of Scottish heritage and Charles was born in Aberdeen; and they both loved reading, poetry and the theatre. 'I think they started corresponding fairly quickly,' says their daughter Mary. 'Then they literally bumped into each

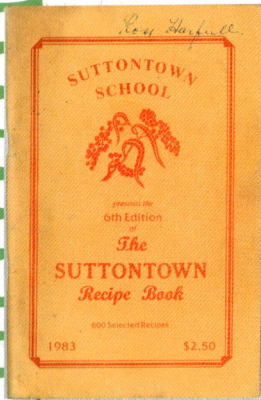

other in Flinders Street in Melbourne just as Dad was about to enlist, so they went and had coffee and cake.'

As the war continued, Jane completed her training at the Crown Street Women's Hospital in Sydney, where she gained qualifications as a midwife. She then took up private nursing, looking after people in their own homes. An inveterate letter writer throughout her life, she kept sending letters to Charles, despite hearing nothing from him after the Japanese over-ran Singapore. But she never gave up hope, and nor did his mother.

'Granny Gray never doubted,' says Mary. 'She had three sons at war, and she told of a dream she had with them all in uniform, standing at various spots on a stairway. Dad went out and then came back just to the edge of the stairway, and then the next one Jim, who was in New Guinea, he stayed there on the stair, and then the next one Ian, went away. Ian subsequently died at El Alamein but she hung onto the fact that Charles was still there on the stairs.'

Above: Jane Clezy in her nurse's uniform (courtesy Mary MacCarthy). Opposite: The first and 1983 editions of the Suttontown cookbook.

Having completed a short course at the Austin Hospital in Melbourne before enlisting, during his capture Charles worked alongside famous Australian surgeon Weary Dunlop, helping to care for the sick, injured and dying. When the men learnt Charles had trained to become a minister, he was also often asked to preside at burials. 'He buried a lot of his friends,' Mary says.

As soon as the camp was liberated in September 1945, Charles wrote to Jane, but he begged her not to come to the port to welcome him home. 'He did not want any of the women in the family to come down and see the ship arriving in Melbourne, because there were some dreadful sights,' Mary says. Instead, his brothers collected him and took him back to their parents' house at Monbulk, east of Melbourne, where he slowly began to put on weight and recover.

Jane mustn't have waited too long to see him, as the couple announced their engagement before the end of October. They were married at St Andrew's Presbyterian Church in Mount Gambier on a perfect summer's day in January 1946, then they lived at Monbulk while Charles trained to become a school-teacher. 'He felt that he could never forgive or forget what the Japanese had done, and that made him unfit to be a minister. But the government had a scheme to assist soldiers to retrain in whatever they wanted, and with his level of education teaching seemed an obvious choice,' Mary says.

Charles was still weak and suffering bouts of malaria when he was given his first teaching appointment in the tiny farming community of Glendaruel, about 30 kilometres north of Ballarat. By then the Grays were a family of four—despite the doctors having feared Charles would never be able to have children—with Mary approaching five years of age and her younger brother, Robert, only three.

They lived in a house attached to the small schoolroom, which accommodated every year level, from kindergarten to two girls tackling their secondary education by correspondence. 'When Mum was doing the laundry in the copper, she could hear Dad talking through the wall,' Mary says. 'If anyone was sick, they would go to the house so Mum could look after them, and she and Dad had to clean the school, and empty the toilets. They did everything.'

Mary remembers these early years as idyllic. Her mother loved gardening and filled the house with fresh flowers. There was no electricity, but Jane made the best of the wood stove and kerosene-powered fridge, turning out roast lamb for Sunday lunch, and baking sponges and biscuits for fundraising stalls. 'She loved food and enjoyed cooking,' Mary says. 'She and her sister Elsy were renowned for their steak and kidney pie, and visiting nephews would always ask for it.'

One thing that Jane never prepared, in any form, was savoury rice. After Changi, Charles could not stand it. 'Creamed rice with raisins was alright but it probably wasn't until the '70s that we would have Chinese fried rice sometimes. Even then he would look at it, and push it around a bit, and not really enjoy it.'

Charles turned out to be a natural teacher, receiving glowing reports from the school inspectors. He soon started applying for larger schools, with the family moving around Victoria often over the coming years. He died in 1978 at the relatively young age of 63, which doctors attributed to the severe malnutrition suffered in Changi. After a few years in Melbourne, Jane returned to Mount Gambier, living with Elsy and helping to care for her brother Bob, in his old age. She died in 2000, at the age of 88.

A keen cook herself, Mary treasures her mother's cookery books, and the recipes handed down through her grandmother Clezy's family. They include a notebook kept by her great-grandmother, Elsy Alexander, which combines traditional recipes with cures for typhoid fever and cancer, and instructions for preparing grafting wax for fruit trees, and French furniture polish.

Unfortunately, Mary's collection doesn't include The "Back to Suttontown" Recipe Book, which Jane and her sister contributed to in the early 1930s.

Organised jointly by the local young farmers' club and the school, the cookbook featured 500 recipes published under the cheekily verbose subtitle: 'From the South-East of South Australia which is famous for everything, including cookery'.

The cookbooks sold for one shilling and sixpence to raise money for the Back to Suttontown celebrations held in May 1933. An initial run of 1000 copies

was printed by *The Border Watch* at Mount Gambier, with the newspaper claiming it was the first cookbook of its kind in the region.

A second edition was put out by the Suttontown Young Farmers' Club in 1936. The Suttontown School Welfare Club took control in 1944, printing a third edition to raise money for a school piano. Another edition, with 100 extra recipes and simply titled the *Suttontown Recipe Book*, followed in 1949. The sixth and final edition was printed 50 years after the first, in 1983.

Apple cake

SERVES 6– 8

This delicious shortcake was a Gray family favourite. Mary remembers her mother making it regularly, as the school residences they lived in usually came with a garden that had apple trees. She suspects the recipe was handed down by Jane's grandmother, who also had ready access to apple trees on the fruit block at Coonawarra. Mary recalls it being made in a shallow cake pan but the early version provided for the Suttontown Recipe Book *is a rustic, free-form apple cake, put together using a clever but simple technique, then cooked on a baking tray.*

INGREDIENTS

Filling:

4 Granny Smith apples, peeled, cored, quartered and sliced

2 tablespoons white sugar

2 tablespoons water

Paste (pastry):

110 g butter, softened

2 tablespoons caster sugar

1 egg, lightly beaten

2 tablespoons cold water

225 g (1½ cups) self-raising flour

METHOD

Preheat the oven to moderate (180°C).

To make the filling, put the apples in a large saucepan with the sugar and water and bring to the boil, stirring to dissolve the sugar. Cook gently for about 10 minutes, until soft.

To make the paste (pastry), beat the butter and sugar together in a large bowl until light and fluffy. Beat in the egg and then the water until combined. Sift in the flour and stir with a knife to form a very soft dough.

Knead the dough lightly, then place it on a long piece of baking paper, dusted with flour. Roll the dough out to form a very long rectangle, about 15 cm wide, with the pastry only a few millimetres thick.

Drain any remaining liquid from the warm apple mixture, then spread it over one half of the pastry. Use the paper to lift the other half over the top of the apples. Leave the apple cake on the baking paper and slide it onto a baking tray. Trim away the excess baking paper, and prick the top of the cake with a fork. Bake for 20–30 minutes, until golden.

- It is very important that the apples are relatively dry to prevent the pastry from going soggy.

- Jane recommended that the apples still be warm when you spread them on the pastry.

- Using the paper to fold over the top layer is a great help because the pastry is very soft.

- The apple cake is delicious warm or cold. Sprinkle it with icing sugar before serving, or cover it with icing and cinnamon if you wish to serve it cold as a slice.

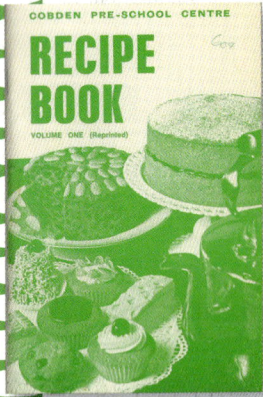

THE BOOK *that* MADE *the* DOUGH

Nookie Teal quite liked the idea of training to become a nurse or a teacher when she left school, but it was wartime and she was needed at home. With so many local men signed up to military service, labour was short on the family dairy farm at Kennedy's Creek, deep in the Otway Ranges of western Victoria. There were eight younger brothers and sisters to care for too.

So Nookie, christened Dorine Howard, gave up the idea and, at the age of fourteen, took over cooking and cleaning for her mother, Molly, so she could spend more time out in the paddock working alongside her husband, Jack.

Nookie remembers her mother being a good cook, particularly when it came to sponges and cream puffs. She made her own potato yeast to bake bread, and Jack kept a productive vegetable garden where he grew plenty of potatoes. 'Where we lived was well into the bush, and there used to be drovers who would bring cattle out to graze on the plains, and you never knew who would drop in for a cuppa or a meal. So there was always a pot of soup on the side of the stove, and biscuits in the tin,' recalls Nookie.

When things picked up after the war, Jack called in a bricklayer from Camperdown by the name of Roy Teal to help him build a new house. 'Roy used to tell our grandkids that I won his heart with my apple pies. He came into the house one day and I had apple pies everywhere, and he counted them up and there were thirteen. The next day he asked me for some more, and there were none left. Just two meals and they were all gone.'

The couple were married in December 1949, a few months after Nookie's 21st birthday, at the Presbyterian church in Cobden where they later settled down to raise a family, while Roy worked at the local cheese and butter factory. Having cared for a large family before she was married, Nookie and Roy only had two children, both boys.

Nookie's sons left home many years ago and Roy died in 1999 but, at the age of 90, she still bakes and makes preserves. 'I have always loved to cook,' she says. Her neighbours in a group of retirement units at Cobden love it when she shares her scones as a special treat, and her grandchildren always ask for some of the latest batch of home-made tomato sauce or chutney when they come to visit.

With her reputation as a capable cook, it's not surprising that Nookie was among those encouraged to contribute recipes when the Cobden Play Centre committee decided in the early 1960s that a cookbook might help fund the cost of building the town's first preschool. The Presbyterian minister had allowed local mothers to hold daily play sessions in the church hall since 1955, but the number of children attending had grown so much there was a pressing need for dedicated facilities.

More than a few people asked, 'Who'd buy that?' when they heard about the *Cobden Pre-school Centre Recipe Book*. 'Quite a large number of people thought it would never happen,' recalls Elizabeth Wilson, who joined the committee a few years later. But they soon had a lovely collection of recipes for soups, main courses, desserts, baked goods, sandwich fillings, preserves, dressings and confectionery. Local businesses agreed to take out advertising, which covered most of the printing costs, and a Melbourne radio announcer even promoted the cookbook during her program.

'The response was astounding,' says Elizabeth. The local post office was inundated with requests, and in no time at all the first 500 copies had sold out, with parcels wending their way across Victoria. Not only was the modest endeavour a success in publishing terms, but it raised enough money to convince the local shire council that the community would be able to sustain a new preschool.

Now part of the Cobden & District Kindergarten, the building was officially opened by Victoria's longest-serving premier, Sir Henry Bolte, in 1967. Hanging on the noticeboard, as he passed by that day, was a copy of the little book with a brief note: 'This is the book that made the dough that made the council say go, go, go'.

The first edition produced in 1961 did so well that a second volume of different recipes was published with equal success in 1968, and later the original book was reprinted due to popular demand in 1971. Elizabeth can't recall how that one fared, but she still uses the copy she bought for 60 cents.

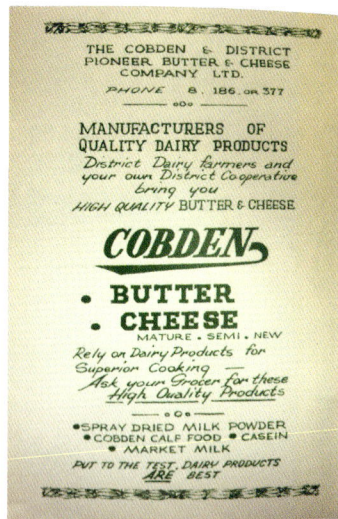

THE COBDEN & DISTRICT
PIONEER BUTTER & CHEESE
COMPANY LTD.

PHONE 8 . 186 *or* 377

MANUFACTURERS OF
QUALITY DAIRY PRODUCTS
District Dairy farmers and
your own District Cooperative
bring you
HIGH QUALITY BUTTER & CHEESE

COBDEN

• BUTTER
• CHEESE
MATURE . SEMI . NEW

*Rely on Dairy Products for
Superior Cooking —
Ask your Grocer for these
High Quality Products*

• SPRAY DRIED MILK POWDER
• COBDEN CALF FOOD • CASEIN
• MARKET MILK

PUT TO THE TEST, DAIRY PRODUCTS
ARE BEST

Above: Advertisement from the cookbook. Below: Elizabeth Wilson (left) and Nookie Teal outside the kindergarten, 2017 (image by Suzy Wilson). Opposite: *Cobden Pre-school Centre Recipe Book*, vol. 1, reprint (courtesy Elizabeth Wilson).

COBDEN & DISTRICT
KINDERGARTEN

Boston bun

Nookie was one of four women to donate this recipe to the cookbook, so it was clearly a district favourite. 'We were asked to submit our favourite recipes, and they had to be tried,' she says. 'My mother made this before I was around. I don't know where she got it—it was just one of those recipes that is cheap and easy to make, and we usually had a little bit of mashed potato left over.'

INGREDIENTS

115 g (½ cup) cold mashed potato

110 g (½ cup) caster sugar

125 ml (½ cup) milk

100 g (½ cup) sultanas

1 heaped cup self-raising flour

pinch of salt

2 tablespoons desiccated coconut

Icing:

125 g (1 cup) icing sugar

15 g butter

1 tablespoon warm water (approximately)

METHOD

Preheat the oven to moderate (180°C). Grease a 20 cm round cake pan and line the bottom with baking paper.

Cream together the mashed potato and sugar until the mixture is free of any lumps. Add the milk, sultanas, flour and salt and stir until combined.

Place the mixture in the sandwich pan and bake for 30 minutes, until golden.

To make the icing, put the icing sugar in a small bowl with the butter, then stir in the warm water, adding enough to form a smooth icing.

Ice the bun once it is cold, then sprinkle with coconut.

LIZ AND NOOKIE'S TIPS

- Nookie says that while you can just put all the ingredients in the bowl and stir, it's better to mix the potato and sugar first, or you might end up with lumps of undissolved mash.

- You don't have to use sultanas — try currants or chopped raisins instead.

- The original version of this recipe suggested topping the bun with cinnamon and sugar, and using plain white icing. Nookie likes coconut, and I like it with pink icing.

Opposite: *The Best of Good Taste*, c. mid-1960s (courtesy Debra Richards).

One ENCHANTED EVENING

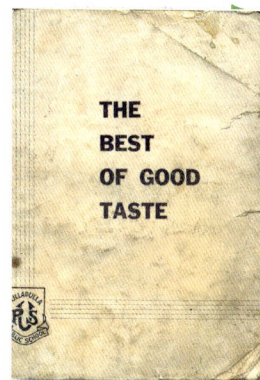

THE
BEST
OF GOOD
TASTE

Ruth Franks was only eighteen when she met the love of her life one night at a party in 1953. Just like the lyrics of 'Some Enchanted Evening', the apprentice hairdresser from Kogarah spotted a good-looking stranger across a crowded room and was instantly smitten. Bruce Richards was equally taken with the gorgeous blonde, dressed in a button-up skirt and scoop-necked peasant blouse. According to their daughter, Debra, he then proceeded to lure her with his mellifluous baritone, when he was asked to sing the romantic show tune that captured so perfectly the magic of that night.

After the party, Bruce escorted Ruth to her home in southern Sydney and asked her for a date the very next evening. Determined to make a good impression, he spent all his money hiring a taxi and taking her to Chequers, one of Sydney's most exclusive cabaret night clubs. 'Mum mistakenly thought he was loaded. Little did she know, he then had to walk all the way home to Penshurst,' says Debra. 'He asked her out again the following night. This time it was public transport to the pictures at the Savoy in Hurstville but by then it didn't matter—they were in love.'

Six weeks later Ruth and Bruce became engaged. Ruth's mother, Zoe, thought her daughter was too young, but she gave permission anyway, knowing the wedding would have to wait because Bruce was about to start a two-year stint working in New Guinea as a fitter and turner. She wasn't very pleased when he showed up within six months, having broken his contract. The young couple tried to convince Zoe they should marry straight away, but she wouldn't budge, so Bruce went back.

Determined not to give up, he sat down and wrote a 29-page letter to his future mother-in-law, stating the case about why he and Ruth should wed immediately. Zoe wrote a 31-page letter back explaining why they shouldn't. The wedding eventually took place in 1955, at St Aidan's Anglican Church in Hurstville Grove, on the wettest April day in 80 years.

The newlyweds went to Queensland for their honeymoon. It was meant to be a two-week trip but, unbeknown to Ruth, Bruce was planning an extended working holiday while they got to know each other better. Travelling north on an old BSA military motorcycle, they ended up in Townsville, where Bruce cut sugar cane while Ruth worked as a housemaid and waitress in a local hotel.

It was 1961, and they were living in Sydney with two young children, when Bruce accepted temporary work in Ulladulla. He was only planning to stay six months, but Ruth had other ideas. Having fallen in love with the picturesque town on the southern New South Wales coast, she told her husband firmly that they were staying. Bruce agreed, but he wasn't keen on her finding paid employment outside the home while they had young children, so she joined the CWA instead, and never looked back.

Over the next 50 years Ruth became increasingly involved in community organisations and projects, not just as a willing volunteer, but often as the instigator. She was president of Meals on Wheels for eight years, served on the Shoalhaven Arts Council, and a range of other committees connected to schools, recreation facilities and community events, the Anglican Church, elder care, the show society, and various council task forces and working parties. She loved to sing and perform with the Milton Follies amateur theatre group, and the Milton Ulladulla Entertainers, which she helped form to raise money for local charities.

As a community activist, Ruth wrote letters to the editor and lobbied energetically for upgrades to the harbour and civic centre, and changes to a local shopping complex. When she was awarded a Medal of the Order of Australia (OAM) in June 2012 for her service to the community, Ruth commented that it reflected her 'dogged determination to see projects through and to stand up and speak out if I think something's not right'.

Among the people who nominated her was Marg Rudd, one of the first friends she had made in Ulladulla. They met after Ruth went to the one-stop shop run by Marg's parents, Viv and Agnes Bland, to buy some ingredients for Debra's fifth birthday cake. It turned out that Marg had a daughter about the same age. They both had husbands named Bruce too, and younger sons only eight months apart. 'It was really eerie,' Marg says.

The two women became lifelong friends and worked alongside each other on many committees and projects, including establishing the town's first preschool, which was run from Marg's house until they got access to a local hall. Ruth stayed involved in the facility long after her children, Debra, Blake and Gavin, were too old to attend. As they grew, she also joined the Ulladulla Public School P&C Ladies Auxiliary, and later the high-school equivalent.

A few months after being awarded the OAM, Ruth was presented with a 50-year service medal by the CWA. Since joining the Milton District Younger Set in 1961, she had served in many different roles at branch and group level, even being named Country Woman of the Year in 1978. 'She embraced the organisation and it embraced her, even though she mistakenly thought to be a real CWA lady you probably needed to be able to knit a sheep,' Debra jokes. 'She loved the camaraderie, the friendship, the commitment and the contribution of the CWA to the national agenda.'

For all those reasons, Ruth decided to attend the CWA national conference held in Hobart in August 2012. The conference had been in progress a few days at the Wrest Point Casino when Ruth headed back to her nearby motel room to freshen up before joining other New South Wales delegates for dinner. She took time to make her daily call to Bruce, excited about becoming a great-grandmother for the third time just the day before. 'I love you,' they said to each other, as usual, before ending the call.

Ninety minutes later, Ruth was dead. In a tragic accident that shocked her family, friends, colleagues and community to the core, she was hit by a car while crossing busy Sandy Bay Road, on her way back to the casino. A passing medical practitioner and nurse performed CPR but Ruth died at the scene.

Eight days later, on what would have been her 77th birthday, more than 700 people turned out for Ruth's funeral in Ulladulla. Attempting to capture the

Below: Ruth Richards at the time she was awarded an Medal of the Order of Australia, 2012 (courtesy *Milton Ulladulla Times*).

palpable sense of loss, a local newspaper wrote of the gaping hole her death had created, robbing the town of a treasured community worker and tireless activist. 'Mum lived by the mantra— "it is better to wear out, than rust out",' Debra told mourners when she was giving the eulogy. 'In the end she did neither. She moved too fast with too much energy to ever rust out and she still had so much to do.'

Lemon cheese tarts

MAKES 12

INGREDIENTS

2 eggs, lightly beaten

110 g (½ cup) caster sugar

3 tablespoons lemon juice, strained

grated zest of 1 lemon

30 g butter, chopped

12 sweet shortcrust tartlet cases, pre-baked

1 tablespoon icing sugar

Sometime in about the mid-1960s, when Ruth was president of the Ulladulla primary school auxiliary, the organisation published a cookbook of 'tried and tested' recipes donated by local homemakers and selected for their variety, economy and simplicity. Marg is not too sure how much money The Best of Good Taste *raised, but it was successful enough to be followed by a second volume in 1974. Among the recipes in the first edition were these tarts made with a lemon filling, using whole eggs.*

The recipe was provided by Agnes, who had a reputation as a good cook, unlike Ruth who was not really known for her prowess in the kitchen—although she did try to make things interesting. 'We didn't have a lot of money, but she would make the most of what we had,' Debra says, recalling school sandwiches made with unusual combinations, such as pineapple and raisins.

METHOD

Put the eggs in a large metal bowl and whisk in the sugar, lemon juice and zest. Add the chopped butter. Place the bowl over a saucepan of simmering water and whisk until the mixture reaches the consistency of thick custard.

Spoon the filling into the pre-baked pastry cases, while it is still warm.

Dust with icing sugar to serve.

LIZ'S TIPS

- Make your own shortcrust pastry cases using your favourite recipe, or cut them from two sheets of shop-bought shortcrust pastry.
- You don't need to whisk the filling continuously, after the sugar has dissolved and the butter has melted. However, keep a close eye on it, as once it starts to thicken it will change quickly and you want it to cook evenly, without lumps forming.
- Once the tarts are cool, store them in the fridge, sitting them on some paper towel in a sealed container.

LOVING *to eat* JEWISH

Henry Nissen was a champion boxer, but it was his skills in another arena that generated headlines 50 years ago for Melbourne's oldest Jewish school.

In 1968, the boxing legend agreed to help Bialik College promote a groundbreaking collection of Jewish recipes, by taking part in a latke-eating competition. In two and a half minutes, he chomped his way through two dozen of the traditional potato pancakes, made using about one and a half kilograms of potatoes, and was proclaimed Australia's Latke Eating Champion.

Nissen and his twin brother, Leon, were born in a refugee camp outside the notorious Belsen concentration camp in Germany in 1948, and came to Australia with their Jewish parents the following year. As a child, Henry attended the college kindergarten, which was the first educational establishment in Australia to use Hebrew as a language of instruction. As a young man, he won 39 out of 49 amateur flyweight fights and a gold medal at the 1969 Maccabiah Games, before turning professional and claiming the Commonwealth title in 1971. Much admired in Melbourne for his efforts since, as a youth social worker, Henry was quite happy to assist his old school.

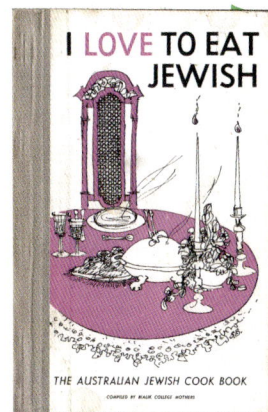

Above: The *I Love to Eat Jewish* cookbook, second edition. Left: Some of the women who contributed recipes and helped compile the cookbook, photographed during the school's 70th anniversary celebrations, 2012 (image by Saville Shulman Photography, courtesy Bialik College).

I Love to Eat Jewish was put together by a group of mothers to raise funds for the college building fund. They settled on the idea after noticing there did not seem to be any Jewish recipe books using familiar measurements and ingredients readily available in Australia. Not only were families associated with the school becoming more interested in traditional recipes, but the women were keen to share with the wider community, treasures handed down from mother to daughter, dating back to 'biblical times'.

The cookbook includes favourite recipes for both everyday meals and religious festivals, reflecting Jewish dietary laws, which prohibit eating pork and shellfish, and combining meat with dairy. The first section is labelled 'Forschpeisen', and features entrees and herring dishes. Then there are soups, fish, meat and poultry recipes, vegetables and salads, a special section for kugels (baked puddings), desserts, nosherei (snacks or nibbles), baking, and finally a section for Pesach, or Passover. One of the most important events on the Jewish calendar, this eight-day festival commemorates the exodus of the Israelites from Egypt and their liberation from slavery. During this period, leavened food and certain grain-based foods are also prohibited.

The recipes found in *I Love to Eat Jewish* were donated by parents associated with the college, who came from diverse cultural backgrounds, often reflected in the recipes they chose. Contributions also came from parents linked to the GK Korsunski Carmel School in Perth, who heard about the project and wanted to participate.

The final 136-page, hardcover cookbook was launched at an exclusive luncheon held at the private home of Mr and Mrs J. Ashkanasy. Malca Pratt, the wife of Israel's ambassador in Australia, flew from Canberra to do the honours before a crowd of about 200 guests. The first edition sold out within seven days and the cookbook was reprinted immediately, with a third edition following in 1971. Copies found their way onto bookshelves across Melbourne, and further afield too, as it became one of the main 'go to' cookbooks in Australia for Jewish food.

In 1999, the college produced a second book, *With a Passion: a celebration of food Bialik style*, and the original cookbook was reprinted in 2012 as part of the school's 70th anniversary celebrations, when it also featured in a special exhibition.

Thinking about why it was so successful, one of the women involved strongly believes that a key reason was making sure each recipe was attributed. 'Everyone was very excited to see their names, and they bought copies as gifts,' says Julette Alexander.

Julette knew nothing about cooking when she became part of the informal committee responsible for compiling *I Love to Eat Jewish*, but she had seen similar community cookbooks in South Africa, and knew they were popular.

Julette grew up in Cape Town, where her father established an electrical business after escaping from Poland before the Second World War. As was the case for most white families living in South Africa at the time, the household employed staff who looked after all the cleaning and cooking. 'I would come home from school, get undressed and drop the clothes on the floor, and someone would pick them up,' she confesses. 'I knew nothing about cooking, and my mother couldn't cook. My father said that my mother was not allowed to go into the kitchen. She knew how to make an omelette, and that was it.'

Julette had to become more self-reliant after emigrating to Australia in 1960 with her husband, Joe, and their six-month-old daughter, Kim. A second child, Mara, was born in 1964, and eleven months later came Peter—later to become famous for his designer pyjamas. In the early years, Julette often phoned Cape Town seeking recipes and advice from Katie, her family's cook. She turned to the same place when the cookbook committee needed particular recipes to fill some gaps. 'Every recipe was tested by women who could cook, and we all tasted them,' Julette says. 'It was a lovely time for us all. There was no-one in charge, we just all worked together.'

Below: Bialik College's first class in 1942, making it Melbourne's oldest Jewish school and the first educational establishment in Australia to use Hebrew as a language of instruction (courtesy Bialik College Archives).

Latkes

INGREDIENTS

7 medium potatoes

1 small onion (optional)

2 eggs, lightly beaten

3 tablespoons plain flour

1 teaspoon salt

½ teaspoon baking powder

¼ teaspoon white pepper

This recipe for latkes was provided by Roma Kausman. I don't recommend that you try to beat Henry's record, but they make a delicious snack served in the traditional way, with apple sauce and sour cream.

METHOD

Peel and grate the potatoes and onion (if using), then squeeze out any moisture.

Place the vegetables in a large bowl and stir in the eggs. Add the flour, salt, baking powder and pepper and stir until thoroughly combined.

Drop heaped dessertspoonfuls into a large, well-greased frying pan and cook over medium heat until golden brown on both sides.

Drain on paper towel, then serve.

HE'S LATKE CHAMP, TOO!

● Henry Nissen, well-known bantamweight boxer, recently downed two dozen latkes — equal to 3 lb. potatoes—to win the Australian latke-eating championship from his challenger, Tim Hargreaves.

The championship was organised by the Bialik College Parents' Association to publicise a new book of recipes entitled "I Love to Eat Jewish."

The book will be sold to raise funds for the College.

LIZ'S TIPS

- Potatoes with higher starch content make the best latkes, such as sebago or kennebec.
- To make a traditional apple sauce, combine 4 tablespoons lemon juice with 100 ml water and 1 tablespoon sugar. Bring to the boil, then stir in two apples that have been peeled, quartered and sliced, a cinnamon stick and a few large pieces of fresh lemon peel. Cook until the apples are soft and thick. Remove the cinnamon stick and the peel, then set the sauce aside to cool.

Left: Champion boxer Henry Nissen winning the latke-eating competition that helped promote the cookbook, 1968 (courtesy *Australian Jewish News*).

RECISES *for* REJOICING

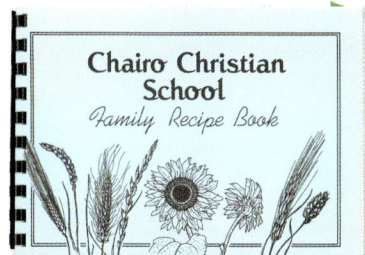

Sprawling across four separate campuses in Victoria's Gippsland region, Chairo Christian School has more than 1650 students and 250 teachers, but it was a completely different story the day it opened. The independent school started in 1983 with just nineteen students.

'There was one teacher and one classroom,' recalls Maggie Donald, whose two daughters were among the first intake. 'It was started by a group of about ten Christian families that wanted their children to have a Christian education. We did a lot of research, and we decided we wanted an independent school, not reliant on a church or government for funding.'

They began by buying an old state school building on Lardners Track, in the tiny rural community of Drouin East. They all lived within less than a twenty kilometre radius, so the location was ideal. One of the parents suggested they name it Chairo—a word from the New Testament of the Bible, meaning 'to rejoice'.

Getting the school off the ground involved frequent working bees, with the parents devoting many hours to renovating the building and grounds, as well as maintaining them. Everyone chipped in to make it work. 'It was just like one big family; they were great times,' Maggie says.

Besides lamington drives, selling bricks that were used in the renovations, annual auctions and a host of other fundraising efforts, in 1988 the school pub-

Above: Chairo Christian School Family Recipe Book, 1988. *Below:* The first day of the new school at Drouin East, 2 February 1983 (courtesy Chairo Christian School).

lished *The Chairo Christian School Family Recipe Book*. A small collection of straight-forward, economical but tasty dishes, the recipes were provided by families and friends, and compiled by one of the parents, Lyn Smith, who also typed them up.

Maggie contributed some recipes and so did her sister, Kath Jarred, who had a child at the school for a couple of years. Kath also helped to teach craft and provide additional support for a disabled student.

The sisters are amazed at how the school has grown since their children attended.

The original site still caters for preschool to year four, and there are middle and senior schools nearby on additional land bought in 1994. A new campus opened at Pakenham four years later. Chairo took over an existing school at Leongatha in 2014 and, in 2018, was due to absorb another campus at Traralgon. 'They have just grown in leaps and bounds,' says Kath.

~~~~~~~~~~~~~~~~~~~~~~~~~~~~~~~~~~~~~~~

Baked steak cake

SERVES 4–6

This recipe is a twist on the classic meatloaf found in just about every Australian community cookbook in the 1970s and early 1980s. I chose it from all the others because of its unusual topping, which takes only moments to make and comes up light and golden. For an economical outlay, this recipe also provides more than enough to feed at least four people.

The recipe was contributed by Kath. 'It's one from my mum. She was a good cook, but you didn't have fancy meals in those days and I'm still that way. I prefer to cook something wholesome,' says Kath, who is also described by her sister as an expert cook.

INGREDIENTS

Meatloaf:

700 g beef mince

90 g bacon, chopped

1 onion, coarsely grated

120 g grated cheddar cheese

2 teaspoons Worcestershire sauce

2 teaspoons tomato sauce

1 garlic clove, finely chopped

½ teaspoon salt

½ teaspoon freshly ground black pepper

pinch of cayenne pepper

Topping:

150 g (1 cup) self-raising flour

½ teaspoon salt

pinch of cayenne pepper

2 eggs, lightly beaten

250 ml (1 cup) milk

100 g (1 cup) grated cheddar cheese

30 g butter, melted

1 heaped teaspoon finely chopped parsley

METHOD

Preheat the oven to moderate (180°C). Grease a shallow, 23 cm square cake pan.

To make the meatloaf, put all the ingredients in a bowl and mix them together with your hands. Press the meat mixture into the prepared pan.

To make the topping, sift the flour, salt and cayenne pepper into a large bowl. Make a well in the centre and add the eggs, milk, cheese, butter and parsley. Whisk together until smooth, then pour over the meat.

Bake for about 50 minutes, until the top is set, crispy and brown. Serve either hot or cold.

KATH'S TIPS

- Use premium-quality beef mince, which is lower in fat.
- Leave the meatloaf to sit for a few minutes after you take it out of the oven, and then gently tip the pan to pour off any juices that have settled in the bottom.

RECEPY FOR SUCCESS

Kirstie Martin may only have been about seven at the time, but *Newport School Cookbook* compiler, Philippa Waugh, was so impressed with her effort to write a recipe without any obvious parental assistance, that she included it verbatim. Kirstie's orange jelly dessert was one of 99 children's favourites featured in the spiral-bound collection, published in 1987 as the Sydney school approached its centenary. Here it is exactly as published:

"Recepy"

(As written by Kirstie)

Cut a orange in half, take the bits of orange inside of it out. Make some frout (fruit) salid. Put the frout salid in the orange skins. Pore some jelly in it. Put it in the frige for a day. When you eat it put some ice creme on it then sprinkl some hundreds and thousins on it and then it is made.

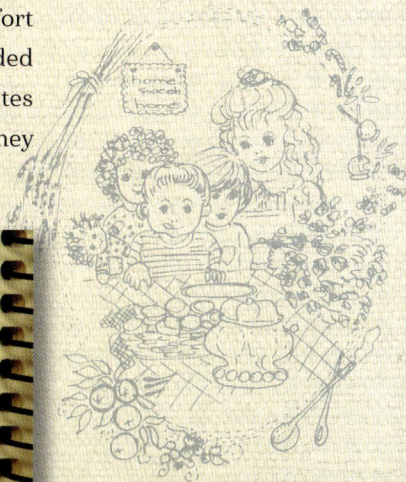

COUNTRY

Women's

WISDOM

BUNDABERG *takes* FLIGHT

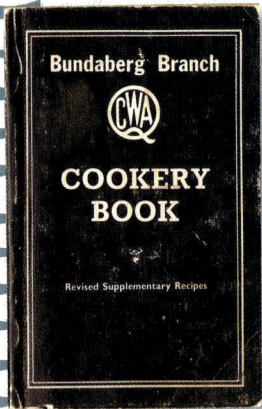

Pandemonium broke loose when aviator Bert Hinkler landed in his home-town after completing the first solo flight from London to Australia in 1928. The official end-point for measuring success was Darwin, which he reached in a record-breaking fifteen and a half days. But for Hinkler the real destination was always Bundaberg, where his mother and siblings were waiting.

Thousands of people turned out to greet the Queensland pilot, with some newspaper accounts putting the number at around 20,000. When they spotted his tiny Avro Avian approaching the local recreation ground shortly after four o'clock on the afternoon of 27 February, motor car horns, sirens and the roar of the huge crowd merged to create a 'terrific din'. As the plane's wheels touched down people rushed onto the rain-sodden field, frantic with excitement. They overwhelmed the official party and dragged Hinkler from the cockpit, hoisting him onto their shoulders.

He may have stood only 162 centimetres (five foot four inches) tall, but the 36-year-old pilot was now a giant in the international world of aviation. The new national hero was feted for weeks to come, with special receptions, dinners, awards, and even a gift of £2000 from the Australian government. In a wave of public adulation and commercial opportunism, Hinkler soon found his name associated with all sorts of objects such as hats, beers and sauces, and a two-tiered cake filled with dried fruit and topped with lemon icing.

Clockwise from top: Crowds rush onto the Bundaberg recreation ground to greet Bert Hinkler, 1928 (courtesy Hinkler Hall of Aviation Memorabilia Trust); Hinkler climbing into the cockpit of a plane, c. 1930s (State Library of Victoria); *The Queenslander* celebrates Hinkler's achievements, 8 March 1928 edition (State Library of Queensland); Hinkler with his plane, and being welcomed home by his mother, Frances (courtesy Hinkler Hall of Aviation Memorabilia Trust).

The cake was devised by Bundaberg members of the Country Women's Association to celebrate his achievements. Seven days after he landed, the branch organised a special gathering attended by about 300 women, at the local rowing club pavilion. Even though the star of the moment was present, the principal guest of honour was his mother, Frances, who was later made an honorary member of the Queensland CWA, along with Hinkler's wife, Nancy. In a show of female solidarity, the branch gave Frances a cheque for £50, praising her for maintaining a brave and cheerful spirit despite the anxious moments she had experienced during her intrepid son's adventures.

The Hinkler cake may well have been served at the event. The recipe certainly existed by the end of March, when it was published in Rockhampton's *Morning Bulletin*, but it became even better known after appearing in the *Q.C.W.A. Bundaberg Branch Cookery Book*.

First published in late 1928, the cookbook was conceived to raise money for a new hostel, which provided accommodation to boys from the bush so they could attend high school. The hostel was officially opened by Bert Hinkler in June that year. It was just one of several projects initiated by the Bundaberg branch, by then recognised as one of the largest and most energetic in the state.

Established in July 1924, within a few months the branch had signed up 200 members and opened rooms in Targo Street to provide a place where country women could rest and attend to their children while travelling through town, visiting for their weekly shopping expeditions, or waiting for their husbands.

Among the first of their kind established by the CWA in Queensland, the rest rooms made a huge difference to women's mobility and comfort. Before the facility opened, there were no public conveniences in Bundaberg, or many other country towns. Instead, women had to go to the expense of renting a room in a hotel for an hour or two. The need was proven in 1928, when more than 9000 visits were recorded.

The CWA was so prominent in Bundaberg that local papers routinely devoted whole columns across several pages to covering its activities. In 1932, the *Daily Times* described it as a 'valuable link in the chain of this great sisterhood movement, which has spread throughout Queensland', praising the association's endeavours to draw country women together and assist one another in a spirit of mutual cooperation essential to the 'progress and happiness of Rural Australia'.

For most of its early years, the Bundaberg branch was led by two women from the same high-profile family. The Gibsons were shareholders and managers of Gibson and Howes Limited, which owned the Bingera sugar mill and plantation, about twenty kilometres south-west of the town, placing them among the social and economic elite of the district.

Established by the Gibsons in the 1880s with financial backing from the Howes family, Bingera was regarded as a 'show sugar place', attracting a steady stream of high-profile dignitaries, from prime ministers and premiers to a touring English soccer team. With a population exceeding 600 people in 1911, it had more than 120 houses where employees and company officials lived with their families, its own hall, bakery, butcher shop and general store, and even a CWA sub-branch.

Jean, known as Jeanne, was married to the company's managing director, William Gibson. Recognised as a highly capable woman, she was president of the CWA 'mother' branch in Bundaberg, when it decided to publish the cookbook. The small committee tasked with making it happen was led by Mary Gibson, who was foundation president of the branch and responsible for overseeing the hostel.

Originally from England, Mary was married to William's cousin Dr Arthur Gibson. A future chairman of the International Society of Sugar Cane Technologists, Dr Gibson was director of the Queensland government's sugar research bureau and then general manager of Central Sugar Mills before returning to Bingera to assist and, later, succeed his cousin.

Jeanne's grandson, Ian Gibson, recalls Mary being a small woman who had to fight for her place in the family. 'At that time there were three Gibson ladies—Aunty Mary, Aunty Birdie, and my grandmother. My grandmother and Aunty Birdie were very strong, dominant women. They were pretty powerful ladies in the district,' says Ian, recalling shop managers rushing to welcome his grandmother when she entered their premises. 'Aunty Mary would have to stand up to them and make her space. She was a good organiser and a real fighter—she didn't lose influence because of her size. She had plenty of fire in her,' he adds.

While Ian does not remember his immediate family talking about Mary's role in creating the cookbook, he was certainly given a copy when he got married in 1960. 'Everyone had to have a Bundaberg CWA cookbook,' he says

Above, from top: Jeanne Gibson, president of the Bundaberg branch when the cookbook was compiled; and Mary Gibson, who led the committee that compiled the cookbook (State Library of Queensland).

279

matter-of-factly. 'It's always been a highly regarded publication because of the simplicity of the recipes.'

In terms of fundraising, the cookbook exceeded expectations from the beginning, despite the impact of the Depression. Advertising more than covered the cost of printing the first edition of about 3000 copies, which sold for two shillings and sixpence each. By May 1930 it had raised more than £300, with about 500 copies still in hand.

In 1931, the branch added more recipes and bravely ordered a second edition of 10,000 copies. A new monthly sales record of £200 was reached in August that year, boosted by delegates selling copies at the CWA State Conference in Townsville. By the following year, orders were coming in daily from across Australia and overseas, and the cookbook had won kudos from businessmen as 'rather a masterstroke of finance'.

Apart from supporting the hostel, profits also went towards the cost of building new rest rooms in Quay Street, incorporating an assembly hall, offices,

Below: CWA members gather in the Bundaberg Botanic Gardens, home of the Hinkler Hall of Aviation, to celebrate the organisation's 95th anniversary in Queensland, 2017 (image by Wendy Driver).

kitchen and playground, which the CWA opened, debt free, in 1936. Future profits were then accumulated in a fund and invested, raising enough money to pay an attendant and cover upkeep, as well as make donations and loans to other branches.

Although the boy's hostel no longer operates, money from the fund continues to maintain the CWA clubrooms as well as supporting other worthy local causes. By 2015, more than 128,000 copies of the book had been sold, with strong sales still being recorded after almost 90 years. 'It's just amazing to see the orders streaming in,' says long-term member Edna Buck. 'Whenever I clear out our mailbox, there is almost certainly at least one cheque or money order to pay for books. It is still being sent off regularly to all parts of the country in boxes of tens and twenties, sometimes more,' she says.

~~~~~~

Hinkler cake

This old-fashioned cake is not baked very often these days, even in Bundaberg, partly, I suspect, because the original recipe misses some key information, such as quantities for the fruit filling, the pan size and cooking time. However, it is delicious and deserves to be more widely known. The revised version provided here with more detail has the tick of approval from Edna and her CWA friends.

INGREDIENTS

120 g self-raising flour

2 teaspoons caster sugar

pinch of salt

60 g butter, chopped

2 tablespoons milk
  (approximately)

75 g (½ cup) currants

45 g (¼ cup) raisins,
  chopped

80 g (½ cup) chopped dates

Sponge mixture:

60 g butter, softened

110 g (½ cup) caster sugar

2 eggs

150 g (1 cup) self-raising flour

4 tablespoons milk

METHOD

Preheat the oven to moderately hot (190°C). Grease and line the base of a large, shallow, square cake pan (approximately 22 cm).

Put the flour, sugar and salt in a bowl. Rub in the butter until the mixture resembles fine breadcrumbs. Make a well in the centre and add the milk. Mix with a knife until it forms a soft dough.

Turn the dough out onto a floured board and knead it very gently until smooth. Roll the dough out to fit the cake pan, then place it in the pan, moulding it gently with your fingers to fit into the corners. Sprinkle over the currants, raisins and dates.

To make the sponge mixture, cream the butter and caster sugar in a large bowl, until light and fluffy and the sugar is dissolved. Add the eggs, one at a time, and beat until combined. Add the flour, alternately with the milk, and beat until combined.

Lemon icing:

185 g (1½ cups) icing sugar

15 g butter, softened

2 tablespoons lemon juice
  (approximately)

Spread the sponge mixture over the fruit and bake in the oven for 30 minutes, or until golden.

Allow the cake to cool in the pan for a few minutes, then turn out onto a wire rack to cool completely.

To make the lemon icing, put the icing sugar, butter and lemon juice in a small bowl and mix until smooth, and of a spreading consistency.

When the cake is cool, ice the top with the lemon icing.

LIZ'S TIPS

- You can use a food processor to mix the butter into the dry ingredients.
- Adapt the ratio of dried fruit to suit your preference.
- Another version of this cake, named after famous pioneering English aviator Amy Johnson, includes jam spread over the base before the dried fruit is added. Blackberry jam enhances the flavour of currants beautifully, if you want to give it a try.

Opposite: *The C.W.A. Cookery Book and Household Hints*, 52nd edition 2003 (courtesy Trish Medlen).

The SCHOOL of EXPERIENCE

The modest nature of rural women almost prevented Western Australia's best-loved community cookbook from getting off the ground.

The Country Women's Association of Western Australia decided to publish *The C.W.A. Cookery Book and Household Hints* during a conference in August 1931, after delegates supported a motion from the branch at Nungarin, in the state's north-eastern wheatbelt. Aside from raising funds, the CWA hoped the cookbook would result in an exchange of economical ideas and experience, which would make life easier for its members during the hard years of the Depression.

The association appointed Agnes Barnes to edit the publication, and sent out a call via its branches for favourite recipes and useful tips garnered from personal experience. Agnes wanted anything and everything that had helped women to overcome the various problems and daily challenges confronted in and around the home, during their life on the land. After a year, only 23 branches had responded and there was nowhere near enough material to make the idea work. Agnes came to the conclusion that modesty was the issue. 'Of course you all know that members of the CWA have unbounded faith in one another as well as a fair amount of confidence in themselves, ... nevertheless, they are modest to a degree,' she told listeners during a speech broadcast by the ABC in 1942. 'Each apparently was holding back, supposing that the other had something better to offer. Once the ice was broken, and it was realised that each had something of worth to give, contributions flowed in, in an unbroken stream.'

By May 1933, the project was back on track. In fact, the personal pleas for support made by Agnes were so successful that she was soon dealing with the opposite problem—too many contributions. About 800 women had provided enough material to fill 700 pages, way more than was practicable for a book the executive had decided must not cost more than two shillings and sixpence. Finding the pruning process 'heart breaking', Agnes reworked the contents, 'giving a just portion to all contributors'.

She was ably assisted by her youngest daughter Patricia, who completed a secretarial course so she could help with the typing; and a small committee, which included noted writer, botanical artist and champion equestrienne

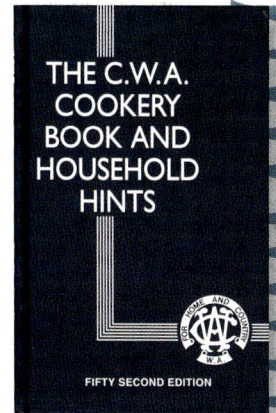

You could have left me the C.W.A cook Book !!

Above, from top: Members of the Ord Valley branch of the CWA (image by Ben Broadwith); and a cartoon by Peg Vickers summing up the value of the cookbook. (courtesy CWA of WA.)

Emily Pelloe. A tall woman with a quiet manner and a warm smile, Emily created a women's interest column for the *West Australian* in the 1920s under the pen name Ixia, as well as answering readers' questions about cookery, dress and health.

Publication of the cookbook was further delayed when the CWA struggled to find enough money to cover the printing costs. However, they managed to strike a deal with E.S. Wigg & Son, who agreed to publish the book on a royalty basis, paying the association threepence for every copy sold, or 10 per cent. Special cloth-bound, hardcover copies would be sold for five shillings.

Five years after the initial decision, the new cookbook was released at the CWA's conference in August 1936. Within a fortnight, 1000 copies had been sold. By May 1937, the entire edition had sold out and a revised version was on the way. By the time Agnes made her broadcast during another era of austerity, as war gripped much of the world, it was in its fifth edition, with copies having gone to homes across Australia, and as far afield as Canada and Britain.

From the start, reviewers praised the cookbook's carefully selected contents, and the generosity of CWA members in sharing their knowledge, skills and ingenuity with the general public. In the book's foreword, state president,

Clare Burt, wrote that it almost seemed unnecessary to suggest that the little book was something special, given that people realised 'Australian women are among the best cooks in the world'. Building on the theme in her preface, Agnes wrote that country women 'are specialists in those things that matter most in the Home, and that preserve the health of their flock. Hard times have made them economists—necessity has made them adaptable. Home lovers and Home builders, their School is the School of Experience—the training that leads to perfection.'

A major contributing factor to the success of the book was no doubt its editor, a capable cook who had raised six daughters and was in her late fifties when she took the project on. Christened Agnes Kirkwood Burns Patrick, she was born in Ayrshire on the west coast of Scotland in 1874, and emigrated to South Australia as a child with her parents, William and Jane.

When Agnes was about 23, the Patricks moved to Cue, in the remote Murchison area of Western Australia's mid-west, where she met James Barnes, a storekeeper from Northern Ireland. They married in 1900 and then ten years later settled at Doodlakine, about 200 kilometres east of Perth, where the family ran a hardware store until James died after an operation in 1926.

Active in the community, Agnes was inaugural president of the CWA's Doodlakine–Baandee branch when it started in 1925. She continued on in the role after her husband's death, and became a well-known public figure once the cookbook was published, helping to judge cookery competitions, and providing cooking advice via the *Perth Daily News* and its Women at War column.

Agnes was awarded honorary life membership of the CWA about two years before she died in January 1949, but the cookbook that she devoted so many hours to, lives on, marking its 57th edition in 2017. The publication has changed a little since the first edition, with measurements converted to metric in the 1970s, and the names of contributors dropped out. However, the iconic cover and style remains the same.

'At one stage people wanted to put photos in there and update it, but the idea didn't get a guernsey at all,' says state president, Heather Allen, who is overseeing the CWA at a time of resurgence, with new branches opening to cater for a growing number of younger women wanting to learn traditional skills such as baking, preserving and handicrafts. 'We sell a lot every day at the Royal Perth Show, and at field days, and we have people come up to us and say, "We love ours and we want to buy one for our grandchildren". It just keeps selling.'

Above: Cookbook editor Agnes Barnes. Below: CWA members celebrating the cookbook's 60th anniversary in 1996. (courtesy CWA of WA.)

Treacle scones

MAKES ABOUT 8

There is no contributor's name under this recipe in the CWA cookery book but I'm betting it came from Agnes herself. These lovely scones are traditional fare in Scotland, where she was born. Although they are flatter than the type of scones most of us know, one bite and you will soon see why they were so popular—if the delicious warm, spicy aroma coming from the oven doesn't convince you first!

INGREDIENTS

225 g (1½ cups) self-raising flour

½ teaspoon ground cinnamon

½ teaspoon bicarbonate of soda

pinch of salt

60 g butter

1 teaspoon caster sugar

1 heaped tablespoon treacle

125 ml (½ cup) buttermilk

METHOD

Preheat the oven to moderately hot (190°C). Line a baking tray with baking paper.

Sift the flour, cinnamon, bicarbonate of soda and salt together in a large bowl. Rub in the butter until the mixture resembles fine breadcrumbs. Stir in the sugar.

In a small bowl, whisk together the treacle and buttermilk until combined. Make a well in the centre of the dry ingredients and add the buttermilk mixture. Stir together using a knife.

Put the scone dough on a lightly floured board, then knead very lightly until it comes together. Press the dough flat with your hands, until it is about 1 cm thick. Use a plain round cutter (approximately 6 cm) to cut out the scones, then place them on the baking tray. Bake for about 10 minutes, until golden and they sound hollow when tapped on the bottom.

Below: CWA state president, Heather Allen, with a batch of treacle scones (image by Peter Allen).

LIZ'S TIPS

- Sift the dry ingredients together twice to make sure they are thoroughly blended.
- Warm the treacle a little before you mix it with the buttermilk, so it is easier to blend.
- Handle the dough lightly, as you would for any scone.
- These scones are best served warm from the oven, with lashings of butter. The spice flavourings are complemented brilliantly by a sharp orange or cumquat marmalade, or try them with honey.

CROWNING *glory*

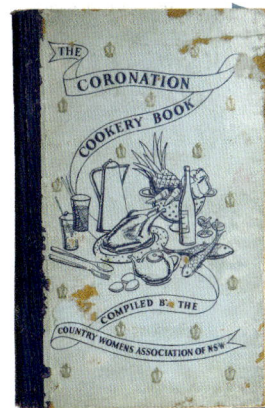

Jessie Sawyer and Sara Moore-Sims were busy putting the finishing touches to a new cookbook for the Country Women's Association (CWA) when news broke of King Edward VIII's scandalous intentions to abdicate and marry an American divorcee. The royal crisis may have seemed well outside the purview of the country women's organisation, except that it was planning to name its publication *The Coronation Cookery Book*. The collection of recipes and household hints was due to be released in 1937, around the time the new King was meant to be crowned in a spectacular ceremony at Westminster Abbey.

There is no hint of the reason, but Jessie asked for alternative suggestions about what they might call the cookbook when she addressed a large meeting in Grenfell in November 1936, as president of the CWA of New South Wales. All the *Grenfell Record* says in an extensive report about the gathering, is that Jessie told the crowd 'they could not call it the "Coronation Cookery Book" as had been suggested'.

The meeting coincided with growing speculation that the King was planning to renounce the throne for Mrs Wallis Simpson, creating an unprecedented calamity for the British monarchy. He confirmed people's worst fears a month later in a radio broadcast. However, within days an official proclamation confirmed the coronation ceremony would go ahead as previously planned, with the King's younger brother, the Duke of York, taking his place.

Along with the rest of the Commonwealth, the news must have reassured Jessie and Sara, who were both stalwarts of the CWA from its earliest days. A dynamic leader who had a significant impact on the organisation, Jessie Sawyer was described on her election in 1928 as an 'excellent example of one of the finest types of Australian womanhood'.

Jessie was originally from the Junee district in the Riverina. Her Scottish-born father, John (A.J.A.) Beveridge, was a well-known pastoralist who hit the headlines in 1879, when he was taken prisoner by Captain Moonlite during a chain of violent events, which eventually saw the notorious bushranger captured, trialled and hanged.

Jessie was in her early forties, married to a grazier from nearby Bethungra, and the mother of five grown children, when she attended an historic conference held in Sydney in April 1922. The three-day event was convened to discuss

Above: *The Coronation Cookery Book*, first edition. Below: State president and co-compiler Jessie Sawyer (courtesy CWA of NSW).

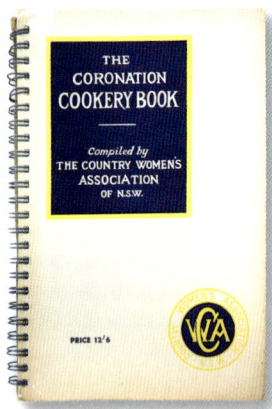

the needs of rural women, and to form the first Country Women's Association in Australia. Jessie was one of three vice presidents elected on the final day.

When she became president of the organisation six years later, Jessie mapped out an ambitious program to visit every branch, no matter how small. During her ten years in office, she lived true to the promise, covering more than 241,000 kilometres on CWA business, usually at her own expense, as she strove to build a strong network to support women on the land and give them a voice. Often she travelled by train, even resorting to catching freight services, so she could reach out-of-the-way branches. Jessie's efforts paid off, with membership growing from about 7000 to more than 18,000 during her tenure.

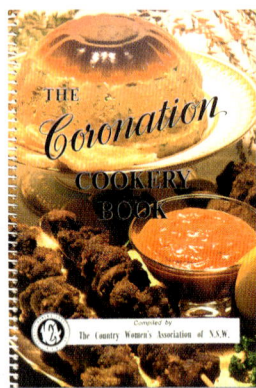

Described by her supporters as a 'woman of unflagging spirits and splendid constitution', Jessie was also noted for what *The Australian Women's Weekly* described as an impressive but unconventional manner of public speaking. 'She speaks directly and to the point, and has little time for any members who try to beguile her into bypaths away from the subject in hand,' the magazine wrote in 1936, reporting on the astonishing fact that, after years of uncontested elections, two candidates were planning to run against her at the next annual general conference. One of them was a kinswoman, Ada Beveridge, who was married to Jessie's cousin. In the end, Ada took over from Jessie when she stepped down in 1938, leaving some members in tears. The same conference decided that in the future no state president should hold office for more than three years.

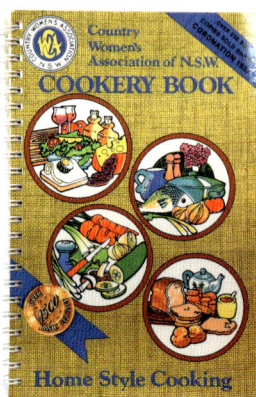

Jessie was given an OBE in 1934. She remained active in the organisation, and also served on the New South Wales Divisional Council of the Australian Red Cross Society until her death in 1947. Three years later, the CWA renamed in her honour its holiday cottage at Batlow, which provided rest in a cool mountain climate for exhausted country women.

Jessie's partner in the cookbook venture was another 'big-hearted' woman, with exceptional organisational skills. Sara Moore-Sims, nee Coulter, was the granddaughter of well-known Sydney businessman James Forsyth, an Englishman who came to Australia during the 1850s goldrush, and set up a tannery and boot-manufacturing business. Sara's husband, Thomas, was a grazier from Kamilaroi station in the Moree district, which became her home after they married in 1907.

Not long after the CWA was formed, Sara hosted three meetings in one day at the station, so as many local women as possible could hear about the organisation's work from a visiting official. Apart from being president of the Mallowa

branch, she also served on the State Executive for several years, and threw herself into supporting metropolitan branches during the summer months, when her family moved to Sydney to escape the outback heat.

In 1923, Sara helped find a property at Dee Why in northern Sydney, which could be used as a seaside holiday house for outback women and children in need of respite, or visiting the city for medical appointments. Her husband acted as one of the guarantors so the CWA could secure a loan to buy Keera House, and Sara served as a trustee until her death.

When the organisation was looking for ways to raise funds for its work, Sara proposed a beautiful towns competition. One of the most successful money-raising schemes initiated by the CWA in its early years, it raised more than £3000. She also played a leading role in persuading the organisation to create the Younger Set, a network of branches for younger women.

However, her most significant contribution was undoubtedly *The Coronation Cookery Book*, which Sara compiled at the request of the executive committee, despite being gravely ill and at times in great pain. Recognised as an outstanding and experienced cook, she had apparently been collecting recipes for more than ten years by the time the executive asked for her help in May 1936.

The Instant
that IS Coffee
Bushells
INSTANT
COFFEE
100%
PURE
COFFEE

The New South Wales organisation was already known for a series of elegant calendars, featuring cake, pudding and luncheon recipes for every day of the year. However, this new venture was to be 'the best and most helpful' cookbook yet published, with all kinds of recipes, household hints and home remedies contributed by members.

In November 1936, a quote was accepted from the Sydney printing house Publicity Press Pty Ltd, to produce 20,000 copies for £635. With the King's coronation just days away, in May 1937 the *Sydney Morning Herald* featured a photograph of Sara checking proofs. They even gave a sneak preview of four recipes—two fruit cocktails made with raisins and prunes, oysters in bacon, and almond potatoes.

When the first edition of *The Coronation Cookery Book* was released the next month, one newspaper described the 284-page publication as the 'best crown's worth of recipes on the market'. Bound in a hard cover designed by Sara's daughter, Sylvia Dryhurst, the contents ranged from tips on designing a cool kitchen and making wool mattresses, to basic recipes for everyday meals and special sections on canapés and souffles. 'They have overlooked no possibilities and if any woman does feel like giving an elaborate dinner party to titled guests, even that may now be accomplished (like the man on the flying trapeze) with the greatest of ease,' praised the *Macleay Argus*.

The *Sydney Morning Herald* was particularly tickled to read the words of warning leading into the poultry section: 'No mean woman can cook well: it calls for a generous spirit, a light hand, and a large heart'.

Sara Moore-Sims died at the age of 57, five months after the cookbook was released. Paying tribute to her friend and colleague two years later, Jessie wrote that she would always feel great sadness that Sara had not lived to see the splendid result of her great work.

By 1950, more than 100,000 copies had been sold. The sixteenth and last edition of the cookbook was published in March 2006, bringing the total number of copies printed to 205,500. Much of the content lives on today as *The Country Women's Association Cookbook: seventy years in the kitchen.*

Green tomato pickles

MAKES ABOUT 7 CUPS

This recipe comes from the 1938 edition of The Coronation Cookery Book. *I tried several different versions from different cookbooks after a very cool summer in the Adelaide Hills, when I ended up with a large amount of unripened tomatoes from my vegetable garden. This is my favourite. It has an interesting mix of spices and a lovely colour because of the turmeric, which works well with the pale green of the tomatoes.*

METHOD

Put the tomatoes in a large non-reactive bowl and sprinkle the salt between the layers. Stand overnight, or for 12 hours. Drain off the liquid and rinse the tomatoes thoroughly.

Put 375 ml (1½ cups) of the vinegar, the treacle and the allspice in a large heavy-based saucepan, with the whole cloves and peppercorns tied up in a piece of muslin. Bring the mixture to the boil, stirring until the treacle has dissolved.

In a small bowl, mix the mustard powder, ginger, curry powder, brown sugar, flour and turmeric into a smooth paste using the remaining vinegar. Stir into the boiling vinegar mixture, then keep stirring until the mixture thickens.

Add the onions and tomatoes and boil gently for about 20 minutes, stirring frequently to keep it from burning. Remove the bag of spices.

Spoon the pickles into warm sterilised jars and seal while hot.

INGREDIENTS

1.8 kg green tomatoes, thinly sliced

1 tablespoon salt

500 ml (2 cups) malt vinegar

2 heaped teaspoons treacle

1 teaspoon allspice

1 teaspoon whole cloves

1 teaspoon whole peppercorns

2 teaspoons mustard powder

1 teaspoon ground ginger

1 teaspoon curry powder

190 g (1 cup, lightly packed) brown sugar

35 g (¼ cup) plain flour

2 teaspoons turmeric

450 g onions, thinly sliced

LIZ'S TIPS

- For smaller tomatoes, simply slice them across, but you may need to halve or quarter larger tomatoes first.

- A large, wide, heavy-based saucepan is best for making these pickles.

- If you don't have any muslin, use a clean cotton hanky.

- Use a good-quality malt or brown vinegar.

- This makes a very dry mixture, so you will need to keep a close eye on it once you add the tomatoes and onions. If the mixture becomes too dry, add a splash of extra vinegar.

- To sterilise your jars, wash them in hot soapy water and rinse thoroughly. Place them on a tray in a cold oven, making sure they are not touching, and set the oven to very slow (120°C), then leave for 30 minutes.

- These pickles need at least 2 or 3 weeks stored in a cool, dark place to develop their flavour. Enjoy them with cold meats, a ploughman's lunch, or some sharp cheddar cheese.

COOKERY TREASURES *from the* ESK VALLEY

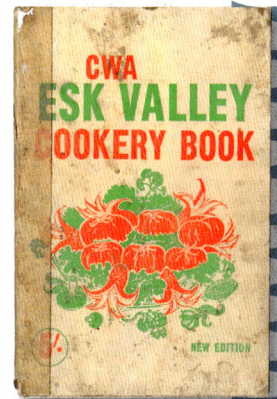

Just a few days before she died at the age of 96, Joan Lane was still taking an active interest in current affairs and writing letters to the editor. As a leader within the Country Women's Association in Tasmania, she believed strongly in giving women a voice, and experience gave her the confidence to speak up when she thought it was necessary.

At a meeting of the Esk Valley group of the CWA in 1950, Joan harnessed that assurance to propose that they publish a cookery book. Her eldest daughter, Eve Prendergast, suspects it was as much about helping other women, who had married recently and moved to the area, as it was about raising money. In the end *The Esk Valley Cookery Book* achieved both, selling more than 400,000 copies and generating many thousands of dollars in profit.

Joan spent her early life in the now-extinct mining community of Magnet in north-western Tasmania, where her father, Norman Gaunt, worked as an accountant with the mine for more than ten years. The family later moved to Launceston, where Joan completed her schooling, receiving a scholarship to study at the Methodist Ladies College. 'She really wanted to go to university and do law but family circumstances didn't permit that so she did commercial studies,' says Eve.

Once qualified, Joan compensated by finding work as a secretary at a law firm in Hobart. After war broke out in 1939, and so many of the men employed there enlisted, she found herself working at a much higher level than usual, helping to prepare cases for the courts.

Joan was in her mid-thirties when she and Staff Sergeant George Lane married in May 1944. Originally from Victoria Valley near Ouse, George ran a business in Bothwell with his brother before the war. He was rejected for overseas service because he had flat feet, but he was accepted into the army and worked in the stores and supply section of a military camp hospital at Campbell Town. Then, at the end of the war, he was sent to the Philippines with forces assigned to repatriate Australian prisoners of war.

After George was discharged, he and Joan took up an opportunity George heard about while he was based in Campbell Town, and bought into a local business in partnership with the Eadie family. Known as The Busy Store, it sold everything from trucks and motorcycles, to drapery, hardware, groceries and

Above: *The Esk Valley Cookery Book,* with the original cover design by Lynette Gall, c. 1950s. Below: Joan Lane with the life membership badge she was awarded by the Campbell Town Ross Public Hospital Auxiliary for her voluntary service, August 2000 (Image by Drew Fitzgibbon, Newspix).

fresh produce. The two families ran the business until the 1970s, when it was sold and the Lanes opened a newsagency instead. They spent the rest of their lives in Campbell Town, Joan dying in November 2007, followed by George eight months later.

Eve remembers her parents being actively involved in the community for most of their lives, both receiving awards recognising their contributions. For Joan, much of her spare time and energy was devoted to the Catholic Women's League, the Red Cross, a mother's club that set up a child health centre in Campbell Town and, of course, the CWA.

Below: An illustration of a homestead on the Nile River, Esk Valley, from the 1976 edition of the cookbook. Opposite, from top: The 1976, 1986 and 1999 editions of the cookbook.

'She was very interested in everything that was going on, not only locally but in the world. She had been holding executive positions in clubs for years, so she was a person who could speak up, but she would always listen to other people and what they were saying. She was genuinely interested in building the community and a place for women to have a voice, although Dad was always head of the house,' Eve says. 'Two or three days before she died, she had the Catholic parish sister help her write a letter to the paper about the need for more rail transport for freight in Tasmania, to take the load off the roads. So she was involved and interested until she died.'

Joan didn't talk much about her role in creating *The Esk Valley Cookery Book*, although she gave a copy to Eve when she got married in 1967, ticking the recipes that she used often as a guide to get her daughter started. 'She was a great all-round cook, and she had thousands and thousands and thousands of recipes,' Eve says.

'Dad always came home from the store at lunchtime and we had the main meal in the middle of the day, and we always had dessert. Dad liked cakes so we always had them too. Mum made everything from scratch. Dad grew vegetables, and we had a garden with beautiful plum and apple trees, and raspberries galore, and the produce was always preserved. I even have vague memories of her pickling beans in layers of salt.'

When Eve was married with children of her own, a favourite treat was visiting the Lanes for evening meals, which the family called 'choose teas'. 'The table was always full of a variety of things, and everyone could choose what they wanted to eat,' Eve explains.

Once the CWA endorsed Joan's idea of creating a cookery book, a small committee was set up under the leadership of Gladys Paterson to make it happen. The inaugural president of the Esk Valley group, when it was formed in 1947, Gladys was the daughter of Tasmanian premier Sir Walter Lee. She and her husband, Mervyn, lived on a property near Longford, which had been in the Paterson family since the 1880s.

In the 'true spirit of association', work soon began collecting treasured recipes from members of the ten CWA branches covered by the group, in the state's north and northern Midlands. When research revealed it would cost £80 to print 1000 copies, the branches also set to work raising funds to cover the production costs; a concert at Longford in September 1950 generated more than twenty pounds.

A competition was also run among group members to generate the cover image. It was won by Lynette Gall from the Newstead branch, who created a bold modern representation of a bowl of salad. A third-generation CWA member, she was only eighteen at the time. As Lynette Wilson, she went on to establish a notable career as an artist and art teacher, and was made a life member of the Art Society of Tasmania before her death in 2014, in recognition of her outstanding contribution to the society.

Released before the end of 1950, the first edition of *The Esk Valley Cookery Book* sold out within four months, with 1500 copies raising more than £120. The response was so pleasing that the group decided at its annual meeting in June 1951 to print another 1500 copies, increasing the cover price from three shillings, to three shillings and sixpence, to offset increased printing costs.

The response was so favourable again that group secretary, Mrs K. Herbert, began work on a fully revised and expanded edition, released in late 1953. The CWA also negotiated for it to be published on their behalf by Southdown Press, the owners of *New Idea* magazine, with the company taking over responsibility for printing and distribution across Australia, paying the CWA a royalty of five per cent for every copy sold.

Initially the profits were handed out as they were generated but, in 1966, the CWA set up a special cookery book account and invested the proceeds. By the 1980s, it had accumulated $14,000, earning sixteen per cent interest.

Then, in 1983, Southdown Press decided to pull the cookbook from the national market and return all the unsold copies. Fearing this marked the end of their iconic publication, the CWA managed to convince them to publish a completely new and revised edition, with metric measurements. A special

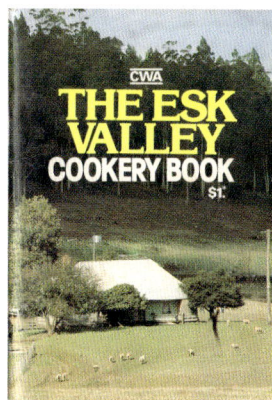

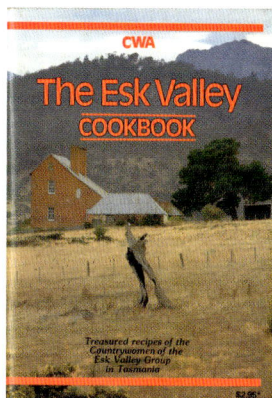

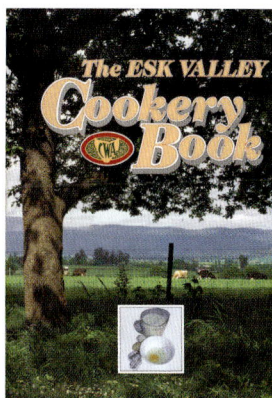

committee was formed to tackle the mammoth task of converting all the recipes. The new-look *Esk Valley Cookbook*, with more recipes and another new cover was released in 1986, this time with the names of recipe donors removed.

The book changed significantly again in 1999, when it was reprinted as a much larger A4-sized publication, with a new microwave recipe section and colour photographs. Members did not realise it at the time, but this edition was to be the last. Five years later, the CWA was restructured in Tasmania, resulting in the Esk Valley group being closed. Responsibility for selling the remaining copies was handed over to the Cressy branch, who decided there would be no more reprints.

Cheese and bacon savories

SERVES 2

This recipe for Cheese and bacon savories [sic] was a favourite in the Lane household at weekends, usually eaten while the family sat around an open fire. 'Mum used to make them often on a Sunday night, and we loved them,' Eve says. Served with a bowl of soup, the toasties make a quick and easy snack, and a perfect way to use up slightly stale bread.

INGREDIENTS

4 thick slices of stale bread

2 bacon rashers

1 egg

100 g (1 cup) grated cheddar
  cheese

METHOD

Preheat the oven to moderate (180°C). Line a baking tray with baking paper.

Cut the bread into thick fingers. Cut the bacon into strips and place a piece on each finger of bread.

Lightly beat the egg in a small bowl, then stir in the cheese. Spoon the egg mixture over the bacon.

Bake for 10–15 minutes until golden brown. Serve hot.

LIZ AND JOAN'S TIPS

- The original recipe suggests removing the crusts from the bread.
- Consider seasoning the toastie with freshly ground black pepper or a pinch of paprika before baking.

Right: Illustration from an early edition of the cookbook.

COOKING *with* COURAGE

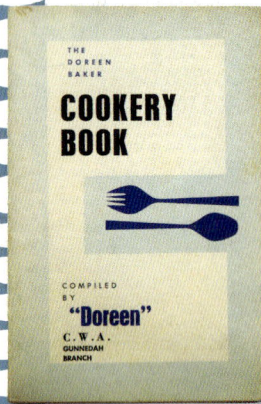

At an age when most teenage girls are dreaming about falling in love and the freedom of finally leaving school to become independent adults, Doreen Baker was coping with the devastating reality that she was blind.

Doreen permanently and completely lost her eyesight when she was seventeen, after surgery to remove a brain tumour. Filled with admiration for her courage, nurses at the Royal Prince Alfred Hospital in Sydney sat at Doreen's bedside, holding her hand and weeping as she fought to survive. 'They didn't tell us this until later, but they put her into a room where they only put people who were dying,' recalls her older sister, Isobel Bond.

By all accounts, Doreen did not despair when she woke to find that she could no longer see. Isobel cannot recall ever seeing her unhappy, and nor can her older sister, Lorna Riley. 'I never saw her down in the dumps,' says Lorna.

'She really was a particularly resilient person,' adds cousin Judy Baker. 'She just went about her life, and she was always patient and cheerful.'

Doreen's surgeon was so impressed by her plucky determination, that he bought her a typewriter, and the two stayed in touch even after she returned home to the family wheat and sheep farm near Gunnedah.

Back in familiar surroundings, Doreen became more and more self-reliant. Encouraged by her capable mother, Clarice, she was soon moving around confidently with the aid of a white cane, and she quickly mastered how to read braille with her fingertips. She sewed and mended her own clothes, and made her own bed. She helped with the housework, doing all the dusting, cleaning the bathroom, wiping the dishes and setting the table at mealtimes.

Using a special pack of playing cards marked with braille, Doreen played a mean game of poker, and she loved going fly-fishing with her father, Connie. By her early twenties, she was recognised as an accomplished artist, noted for her beautiful basketry, handweaving, rug making and needlework. She also became an expert knitter, relying on her sensitive touch to create intricate patterns. 'If I liked I could still be sitting in a corner, but I wouldn't be getting any fun, would I?' she told the rural weekly newspaper, *The Land*, when they featured her inspiring achievements in a 1953 edition.

Urged on by her mother to keep active, in the 1960s Doreen set up a small business making three-dimensional greeting cards for the blind, which found

Clockwise from top: Jules Sebastian with Elaine Kennedy at the high tea celebrating the opening of the refurbished Doreen Baker kitchen, 2014 (courtesy Sebastian Foundation); Doreen Baker with her 'talking book' as pictured in her cookbook; the celebration high tea, and the door leading into the refurbished kitchen (courtesy Sebastian Foundation). Opposite: *The Doreen Baker Cookery Book*, 1967 (State Library of NSW).

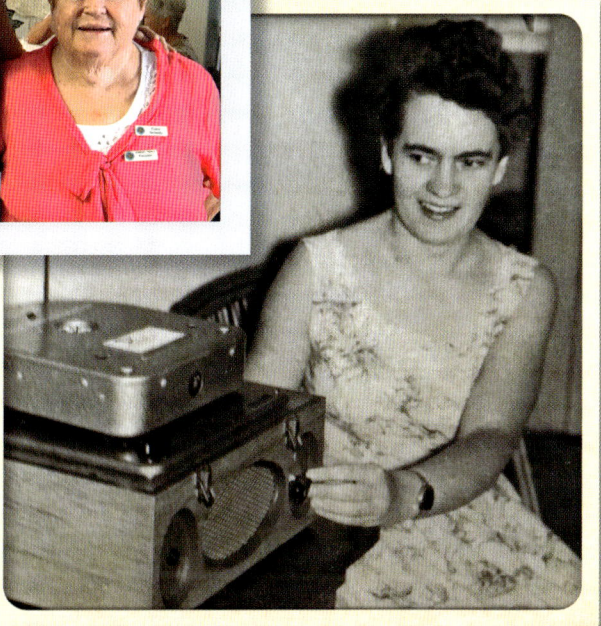

The
Doreen Baker
Community
Kitchen

Donated by
THE SEBASTIAN FOUNDATION
and
FREEDOM KITCHENS

a ready market in Sydney. But it was her endeavours as a cook that helped ensure her name would be remembered in Gunnedah, at least by members of the CWA.

Clarice was a prize-winning CWA cook and she shared her knowledge and passion with Doreen. Rather than having to memorise recipes or have someone read them out to her, Doreen transcribed her favourites into braille, using a pin and a special frame to laboriously pick out raised dots on thick sheets of brown paper.

To help her manage in the kitchen without assistance, the Bakers bought an oven with grooved switches marking the temperature settings. They also set up kitchen scales that measured ingredients by counter-balancing them against a tray of weights. Doreen would select the required weight and place it on a tray on one side of the scales. She then held her hand under the opposite tray while she added the ingredient, until she felt the tray descend.

Doreen became so proficient at cooking that she won prizes at the Gunnedah show, and in The Land Cookery Competition run annually by the CWA in New South Wales. Her mother was an enthusiastic member of the organisation, and took her daughter with her to meetings from a young age.

Formed in 1922, the Gunnedah branch had long been an active force in the community. Members raised enough money to open rest rooms in the town's main street within a few years of setting up and, with support from neighbouring branches, they established a rest home to provide respite care.

In 1966, the branch built new premises in Barber Street, at a cost of more than £10,000. The facility included a baby health centre, which was partly funded by a government subsidy, but branch members had to find the remainder. A public appeal supported by a local radio station and service clubs helped, and so did a loan from the CWA of New South Wales.

Later on, money was needed to pay off the loan, so one of the vice presidents of the Namoi group that included the Gunnedah branch, Mrs A.R. Edmonds, suggested a cookery book. Doreen offered to compile a collection of her favourite recipes, and set to work typing them up herself. In her foreword to the book, branch president Dorothy Dickens described it as a remarkable achievement, 'yet not so remarkable to those who know Doreen's many talents, both culinary and artistic, combined with immense courage and selfless interests in her surroundings and the people with whom she meets'.

A small committee worked with Doreen to produce the book, and her brother-in-law, Neville Riley, was co-opted to design the cover. After being approached by members, local businesses placed advertisements to cover the initial printing costs.

The Doreen Baker Cookery Book was released in September 1967. According to a story in *The Australian Women's Weekly*, a total of 2000 copies were printed at first, selling for 60 cents each. Former branch president Elaine Kennedy, who has been a CWA member for almost 50 years, says that eventually 4000 copies were sold. A review of the project in 1968, showed that it had raised $1944.49, with only 750 copies remaining.

Doreen died in 1970, at the age of 40, from breast cancer. To celebrate her life and contributions to the CWA, the Gunnedah branch gave her name to the official honour board they were about to hang in their club rooms. However, that was not the end of the story.

More than 40 years later, the branch heard about an opportunity to apply for funding to renovate its kitchen. It hadn't been updated since 1966 and no longer met food-handling regulations. Thinking they had little chance, given the likely number of competing applications, members took photos and wrote a letter outlining their need, and the work of the local branch and its 43 members, producing meals and catering for other community groups as well as their own events. 'We were quite surprised when they told us we had won,' says Elaine, with considerable understatement.

Below: Members of the CWA's Gunnedah branch celebrating their 95th birthday, 2017 (courtesy Gunnedah CWA).

Within months the Gunnedah branch had a brand new kitchen, courtesy of the Sebastian Foundation, a philanthropic organisation established by Australian singer Guy Sebastian and his wife, Jules. In December 2014, Jules Sebastian was guest of honour at the opening of the new facility, which the CWA decided to name the Doreen Baker Community Kitchen. The occasion was celebrated in true CWA tradition, with a special afternoon tea.

The kitchen and her cookery book are not the only tangible reminders of Doreen's inspiring life. Back in the 1950s, she carefully wove a large cane basket, about a metre long and half a metre wide, with low sides and large handles that met over the top. Painted white and softly lined, it was used by Doreen's sister Isobel as a bassinet for her babies. Many years later Isobel lifted it down from the top of the wardrobe where it had been put for safekeeping, and showed the basket to her granddaughter, Hannah, who took it home to restore. The bassinet was being made ready to repeat life's cycle and provide a safe place to sleep for her own baby, due in September 2017.

Sago fruit pudding
SERVES 4–6

I chose this rich, moist pudding recipe from Doreen's cookbook because it is very similar to the one my family makes every year for Christmas. It was introduced to us by my sister-in-law, Anne, who in turn was shown how to make it by her mother, Jeanette Telford. Originally from Lameroo in the South Australian Mallee, Jeanette was well known in the Mount Gambier community where I grew up, because of her volunteer work as a singing teacher and choral society conductor. Awarded a Medal of the Order of Australia for her contribution to the town's musical life, she was also a life member of the CWA.

INGREDIENTS

2 tablespoons sago

250 ml (1 cup) milk, plus
1 teaspoon extra

85 g (1 cup) raisins, chopped

60 g (1 cup) fresh
breadcrumbs

100 g (1 cup lightly packed)
dark brown sugar

1 teaspoon bicarbonate
of soda

1 tablespoon melted butter

METHOD

Soak the sago in the milk overnight. The next day stir in the raisins, breadcrumbs and sugar. Dissolve the bicarbonate of soda in the extra milk, then stir it into the pudding mixture. Lastly, add the melted butter.

Pour the mixture into a buttered, 1.5 litre (6 cup) pudding basin. Put a saucer or small plate upside-down in the bottom of a large saucepan, then stand the basin on top of the saucer. Add just enough hot water to the saucepan to come halfway up the side of the basin, cover, then steam for 2½ hours.

Turn the pudding out onto a large plate and serve with custard, ice cream or cream.

LIZ'S TIPS

- I usually double the quantities. The mixture still fits in a standard 1.5-2 litre (6-8 cup) pudding basin, but you will need to steam it for 3 hours.

- Doreen's recipe included an egg, but having tried both methods I prefer it without, and I've cut back on the amount of sugar too, to better suit modern tastes.

- The sago should be slightly soft after soaking it overnight and starting to become translucent. Some modern brands of sago do not do this, so you may need to heat the milk the next day before you add the other ingredients, to start the process. Do not cook the sago completely; take the milk off the heat as soon as the sago starts to become translucent.

- If you can't get sago, seed tapioca works fine.

- Experiment with different combinations of dried fruit. My favourite is half dates and half raisins.

- Use bread that is 2 or 3 days old to make the breadcrumbs.

- If the mixture looks sloppy when you put it in the basin, don't worry — it is meant to be sloppy.

- The pudding can be made a few days in advance and kept in the fridge. Reheat by steaming again for about $1^1/_2$ hours. It also freezes well. Just cut off slices as you need them, and heat gently in a microwave oven.

steamed pudding goes with **Mums** custard!

. . . smooth as whipped cream!

REFERENCES AND FURTHER READING

Note: The chapters in this book use the popular titles of the community cookbooks featured, as they appear on the covers. However, libraries mostly catalogue them according to the wording on the title page, which is given below. Publication dates are often missing from the cookbooks, which has led to some discrepancies in dates cited by the National Library of Australia, compared to the findings of extensive original research carried out by the author.

INTRODUCTION

Books Henry Coldham (Mrs), *A Voice from the Bush: a book of tested recipes, in aid of All Saints' Church, Clermont, Queensland* (Rockhampton: Morning Bulletin, 189–?). Elizabeth Driver, *Culinary Landmarks: a bibliography of Canadian cookbooks, 1825–1949* (Toronto: University of Toronto Press, 2008), pp. 276–7. Maria J. Moss, *A Poetical Cook-book* (Philadelphia: C. Sherman, Son & Co, 1864). **Documents** Sarah Jane Shepherd Black, '"Tried and Tested": community cookbooks in Australia, 1890–1980', PhD thesis, University of Adelaide, 2010. **Newspapers** *Argus*, 24 October 1888, p. 1. *Capricornian*, 11 August 1888, p. 18; 10 January 1903, p. 39. *Sydney Morning Herald*, 3 September 1887, p. 1. **Internet** Amanda Moniz, 'First Community Cookbook Written for Fun, Started a Trend', American Food Roots, June 2014 <www.americanfoodroots.com/features/readings/first-community-cookbook-written-fun-started-trend/>.

RECIPES FOR SAVING SOULS
Our history in recipes
Cookbook Presbyterian Women's Missionary Union of Victoria, *Home Cookery for Australia: all tested recipes/compiled and issued under the auspices of the Presbyterian Women's Missionary Union of Victoria*, 1st ed. (Melbourne: Gordon & Gotch, 1904). *P.W.M.U. Cookery Book of Victoria*, 5th ed. (Melbourne: Brown Prior, 1923). A.M. Campbell, *P.W.M.U. Cookery Book: including pressure cooking*, 10th ed. (Melbourne: Hibbins Taylor, 1955). Ann Gemmell, Val Howat and Gwen Mierisch, *P.W.M.U. Cookery Book: metric edition* (Melbourne: Lothian Publishing, 1973).

Books Fiona Bligh, *From Suet to Saffron: the history of the PWMU cookbook in Victoria 1904–2012* (Preston: Fairfield Press, 2013). **Newspapers** *Age*, 13 September 1977, Epicure section p. 2. *Australasian*, Melbourne, 21 December 1929, p. 17. **Radio** Interview with Fiona Bligh, *Overnights*, ABC, 2 August 2013. **Internet** 'When Did PWMU Begin?', PWMU <pwmu.org.au/index.php/home/history>. Helen McKenzie, Australian Dictionary of Evangelical Biography, 2004 <webjournals.ac.edu.au/ojs/index.php/ADEB/article/view/1008/1005>.

More than she knew
Cookbook Jean Rutledge, *The Goulburn Cookery Book*, 2nd ed. (Sydney: WC Penfold & Co, 1905); 28th ed. (Sydney: Edwards, Dunlop & Co, 1921); 35th ed. (1934); 40th ed. (Sydney: National Trust of Australia, NSW, 1973). **Books** Sally Osborne, *A Small Church in a Small Town: St Philip's Church, Bungendore 1964–2014* (Bungendore: 2015), pp. 9–10. Barry Stephenson, *Bungendore to Captain's Flat—cemeteries, gravesites of the district and deaths during the wars* (Queanbeyan: B. Stephenson, 2003). Ransome T. Wyatt, *The History of the Diocese of Goulburn* (Sydney: Edgar Bragg & Sons, 1937), pp. 111, 131, 152–3. **Journals** Alf Body, 'The Goulburn Cookery Book: a best seller for the diocese', *Diocese of Canberra and Goulburn Anglican Historical Society Journal*, no. 8, October 1989, pp. 18–25. **Newspapers and magazines** *Australian Women's Weekly*, 28 November 1973, p. 81. *Brisbane Courier*, 17 March 1931, p. 17. *Canberra Times*, 22 November 1973, p. 18. *Goulburn Evening Penny Post*, 27 April 1882, p. 4; 1 December 1904, p. 2; 12 November 1921, p. 4; 15 August 1932, p. 2. *Goulburn Herald*, 26 September 1885, p. 4; 15 November 1899, p. 4. *Southern Argus*, 26 September 1885, p. 7. *Southern Churchman*, 1 July 1904; 1 January 1905; 1 May 1905. *Sydney Mail*, 4 June 1924, p. 21. *Sydney Mail and New South Wales Advertiser*, 25 October 1905, p. 1070. **Internet** 'Rutledge, William Forster (1851–1912)', Obituaries Australia <oa.anu.edu.au/obituary/rutledge-william-forster-888/text889>.

No mere trifle
Cookbook Church of England Ladies Guild, Tatura branch, *The Rodney Cookery Book*, 1st ed. (Tatura: Church of England Ladies Guild, c. 1907); 2nd ed. (c. 1912). **Books** William Henry Bossence, *Tatura and the Shire of Rodney* (Melbourne: Hawthorn Press, 1969), p. 247. Eric Percy Evans, *The First*

Decade, All Saints Church of England Tatura: an intimate glimpse of a country parish and its people 1880–1890 (Tatura: Rodney Printers, 1980), p. 35. *Mrs Beeton's Every Day Cookery and Housekeeping Book*, facsimile of original 1865 ed. (London: Bracken Books, 1984). **Newspapers** *Age*, 27 August 1895, p. 6; 21 August 1940, p. 10. *Argus*, 24 April 1900, p. 1; 5 October 1910, p. 13; 21 August 1940, p. 4. *Bendigo Independent*, 30 September 1903, p. 2. *Bendigonian*, 11 July 1918, p. 18. *Dookie and Katamatite Recorder*, 21 January 1904, p. 3. *Weekly Times*, 29 November 1913, p. 2. *Worker*, 1 October 1908, p. 9. **Internet** Michael E. Humphries, 'Zercho, Charles Henry (1866–1962)', Australian Dictionary of Biography <adb.anu.edu.au/biography/zercho-charles-henry-9227/text16307>. 'All Saints Anglican Church', St Kilda Historical Series <skhs.org.au/SKHSchurches/all_saints_anglican_church.htm>.

Einstein and the eclipse
Cookbook Florence A. Moody, *The "Eclipse" Cookery Book of Good and Tried Recipes* (Orroroo: Enterprise Printery, 1922). **Documents** *St Paul's Orroroo 100 Years of Worship 1879–1979*, Orroroo Historical Society collection. **Newspapers** *Advertiser*, 12 August 1922, p. 11. *Border Watch*, 22 September 1922, p. 3. *Express and Telegraph*, 1 August 1922, p. 4; 4 August 1922, p. 1. *Register*, 18 February 1922, p. 6; 4 November 1922, p. 13. **Internet** Geoff Barker, 'Einstein's Theory of Relativity Proven in Australia, 1922', Inside the Collection, Museum of Applied Arts and Sciences, 2012 <maas.museum/inside-the-collection/2012/08/22/einsteins-theory-of-relativity-proven-in-australia-1922/>. Tim Sherratt, '1922 Solar Eclipse in Australia, Testing Einstein's Theory', Physics in Australia to 1945, 1995 <www.asap.unimelb.edu.au/bsparcs/physics/eclipse.htm>.

A different way to read papers
Cookbook St Andrew's Women's Guild, *St. Andrew's Modern Recipe Book: and other useful hints* (Launceston: St Andrew's Women's Guild, n.d.). **Newspapers** *Examiner*, 14 March 1934, p. 7. *Smith's Weekly*, 9 August 1930, p. 16. **Internet** Ted Best, 'Cadbury', The Companion to Tasmanian History <www.utas.edu.au/library/companion_to_tasmanian_history/C/Cadbury.htm>.

Father's delight
Cookbook Church of England in Australia, Diocese of Brisbane, *Fathers' Delights: recipes of the wives of Anglican priests in*

306

the Diocese of Brisbane (Brisbane: Anglican Church Diocese of Brisbane, 1978). **Books** Ralph Wicks, *Felix Raymond Arnott, Bishop and Scholar: a brief account of his life and ministry* (Moorooka: Boolarong Press, 1997). **Newspapers and magazines** *Australian Women's Weekly*, 18 October 1978, pp. 81, 83; 2 April 1980, p. 7. *Queensland Times*, 28 March 1939, p. 6. **Internet** Jonathan Holland, 'Arnott, Felix Raymond (1911–1988)', Australian Dictionary of Biography <adb.anu.edu.au/biography/arnott-felix-raymond-12150/text21483>.

RECIPES WITH AN ARTISTIC FLOURISH

Taking pot luck

Cookbook Mary Lundqvist (ed.), Alan McCulloch (illus.), *Pot Luck: a patriotic party book* (Kew: W.D. Vaughn in conjunction with B.T. Addison & Son for the Women's Auxiliary Social Patriots Organisation, 1941). **Journals** Vane Lindesay, 'Alan McCulloch: cartoonist of distinction', *Latrobe Journal*, Nos 93–94, September 2014, pp. 175–80. **Newspapers** *Advocate*, 30 January 1941, p. 29. *Age*, 31 January 1941, p. 3; 15 February 1941, p. 24; 26 March 1941, p. 5; 29 March 1941, p. 16. *Argus*, 28 December 1935, p. 16; 21 February 1941, p. 4; 20 March 1941, p. 5; 29 March 1941, p. 14; 31 March 1941, p. 6. *Australasian*, 22 March 1941, p. 24; 5 April 1941, p. 32. *Weekly Times*, 24 February 1934, p. 25. **Internet** Rodney James, 'McCulloch, Alan McLeod (1907–1992)', Australian Dictionary of Biography, 2016 <adb.anu.edu.au/biography/mcculloch-alan-mcleod-16351/text28310>. 'About', McCulloch and McCulloch <mccullochandmcculloch.com.au/whistlewood/about/>.

Recipes with harmony

Cookbook Sonia Brodie, *Sounds Delicious: Sydney Philharmonia Cookbook* (Sydney: Sydney Philharmonia Society, 1979). **Internet** 'History', Sydney Philharmonia Choirs <www.sydneyphilharmonia.com.au/history/>.

Singing for their supper

Cookbook Christopher Willcock, *The Melbourne Chorale Christmas Book* (Melbourne: The Melbourne Chorale, 1980). **Newspapers** *Age*, 23 December 1980, p. 15. **Radio** 'Ann James Becoming an Illustrator', *Splash*, ABC, 2014. **Documents** 'Melbourne Symphony Orchestra Chorus to Celebrate 50th Anniversary This October', media release, Melbourne Symphony Orchestra, 24 July 2015. **Internet** 'About Us', Books

Illustrated <www.booksillustrated.com.au/bi_about.php>. 'MSO Chorus', Melbourne Symphony Orchestra <www.mso.com.au/about-us/mso-chorus/>.

Wind beneath their wings

Cookbook *Tasmanian Festival Wind Symphony Cookbook* (Devonport: Mersey Valley Festival of Music, 1986).

Threading the nation

Cookbook Libby Fenwick-Williams, Jean Finnegan and Marlene Greenwood, *Afternoon Tea with the P.H.E.* (Canberra: Embroiderers' Guild, ACT Inc, 1987). **Books** Loma Rudduck and Robert Hyslop, *And So to Sew: a history of embroidery in the Australian Capital Territory* (Canberra: Embroiderers' Guild of the ACT, 1992). **Journals** Dorothy Hyslop, 'The Parliament House Embroidery: a study in project management', *Canberra Historical Journal*, New Series no. 29, March 1992, pp. 14–20. **Newspapers** *Canberra Times*, 2 February 1988. **Internet** 'The Great Hall Embroidery: a story told by one artist and worked by a thousand hands' <www.aph.gov.au/Visit_Parliament/Art/Top_5_Treasures/Great_Hall_Embroidery>. Louise Moran, 'Parliament House Embroidery (1988–)', The Australian Women's Register, 2013 <www.womenaustralia.info/biogs/AWE4886b.htm>.

BUILDING WITH RECIPES

Sea of heartache

Cookbook H. Wharton Shaw (Mrs) and Auburn Methodist Church Ladies' Guild, *600 Tested Recipes*, 3rd ed. (Melbourne: Auburn Methodist Church, 1906). **Books** Auburn Methodist Church, *Jubilee Celebrations, 1889–1939: Auburn Methodist Church, Oxley Road* (Melbourne: E. Whitehead & Co., 1939). **Documents** Heritage Council Victoria, 'Auburn Uniting Church Complex', Victorian Heritage Database Report, 2003. **Newspapers** *Age*, 30 March 1909, p. 5; 31 August 1939, p. 10. *Argus*, 15 February 1909, p. 7; 1 March 1909, p. 1; 11 August 1909, p. 1; 18 September 1920, p. 2; 14 December 1956, p. 20. *Australasian*, 26 February 1909, p. 472. *Ballarat Star*, 9 December 1913, p. 7. *Colonist* (New Zealand), 18 November 1892; 25 August 1909. *Methodist*, 23 October 1926, p. 12. *Register*, 16 February 1909, p. 4. **Internet** 'About us', Auburn Uniting Church Hawthorn, <www./auburnuc.org.au/about-us/>.

A hall full of memories

Cookbook Mechanics' Hall Auxiliary, *The Rainbow Recipe Book* (Rainbow: s.n., n.d.).

Journals Mechanics' Institutes of Victoria, 'Where They Stood', *Useful Knowledge: the magazine of the Mechanics' Institutes of Victoria Inc*, no. 34, August–Winter 2014, p. 21. **Newspapers** *Age*, 11 March 1912, p. 7. *Horsham Times*, 5 January 1912, p. 5; 9 January 1912, p. 3; 30 January 1912, p. 3.

Never judge a book by its cover

Cookbook Jean Horan Kindergarten, *A Collection of Favourite Recipes* (Flinders Park: Jean Horan Kindergarten, 196–?). **Documents** 'A Brief History of the Suburb of Hendon', local history fact sheet, City of Charles Sturt. 'Jean Horan Memorial Kindergarten', *City of Charles Sturt Heritage DPA 2010*, p. 159. **Newspapers** *Advertiser*, 14 September 1929, p. 29; 26 October 1935, p. 27. *Barrier Miner*, 7 February 1941, p. 3. *News*, 6 April 1954, p. 23. **Internet** Suzanne Edgar and Helen Jones, 'Miethke, Adelaide Laetitia (1881–1962)', Australian Dictionary of Biography <adb.anu.edu.au/biography/miethke-adelaide-laetitia-7571/text13215>.

In at the deep end

Cookbook Bairnsdale and District Olympic Swimming Pool Committee Ladies' Auxiliary, *The Mitchell Valley Recipe Book* (Bairnsdale: James Yeates & Sons, c. 1965). **Books** John D. Adams, *Path Among the Years: history of Shire of Bairnsdale* (Bairnsdale: Bairnsdale Shire Council, 1987). **Newspapers** *Age*, 8 December 1930, p. 11. *Gippsland Times*, 11 August 1930, p. 5. **Internet** 'History of the East Gippsland Waterdragons', East Gippsland Waterdragons Swim Club <www.waterdragons.org.au/the-club/club-history. html>.

Party prescriptions

Cookbook Australian Boy Scouts Association, New South Wales branch, Canberra–Monaro Area, Red Hill Group, *Party Prescriptions Compiled for Your Pleasure*, 1st ed. (Canberra: National Printers, 1963). **Internet** Naomi Russo, 'Now and Then: Australia's "six o'clock swill"', Australian Geographic, February 2016 <www.australiangeographic.com.au/topics/history-culture/2016/02/now-and-then-australias-six-oclock-swill>.

RECIPES FOR THE DISABLED

The recipe collector

Cookbooks Alex Edgar (Mrs), *Strathalbyn Cookery Book: over 40 year's [sic] collection, tried recipes* (Perth: Braille and Advancement Society for the Blind of Western Australia, 1921); *Strathalbyn Cookery*

Book No. 2 (1925). **Books** Jan Howell, *From De Grey to Gingin: a history of the Edgar family* (Cottesloe: J. Howell, 1989), pp. 18–21. **Journals** 'A.W. Edgar', obituary, *The Pastoral Review*, 16 December 1927, p. 1185. Wanderer, 'A West Australian Stud Farm', supplement to *The Australasian Pastoralists Review*, 15 February 1901, p. 795. **Sound recordings** Chris Jeffrey (interviewer), interview with Ian Edgar, 1987. **Newspapers** *Daily News*, 10 January 1895, p. 2; 9 April 1921, p. 4; 16 May 1921, p. 5; 11 November 1927, p. 1. *Kalgoorlie Miner*, 11 May 1909, p. 6. *Portland Guardian*, 6 January 1890, p. 4. *Sunday Times*, 30 January 1921, p. 6. *Victorian Express*, 7 June 1890, p. 5. *WA Bulletin*, 26 July 1890, p. 4. *West Australian*, 6 April 1886, p. 3; 31 July 1890, p. 2; 23 February 1921, p. 6; 5 September 1921, p. 8; 10 July 1925, p. 6. **Internet** 'Edgar, Alexander Williamson (1856–1927)', Obituaries Australia <oa.anu.edu.au/obituary/edgar-alexander-williamson-1441/text1441>.

Secret recipes, patent cures and bruised reeds

Cookbook The Wardmaster, *The Everyday and Everyway Recipe Book* (Melbourne: Veritas Publishing Co, c. 1925). **Books** Disabled Men's Association of Australia, *Bruised Reeds* (Melbourne: Disabled Men's Association of Australia, 1928). The Wardmaster, *Secret Recipes* (Melbourne: Veritas Library, 1923). The Wardmaster, *The First Book of Knowledge* (Melbourne: Veritas Library, 1923). The Wardmaster, *Medical Prescriptions: for all diseases and ailments* (Melbourne: Veritas Publishing Co. for Disabled Men's Association of Australia, 1925). **Newspapers** *Age*, 1 November 1947, p. 13. *Sydney Morning Herald*, 2 May 1927, p. 4. **Internet** Photo, Museums Victoria Collections <collections.museumvictoria.com.au/items/1806632>. 'State Library Note', State Library of Victoria <search.slv.vic.gov.au/MAIN:Everything:SLV_VOYAGER1820380>.

Storm in a teacup

Cookbooks New South Wales Society for Crippled Children, *Forget-me-not Biscuit Cook Book: a collection of good and tried recipes* (Sydney: The Harbour Press, 1958). Doris State and Maureen Simpson, *The Cook's Handbook* (Sydney: NSW Society for Crippled Children, c. 1958). **Documents** 'Forty Years of Charitable "Cuppas"', news release, NSW Society for Children and Young Adults with Physical Disabilities, May 1995. *NSW Society for Crippled Children 1957/8 Annual Report*. **Newspapers and magazines** *Australian Women's Weekly*, 17 November 1954, p. 37; 4 January 1956, p. 22; 31 July 1957, p. 13. *Biz*, 18 July 1956, p. 3; 26 March 1958, p. 16; 17 June 1959, p. 17. *Sun*, 24 March 1954, p. 41. **Internet** 'Values Mission and History', Northcott <www.northcott.com.au/support/service/values-mission-and-history/>. Naomi Parry, 'New South Wales Society for Crippled Children (1929–1995)', Find and Connect, 2013 <www.findandconnect.gov.au/ref/nsw/biogs/NE01332b.htm>.

Cooking with Miss Australia

Cookbook Elizabeth Sewell (ed.), *Miss Australia Cookbook* (Sydney: Hamlyn, 1971). **Newspapers** *Canberra Times*, 4 June 1970, p. 22. **Internet** 'Miss Australia: a nation's quest', National Museum of Australia <www.nma.gov.au/exhibitions/miss_australia_a_nations_quest/home>. 'Miss Australia: a short history, excerpts from "Nothing Is Impossible" written by Neil McLeod with additional material from various sources', Cerebral Palsy Australia, 1910 < https://www.cerebralpalsy.org.au/wp-content/uploads/2013/07/Miss-Australia-Booklet-Web.pdf>.

Spam spam spam, wonderful spam

Cookbook St George School for Crippled Children, *Recipes with Wine!* (Rockdale: St George School for Crippled Children, 1970). **Internet** 'The Little Blue Can of the Past, Present and Future', Hormel Foods <www.spam.com/about>.

RECIPES FROM THE FAMOUS
A Royal mystery

Cookbook Frankston Methodist Church, *Frankston Methodist Cookery Book* (Frankston: Frankston Methodist Church, c. 1960). **Books** Carol Ferguson and Margaret Fraser, *A Century of Canadian Home Cooking* (Scarborough: Prentice-Hall, 1992). **Newspapers** *Barrier Miner*, 16 November 1937, p. 4. *Daily Mercury*, 19 August 1939, p. 6. **Internet** Lpeterat, 'Queen Elizabeth Cake', BCFH, August 2016 <www.bcfoodhistory.ca/queen-elizabeth-cake/>.

Cooking with the White House

Cookbooks Mrs Rush Clark, *Star Spangled Cooking with the American Women's Club: a collection of favorite recipes of the members of the American Women's Club of Sydney* (Sydney: American Women's Club of Sydney, 1962). Mrs Lyle Rothenberger and Pixie O'Harris (illus.), *More Star Spangled Cooking with The American Women's Club of the American Society* (Sydney: American Society, 1968). **Books** American Women's Club of Sydney, *The Charity Work of American Women in Sydney and the History of the American Women's Club* (Sydney?: American Women's Club, 1964). **Newspapers** *Sun*, 2 September 1946, p. 10. *Sydney Morning Herald*, 5 December 1946, p. 14; 4 September 1947, p. 14; 29 February 1968, p. 33; 6 October 1983, p. 40; 1 December 1988, p. 13. **Internet** Jennifer Trainer Thompson, 'How to Cook JFK's Favorite Chowder', Boston Globe, 12 January 2016 <www.bostonglobe.com/magazine/2016/01/12/recipes-how-cook-jfk-favorite-chowder/BwXWFjiiDqHNvEB14bPDLL/story.html>.

Binny and the famous men

Cookbook Binny Lum, *Favourite Recipes of Famous Men* (Adelaide: Rigby for the Rheumatism and Arthritis Association of Victoria, 1975), © MOVE muscle, bone & joint health. **Newspapers** *Sydney Morning Herald*, 28 September 1975, p. 118. **Internet** Chris Arneil, 'Binny Lum's Conversation with the Stars', NFSA, <www.nfsa.gov.au/latest/binny-lum-and-stars>. 'Binny Lum', NFSA <www.nfsa.gov.au/collection/curated/binny-lum-0>. Philip Brady and Bruce Mansfield, 'Interview with Binny Lum', 6 December 1992 <www.youtube.com/watch?v=rE_jjOO87fA>. Sharon Terry, 'Star Lifted Profile of Women in Radio', Age, 5 January 2013 <www.theage.com.au/comment/obituaries/star-lifted-profile-of-women-in-radio-20130104-2c9gg>.

Variety with heart

Cookbook CSR Limited, *Variety Club Entertainer's Cookbook* (Sydney: Variety Club of Australia, 1980). **Documents** Variety, *Variety the Children's Charity Annual Report 2008*, p. 3. **Newspapers** *Canberra Times*, 16 October 1983, p. 14. **Internet** Jude French, 'Variety—the children's charity of Australia', 7 December 2016 <www.facebook.com/VarietyAU/>.

RECIPES FOR THE UNDERPRIVILEGED
The Great Cream Puff Dilemma

Cookbook Flo. L. Barnet, *Modern Athens Cookery Book: containing 600 tested recipes signed as tried by the givers* (Gawler: The Bunyip, 1927). **Books** Rodney Cockburn, *Nomenclature of South Australia* (Adelaide: W.K. Thomas and Co, 1908). Gawler Tourist Association, *Gawler: 'the colonial Athens': how to get there, what to do and see* (Gawler: W. Barnet, 1911). **Newspapers** *Advertiser*, 17 October 1927, p. 16. *Bunyip*, 9 September

1927, p. 6; 30 September 1927, p. 9;
21 October 1927, p. 10; 4 November 1927, p. 8;
22 November 1935, p. 10; 13 December 1935,
p. 4; 20 July 1945, p. 2. *News*, 19 August 1936,
p. 4. *Register*, 4 January 1927, p. 12.

Feeding the poor in the land of sunshine
Cookbook A.A. Drummond, *The Blossoms Cookery Book* (Adelaide: Hunkin Ellis & King, 1931). **Books** Whitefield's Institute, *Blossom in 'The Land of Sunshine' Gift Book* (Hindmarsh: Whitefield's Institute, 1930). **Newspapers** *Advertiser*, 18 September 1928, p. 22; 11 March 1929, p. 10; 19 July 1929, p. 12; 19 October 1929, p. 22; 16 January 1954, p. 12. *Mail*, 23 March 1929, p. 18; 20 July 1929, p. 29; 14 June 1930, p. 7; 5 July 1930, p. 6; 4 April 1931, p. 19; 6 June 1931, p. 10; 22 August 1931, p. 22. *News*, 26 August 1927, p. 5; 31 October 1927, p. 9; 15 August 1929, p. 10; 24 March 1931, p. 9; 7 July 1932, p. 9. *Register News-Pictorial*, 3 July 1930, p. 22. *Recorder*, 8 March 1924, p. 1. **Internet** 'About Lady Gowrie', Gowrie New South Wales <gowriensw.com.au/page/about-lady-gowrie>. Susan Marsden, 'Hindmarsh—a short history', Discover South Australia's History, 1985 <www.sahistorians.org.au/175/documents/hindmarsh-a-short-history.shtml>.

Land of apples nonsense
Cookbook Hobart Free Kindergarten Association, *Cookery Calendar from Apple Land* (Hobart: Cox Kay Pty Ltd, Printers, 1929). **Newspapers** *Daily Post*, 1 August 1910, p. 2. *Mercury*, 1 October 1910, p. 6; 21 March 1912, p. 2; 16 May 1933, p. 9; 23 September 1933, p. 6; 29 September 1933, p. 5. **Internet** Elspeth Hope-Johnstone, 'Kindergarten', The Companion to Tasmanian History <www.utas.edu.au/library/companion_to_tasmanian_history/K/Kindergarten.htm>. Gladys Dobson, 'Reminiscences Grandma Dobson', Significant Tasmanian Women <www.dpac.tas.gov.au/divisions/csr/information_and_resources/significant_tasmanian_women/significant_tasmanian_women_-_research_listing/emily_dobson/reminiscence>. I.A. Reynolds, 'Dobson, Emily (1842–1934)', Australian Dictionary of Biography <adb.anu.edu.au/biography/dobson-emily-5985/text10215>. Wendy Rimon, 'Emily Dobson', Significant Tasmanian Women <www.dpac.tas.gov.au/divisions/csr/information_and_resources/significant_tasmanian_women/significant_tasmanian_women_-_research_listing/emily_dobson>.

The Berry Street Girls
Cookbook Foundling Hospital and Infants' Home, *Berry Street Foundling Home Infant Welfare and Cookery Book* (East Melbourne: Berry Street Foundling Home, 1937). **Newspapers** *Age*, 12 June 1937, p. 2. *Argus*, 1 December 1937, p. 8. **Internet** Cate O'Neil, 'The Foundling Hospital and Infants' Home (1906–1964)', Find and Connect, February 2009 <www.findandconnect.gov.au/ref/vic/biogs/E000036b.htm>. 'Our History', Berry Street <www.berrystreet.org.au/our-history>.

Saving children one hundred thousand books at a time
Cookbooks Elizabeth Jolley (ed.), Save the Children Fund University of Western Australia Branch, *Cooking by Degrees* (Crawley: The Branch, 195–?); Save the Children Fund University of Western Australia Branch, *Cooking by Degrees II* (Crawley: The Branch, 1986). **Documents** Sue Graham-Taylor and Wendy Birman, *History of a Book Sale, 1964–2014*, Save the Children Australia University branch, Perth. Barbara Milech and Brian Dibble, *Elizabeth Jolley: a bibliography—1965–2007*, Elizabeth Jolley Research Collection, Curtin University Library, Curtin University of Technology, p. 8. **Radio** Emma Wynne, 'Save the Children Book Sale at University of Western Australia Celebrates 50 years', ABC Radio Perth, August 2014. **Internet** 'Save the Children Book Sale', University News, University of Western Australia, August 2016 <www.news.uwa.edu.au/201608118926/august-2016/uwa-book-sale-friday-19-wednesday-24-august>. J.D. Legge, 'Emeritus Professor Fred Alexander', Academy of the Social Sciences in Australia <old.assa.edu.au/fellowship/fellow/deceased/100075>.

RECIPES AT WAR
Annie carries on
Cookbook Annie J. King, *The Australian Missionary Cookery Book: a collection of recipes simple, practical and up-to-date* (Sydney: Marchant & Co, 1915); *"Carry On": a collection of recipes, simple, practical and up-to-date*, 1st ed. (Parramatta: The Cumberland Argus, 1918). **Journals** Jane Gardiner, 'Annie Julia King', *The Pioneer: Official Newsletter of the Alstonville Plateau Historical Society Inc*, vol. 15, no. 1, March 2015, p. 8. **Newspapers** *Barrier Miner*, 8 March 1948, p. 6. *Evening News*, 12 May 1915, p. 6; 13 May 1915, p. 4. *Mail*, 10 September 1949, p. 40. *Northern Star*, 21 November 1923, p. 4; 30 September 1926, p. 4; 26 October

1944, p. 4; 9 October 1950, p. 4. **Internet** 'John James King', North to the Big Scrub <www.northtothebigscrub.org/kinj1864.htm>. Peter Stanley, 'Belgian Day', National Library of Australia, February 2016 <www.nla.gov.au/blogs/behind-the-scenes/2016/02/24/belgian-day>.

Alice Anderson's astonishing Anzacs
Cookbook Citizens' War Chest Fund, *The War Chest Cookery Book* (Sydney: Websdale Shoosmith, 1917). **Documents** Citizens' War Chest Fund of NSW, *The Citizens' 'War Chest' Report* (William Brooks and Co Ltd, 1917). **Newspapers** *Evening News*, 15 May 1895, p. 4. *Sun*, 1 April 1917, p. 17. *Sydney Morning Herald*, 3 December 1924, p. 12; 7 April 1936, p. 8; 26 June 1951, p. 18. **Internet** Alan Dougan, 'Thomson, Adam (1813–1874)', Australian Dictionary of Biography, <adb.anu.edu.au/biography/thomson-adam-4714/text7817>.

Auntie Cleggett and the Angorichina Hostel
Cookbook Tubercular Soldiers' Aid Society, *The Angorichina Cookery Book: first and second editions by popular request* (Adelaide: Quality Press for the Tubercular Soldiers' Aid Society, 1963). **Documents** Carol Ann Putland, *Tuberculosis and the Australian State: Australia's national anti-tuberculosis campaign 1898–1948: an administrative history of a public health policy*, Centre for Development Studies, Flinders University, 2013, pp. 208–51. **Newspapers** *Chronicle*, 1 January 1927, p. 56. *Daily Herald*, 21 June 1917, p. 4. *Laura Standard and Crystal Brook Courier*, 4 August 1922, p. 3. *News*, 20 June 1925, p. 6; 12 March 1953, p. 13. *Observer*, 9 October 1926, p. 46; 11 June 1927, p. 47. *Recorder*, 6 August 1954, p. 1. *Register*, 8 December 1921, p. 9; 26 July 1922, p. 8; 8 May 1926, p. 12. **Internet** 'Bedford Park', City of Mitcham <www.mitchamcouncil.sa.gov.au/page.aspx?u=1351>. 'Cleggett, Ella', The Encyclopedia of Women and Leadership in Twentieth-Century Australia, 2014 <www.womenaustralia.info/leaders/biogs/WLE0156b.htm>. Susan Marsden, 'Cleggett, Ella (1884–1960)', Australian Dictionary of Biography <adb.anu.edu.au/biography/cleggett-ella-9761/text17245>.

Longreach Red Cross goes all in
Cookbook Australian Red Cross Society, Queensland Division, Longreach Branch, *The Red Cross Recipe Book of the Queensland Red Cross Society*, 1st ed. (Longreach:

Australian Red Cross Society, Queensland Branch, Longreach Division, 1943); 2nd ed. (1946). **Documents** Tom Harwood, 'The Q.A.N.T.A.S. Hangar—it's [sic] life, times and people', unpublished manuscript, 2017, courtesy Qantas Founders Museum. **Newspapers** *Central Queensland Herald*, 17 August 1944, p. 21. *Courier-Mail*, 28 January 1943, p. 4; 12 September 1946, p. 8. *Longreach Leader*, 13 April 1923, p. 3; 26 July 1941, p. 9; 20 December 1941, p. 19; 7 February 1942, p. 3; 9 December 1942, pp. 3, 5; 19 December 1942, p. 11; 6 November 1943, p. 14; 19 February 1944, p. 7; 13 December 1944, p. 20; 6 September 1946, p. 6; 6 August 1948, pp. 13, 16; 4 August 1950, p. 13; 24 November 1950, p. 9; 29 December 1950, p. 10. *Queensland Country Life*, 9 December 1943, p. 6. *Telegraph*, 7 November 1942, p. 4. *Townsville Daily Bulletin*, 7 December 1954, p. 1. **Internet** 'South West Pacific Campaign', Queensland WWII Historic Places, updated 2014 <www.ww2places.qld.gov.au/southwestpacificcampaign/>.

RECIPES WITH A SPORTING EDGE

A guilty pleasure

Cookbook Wakehurst Golf Club, *Wakehurst Golf Club's Selected Recipe Book*, revised ed. (Wakehurst: Wakehurst Golf Club, 197–?).

Doris and the Roosters

Cookbook North Adelaide Football Club Ladies Committee, *Recipe Book* (Adelaide: North Adelaide Football Club Ladies Committee, 1977). **Documents** 'Bereavements', *North Adelaide Football Club Annual Report*, 1999. *Boyce of Experience*, North Adelaide Football Club Archives. **Newspapers** *Advertiser*, 30 October 1999.

Iconic cartoonist has the last laugh

Cookbook Epilepsy Social Welfare Foundation and WEG (illus.), *The Sportsman's Cook Book* (Melbourne: Epilepsy Social Welfare Foundation, 1977?). **Journals** Vane Lindesay, 'WEG: William Ellis Green (1923–2008)', *LaTrobe Journal*, no. 86, December 2010, pp. 131–6. **Documents** George Haddon, 'William Ellis Green (WEG) and Geoff Hook', Melbourne Press Club, 2009. **Internet** Larissa Ham, 'Final Siren for Legendary Footy Cartoonist WEG', *Age*, December 2008, <www.theage.com.au/national/final-siren-for-legendary-footy-cartoonist-weg-20081229-76mh.html>. Joan Kerr, 'William Ellis Green b. 1923', Design and Art Australia Online, 2007. Selma Milovanovic, 'WEG Makes a Mug of a Robber', *Age*, September 2006 <www.theage.com.au/news/national/making-a-mug-of-a-robber/2006/01/17/1137466991594.html>. Sarah Wotherspoon, 'Legendary Cartoonist William Ellis Green—WEG—dies', *Herald Sun*, December 2008 <www.heraldsun.com.au/news/victoria/footy-cartoonist-weg-dies/news-story/3f6a2c7807ab8958e77a692a34fe0d3d>.

Noshie for Neddie Lovers

Cookbook Eleanor Russell, *Noshie for Neddie Lovers: a collection of riders recipes* (Melbourne: Howley & Russell, 1983). **Newspapers and magazines** *The Horse Magazine*, August 2010. **Internet** Fran Cleland, 'Australian Dressage Loses Two Greats', Horse Zone, January 2011 <horsezone.com.au/news/australian-dressage-loses-two-greats-621/#S9cxDFdaB2Fxcxwy.97>. 'Vale—Owen 'Doc' Matthews—Pioneer of Dressage in Australia', Top Horse <www.tophorse.com.au/vale-owen--doc--matthews-pioneer-of-dressage-in-australia__doc_matthews__N>.

RECIPES FOR WELLNESS

The gift that keeps on giving

Cookbook Orange District Hospital Auxiliary, *The Orange Recipe Gift Book*, 3rd ed. (Orange: The Leader, 1939). **Books** Elisabeth Edwards, *In Sickness and in Health: how medicine helped shape Orange's history* (Orange: Orange City Council, 2011). **Newspapers** *Daily Advertiser*, 29 November 1927, p. 2. *Forbes Advocate*, 27 June 1939, p. 2. *Gilgandra Weekly*, 24 September 1953, p. 3. *Leader*, 24 February 1919, p. 3; 30 April 1919, p. 2; 3 September 1920, p. 7. *Lithgow Mercury*, 22 July 1937, p. 5. *Mudgee Guardian and North-Western Representative*, 20 November 1930, p. 9; 19 July 1937, p. 6. *National Advocate*, 19 June 1939, p. 3. *South Bourke and Mornington Journal*, 22 May 1913, p. 3. *Sun*, 25 September 1930, p. 29; 26 May 1932, p. 29. *Sydney Morning Herald*, 24 January 1935, p. 6; 1 October 1930, p. 20. *Wellington Times*, 10 September 1953, p. 12. **Internet** Lisa Cox, 'Orange Hospital Auxiliary Doubles Fundraising Efforts', Central Western Daily, 9 June 2011 <www.centralwesterndaily.com.au/story/789227/orange-hospital-auxiliary-doubles-fundraising-efforts/>.

Cooking with society's elite

Cookbook Cancer Campaign Appeal, Women's Committee, *We Cook at Home*

(Melbourne: Women's Committee of the Cancer Campaign Appeal, 195–?). **Books** W. Alan Dick, *Fighting Cancer: Anti-cancer Council of Victoria, 1936–1996* (Carlton: Cancer Council Victoria, 2001). **Newspapers** *Age*, 24 June 1958, p. 8; 10 July 1958, p. 8. *Weekly Times*, 19 April 1950, p. 64.

Caring at Kaniva

Cookbook Kaniva District Hospital Ladies' Auxiliary, *Recipe Book: compiled by Kaniva District Hospital Ladies Auxiliary*, 1st ed. (Kaniva: Kaniva District Hospital, 19––?). **Newspapers** *Countryman*, 27 July 1928, p. 9. *Horsham Times*, 16 January 1931, p. 4.

Tripping down memory lane with pineapple royalty

Cookbook Valerie Bursill, *The Liberated Cook by the Reluctant Housewife* (Pymble: Muscular Dystrophy Association, 1970). **Newspapers and magazines** *Australian Women's Weekly*, 20 August 1975, p. 66. **Internet** Pineapple Princesses <pineappleprincesses.blogspot.com.au/>. 'Ruby Borrowdale Papers', summary information, State Library of Queensland <onesearch.slq.qld.gov.au/SLQ/SLQ_PCI_EBSCO:slq_alma2114878461O002061>.

From baking with biscuits to Boyup Brook

Cookbook Bruce Rock Hospital Auxiliary, *Country Cooking* (Bruce Rock: Bruce Rock Hospital Auxiliary, n.d.).

Giblet snack anyone?

Cookbook Mental Health Auxiliaries of Victoria, Malvern–Caulfield Branch, *Grub Stakes* (East Malvern: Mental Health Auxiliaries of Victoria, Malvern–Caulfield Branch, 197–?).

RECIPES FROM THE OUTBACK

Alice and the Wangi Club

Cookbook Wangi Club, *Once a Jolly Jumbuck: a mutton cookbook* (Wangi Club, 196–?). **Documents** St Andrew's Uniting Church, 'James Crombie 1881–1942', *Stories from the Honour Boards*, Booklet no. 122, St Andrew's Uniting Church, 2016. **Newspapers** *Courier-Mail*, 21 September 1936, p. 20; 10 December 1937, p. 6. *Telegraph*, 29 December 1939, p. 7; 22 November 1944, p. 4. *Townsville Daily Bulletin*, 24 February 1947, p. 6. **Internet** Blythe Moore, '50 Years of Margie's Memories of Muttaburra's Iconic Sheep Show', ABC Western Queensland, June 2015 <www.abc.net.au/local/photos/2015/06/04/4248661.htm>.

Tucking in with Tara
Cookbook Tara Women's Show Auxiliary, *Tara Tucker Book*, 1st ed. (Tara: Tara Women's Show Auxiliary, 1971); 5th ed. (1981); 7th ed. (1990). **Newspapers** *Dalby Herald*, 19 November 1954, p. 5; *Queensland Country Life*, 25 November 1954, p. 13. **Internet** 'Barbara Giesel', Shop 26 Gallery <shop26art. weebly.com/barbara-geisel.html>.

Up the track
Cookbook Paula Rutt (ed), *Up the Track: guide dog cook book containing recipes donated by professional chefs and friends from associations in outback Australia* (Adelaide: Guide Dogs for the Blind Association of South Australia/Northern Territory, 197–?). **Journal** Royal Guide Dogs for the Blind Associations of Australia 'Keeping in Touch with the Territory Folk— and northern SA', *Guide Dog Magazine*, vol. 9, 1974. **Newspapers** *Advertiser*, 22 March 1952, p. 5. *Chronicle*, 15 June 1912, p. 41; 25 February 1932, p. 18. **Internet** Julie Collins, 'Rutt, Walter Bevan Charles', Architects of South Australia, 2008, <www.architectsdatabase.unisa.edu. au/arch_full.asp?Arch_ID=94>. 'Honouring South Australian Pioneers', Guide Dogs SA/ NT, January 2017 <www.guidedogs.org.au/ blogs/honouring-south-australian-pioneers>.

Taking flight at Kanandah
Cookbook C. Finlayson (compiler), *Historical Cookbook*, 4th ed. (Boulder: Women's Auxiliary, Royal Flying Doctor Service Eastern Goldfields Section, 1981). **Internet** Eric Swann, 'Life Member—the first bestowed', Royal Flying Doctor Service—Esperance Auxiliary <http://www.esperancerfds.com/>, 'RFDS Eastern Goldfields Auxiliary Celebrates 50th Anniversary', Royal Flying Doctor Service, June 2016 <www.flyingdoctor.org. au/news/rfds-eastern-goldfields-auxiliary-celebrates-50th-anniversary/>.

The buffalo hunters
Cookbook Country Women's Association of the Northern Territory, *Buffalo Cook Book* (Darwin: CWA of the Northern Territory, 1981). **Documents** B. Lemcke, D. Foulkes, K. Hedenig and Neil Ross, 'TenderBuff: a healthy and exciting alternative red meat', Agnote no. J29, Department of Primary Industry, Fisheries and Mines, Northern Territory Government, 2006. **Newspapers** *Centralian Advocate*, 8 August 1952, p. 1. *Chronicle*, 25 June 1953, p. 26. *Courier-Mail*, 7 October 1953, p. 1. *Northern Territory News*, 9 June 2016, Lifestyle section p. 21. **Radio** Interview with Judy Anictomatis, *The Guestroom*, ABC Radio Darwin, 4 August 2010.

Making do in a hurry
Cookbook Royal Flying Doctor Service of Australia, Women's Auxiliary of the Air Branch, Alice Springs, *Cookery Book* (Alice Springs: The Auxiliary, 195–?). **Newspapers and magazines** *Australian Women's Weekly*, 31 October 1962, p. 14.

RECIPES FOR THE YOUNG
The invisible woman
Cookbook Congregational Union of South Australia and South Australian Baptist Union, *Green and Gold Cookery Book: containing many good and proved recipes*, 1st ed. (Adelaide: Vardon and Sons, 1924); 7th ed. (Adelaide: R.M. Osborne Ltd, n.d.); 9th ed. (n.d.); 11th ed. revised (1939); 20th ed., revised, war-time finish (n.d.); 41st ed., revised (Adelaide: Rigby Publishers, 1985, reprinted 1987); limited edition (Sydney: New Holland Publishers, 2013). **Books** J.R. Davis, *Principles and Pragmatism: a history of Girton, King's College and Pembroke School* (Kensington Park: Pembroke School Council, 1991), pp. 215–16, 241, 289, 296. **Journals** Julia Pitman, 'The Green and Gold Cookery Book: women, faith, fetes, food and popular culture', *Journal of the Historical Society of South Australia*, no. 35, 2007, pp. 64–81. **Documents** Correspondence between Ethel and Florence Sharman and Pembroke School, 1985–1986, courtesy Pembroke School Archive. **Sound recordings** Interview with Miss Ethel Sharman and Mrs Florence Leslie (nee Sharman), Pamela Runge (interviewer), Australian Federation of University Women SA Oral History Project, J.D. Somerville Oral History Collection, State Library of South Australia, recorded 14 October 1981. Interview with Ethel and Anne Sharman and Florence Leslie, Beth M. Robertson interviewer, South Australian Women's Responses to the First World War, J.D. Somerville Oral History Collection, State Library of South Australia, recorded 1979. **Newspapers** *Bunyip*, 13 May 1938, p. 1. *Chronicle*, 26 November 1953, p. 55. *Evening Journal*, 2 May 1911, p. 2. *News*, 21 March 1924, p. 7; 22 April 1924, p. 4; 16 December 1925, p. 11; 5 January 1926, p. 5; 26 May 1927, p. 6; 25 November 1929, p. 4; 28 January 1930, p. 6; 31 October 1930, p. 10; 17 December 1932, p. 4; 13 January 1936, p. 6; 19 January 1938, p. 8; 6 May 1938, p. 8. *Observer*, 23 February 1918, p. 13; 12 December 1925, p. 84. *Recorder*, 30 April 1936, p. 1. *Register*, 24 March 1924, p. 13.

There was never a doubt
Cookbook Back to Suttontown Fund, *The "Back to Suttontown" Recipe Book: five hundred selected recipes from the South-East of South Australia which is famous for everything, including cookery*, 1st ed. (Mount Gambier: The Border Watch, 1933); *The Suttontown Recipe Book: 600 selected recipes*, 3rd ed. (Mount Gambier: The Border Watch, 1945); 6th ed. (1983). **Newspapers** *Border Watch*, 31 December 1918, p. 4; 23 May 1933, p. 4; 19 May 1936, p. 4; 4 December 1937, p. 1; 28 December 1939, p. 3; 20 June 1944, p. 5; 16 September 1944, p. 4; 20 October 1945, p. 4; 7 February 1946, p. 4; 30 June 1949, p. 13. *Chronicle*, 22 April 1899, p. 4.

The book that made the dough
Cookbook Cobden Pre-School Centre, *Cobden Pre-School Centre Recipe Book*, vol. 1, reprinted (Cobden: Cobden Pre-School Centre Committee, 1971). **Documents** 'From the History Books', *Connecting Cobden Community Newsletter*, no. 12, 19 December 2012.

One enchanted evening
Cookbook Ulladulla Public School Ladies Auxiliary, *The Best of Good Taste* (Ulladulla: Ulladulla Public School, 196–?); vol. 2 (1974). **Journals** 'Vale Ruth Mary Richards OAM', *The Country Woman: official publication of the Country Women's Association of NSW*, vol. 53, no. 5, October 2012, p. 7. **Newspapers** *South Coast Register*, 5 September 2012, p. 1.

Loving to eat Jewish
Cookbook Bialik College Parents Association Mothers Book Committee, *I Love to Eat Jewish: home tested Jewish recipes collected throughout Australia and published*, 2nd ed. (Hawthorn: Bialik College Parents Association, 1968). **Documents** Information prepared for Bialik College 70th anniversary exhibition, 2012, courtesy Bialik College Archive. **Newspapers** *Age*, 13 November 1968, p. 15; 1 October 1970, p. 4. *Herald*, 9 July 1968. *Jewish News*, 9 August 1968. **Internet** 'Ex Boxer Goes Hell for Leather for Youth', *Age*, 24 June 2004 <www.theage.com.au/ articles/2004/06/27/1088274626533.html>. 'History and Vision', Bialik College <www. bialik.vic.edu.au/about-bialik/history-and-vision/>. Russell Jackson, 'Henry Nissen: from boxing hero to champion of Melbourne's most vulnerable', The Guardian, 24 December 2016 <www.theguardian.com/sport/2016/ dec/24/henry-nissen-from-boxing-hero-to-champion-of-melbournes-most-vulnerable>. Adam Kamien, 'Champion Boxer Inducted

into Hall of Fame', The Australian Jewish News, 19 October 2009 <www.jewishnews.net.au/champion-boxer-inducted-into-hall-of-fame/8706>.

Recipes for rejoicing
Cookbook Lyn Smith (compiler), *Chairo Christian School Family Recipe Book* (Drouin: Chairo Christian School, 1988). **Internet** 'History', Chairo Christian School <www.chairo.vic.edu.au/history>.

Recepy for success
Cookbook Newport Primary School, *Newport School Cookbook* (Mona Vale: Newport Primary School, 1987).

COUNTRY WOMEN'S WISDOM
Bundaberg takes flight
Cookbook Queensland Country Women's Association, Bundaberg Branch, *Cookery Book: revised supplementary recipes,* 11th ed. (Brisbane: Watson Ferguson & Co, 1962); *Bundaberg Branch Cookery Book: new and revised recipes* (2015). **Newspapers** *Brisbane Courier*, 26 July 1924, p. 22; 3 July 1928, p. 21; 16 September 1931, p. 16. *Bundaberg Daily Times*, 8 April 1932, p. 3. *Bundaberg News Mail*, 8 September 1956, p. 4. *Daily Mail*, 3 January 1921, p. 7. *Daily Mercury*, 28 December 1932, p. 4; 10 March 1944, p. 2. *Daily Standard*, 8 September 1931, p. 11. *Morning Bulletin*, 29 May 1930, p. 14; 16 April 1932, p. 11; 7 April 1938, p. 4. *Queenslander*, 3 January 1929, p. 52. *Uralla Times*, 1 March 1928, p. 1. *Week*, 14 September 1928, p. 6. **Internet** E.P. Wixted, 'Hinkler, Herbert John (Bert) (1892–1933)', Australian Dictionary of Biography <adb.anu.edu.au/biography/hinkler-herbert-john-bert-6680/text11519>. 'Pieced Together: Queensland CWA Archives', The Fashion Archives, Issue 10., 11 March 2014 <thefashionarchives.org/?pieced_together=queensland-cwa-archives>.

The School of Experience
Cookbook Agnes K.B. Barnes (compiler), *The C.W.A. Cookery Book and Household Hints*, 4th ed. (Perth: Country Women's Association of Western Australia, 1940); 5th ed. (1941); 52nd ed. (Pymble: Angus & Robertson, 2003). **Documents** Speech by Agnes Barnes, broadcast by ABC radio, Perth, 3 July 1942, courtesy CWA Archives. Unpublished research notes compiled by Vivienne Rowney, September 2015, courtesy CWA Archives. **Newspapers** *Albany Advertiser*, 13 August 1936, p. 6. *Daily News*, 5 August 1936, p. 8; 3 December 1936, p. 7; 6 December 1937, p. 7; 6 June 1942, p. 6.

Kapunda Herald, 16 February 1900, p. 2. *Sunday Times*, 24 October 1926, p. 5; 27 August 1933, p. 5. *West Australian*, 10 November 1925, p. 4; 28 August 1928, p. 4; 10 August 1932, p. 18; 5 January 1949, p. 1. *Western Mail*, 13 August 1936, p. 37; 30 December 1937, p. 30.

Crowning glory
Cookbook Jessie Sawyer and Sara Moore-Sims (compilers), *The Coronation Cookery Book*, 1st ed. (Sydney: Country Women's Association of New South Wales, 1937); 2nd ed. (1938); 9th revised ed. (1963); 13th revised ed. (1976); 15th revised ed. (1981). **Books** Helen Townsend, *Serving the Country: the history of the Country Women's Association of New South Wales* (Sydney: Doubleday, 1988), pp. 13–14, 32, 37. **Documents** Executive meeting minutes, CWA of New South Wales, May and November 1936, courtesy CWA Archives. **Journals** Dulcie Hunter, 'The Late Mrs T. Moore-Sims', *The Countrywoman in New South Wales: official journal of the Country Women's Association of New South Wales*, 6 January 1938, p. 34. **Newspapers and magazines** *Armidale Express and New England General Advertiser*, 8 May 1928, p. 4. *Australian Women's Weekly*, 13 April 1935, p. 2. *Daily Advertiser*, 13 November 1937, p. 10; 10 October 1939, p. 4. *Grenfell Record and Lachlan District Advertiser*, 5 November 1936, p. 3. *Gundagai Independent and Pastoral, Agricultural and Mining Advocate*, 2 April 1904, p. 2. *Guyra Argus*, 20 August 1936, p. 2. *Macleay Argus*, 9 July 1937, p. 14. *Methodist*, 20 April 1907, p. 6. *Mudgee Guardian and North-Western Representative*, 11 March 1937, p. 10. *Narrandera Argus and Riverina Advertiser*, 14 February 1941, p. 2. *Newcastle Morning Herald and Miners' Advocate*, 12 August 1937, p. 4. *North West Champion*, 11 November 1937, p. 4. *Richmond River Herald and Northern Districts Advertiser*, 10 November 1936, p. 4. *Sun*, 7 March 1937, p. 2; 27 April 1938, p. 18. *Sydney Mail*, 19 July 1922, p. 21. *Sydney Morning Herald*, 11 May 1907, p. 8; 6 May 1937, p. 27; 23 June 1937, p. 5. *Sydney Stock and Station Journal*, 25 April 1922, p. 2. **Internet** Jane Carey, 'Country Women's Association of New South Wales 1922–)', Australian Women's Register, March 2004 <trove.nla.gov.au/people/459294?c=people - history of group>. 'Country Women's Association', State Library of NSW <www2.sl.nsw.gov.au/archive/discover_collections/history_nation/agriculture/communities/cwa.html>. Julie Gorrell, 'Sawyer, Jessie Frederica Pauline (1870–1947)', Australian Dictionary

of Biography <adb.anu.edu.au/biography/sawyer-jessie-frederica-pauline-11619/text20749>.

Cookery treasures from the Esk Valley
Cookbook K. Herbert, Esk Valley Group, *The Esk Valley Cookery Book: treasured recipes of the Country Women of the Esk Valley*, 3rd ed. revised (Melbourne: Southdown Press, 1953); new ed. (Melbourne: Southdown Press, 195?), 13th ed. (1976); 1st metric ed. (1986); (Devonport: Taswegia, 1999). **Documents** Esk Valley Group CWA Records, courtesy Elizabeth Clark. **Newspapers** *Daily Telegraph*, 23 November 1907, p. 4. *Examiner*, 21 March 1929, p. 11; 1 March 1944, p. 6; 3 May 1944, p. 8; 10 May 1944, p. 6; 28 August 1947, p. 3; 7 May 1949, p. 7; 3 June 1949, p. 8; 27 September 1950, p. 10; 28 June 1951, p. 8; 13 November 1953, p. 13. *Mercury*, 14 August 1954, p. 6.

Cooking with courage
Cookbook Doreen Baker, *The Doreen Baker Cookery Book*, 3rd ed. (Gunnedah: Country Women's Association, Gunnedah Branch, 1968). **Newspapers and magazines** *Australian Women's Weekly*, 17 March 1965, p. 2; 20 September 1967, p. 38. *Land*, 11 December 1953, p. 33. *Sydney Stock and Station Journal*, 7 July 1922, p. 3. **Internet** 'New Heights for High Tea', Namoi Valley Independent, 6 November 2014 <www.nvi.com.au/story/2678405/new-heights-for-high-tea/>. 'The CWA Gunnedah Kitchen Project', The Sebastian Foundation, <thesebastianfoundation.org/our-heartbeat/how-we-do-it/the-cwa-gunnedah-kitchen-project/>. Annette Turner, 'A Recipe for Success', Snippets: little stories from the Country Women's Association of NSW, December 2014 <cwaofnsw.wordpress.com/tag/doreen-baker/>.

RECIPE INDEX

ACKNOWLEDGEMENTS

Much like the cookbooks I have written about, this book would not exist without the very willing assistance and enthusiastic support that I have received from dozens of community groups and volunteers across the country. Many people living busy lives willingly stepped up to help dig out the records and information I needed, when time, cost, distance and logistical challenges made it difficult for me to do it all myself. They stuck with me through months of detective work and endless fact checking, patiently responding to my every email, offering cheerful encouragement, and sharing in the excitement of what we uncovered.

Then there were the professional librarians, archivists and other staff who helped me access both public and private collections of cookbooks and other pertinent resources. In some of the larger libraries, they dragged out hundreds of books, sometimes in just a few days, bending the rules to help meet my tight schedules. The work of such people often goes unappreciated in today's manic, digital world, but libraries and historical archives and the treasures they keep are vital to our sense of who we are, and the country and communities we live in.

Once again, a large team of volunteer cooks contributed their time, pantries and waistlines to testing recipes. While it is impossible to mention every single individual, I would like to thank Kay Long in particular. She not only baked, but spent hours carefully arranging the end results and taking beautiful photographs for me, for no financial reward. Many other people also volunteered their services as photographers, or provided treasured images that have been vital in bringing the stories to life, and have been duly credited alongside their contributions. Thank you one and all.

My personal thanks also goes to my family and friends for their ongoing love and support, to my agent, Fiona Inglis, for her wise counsel, and to the remarkable team at Allen & Unwin, in particular Claire Kingston, who continues to show faith in me and my books; editor Ariana Klepac, whose skill and attention to detail took the whole book to a new level; and the astoundingly calm, efficient and supportive Siobhán Cantrill, who shepherded the book so capably through editing and production.

Last, but not least, I give special thanks to the extremely talented designer Liz Nicholson. This is the third occasion on which I have been lucky enough to work with Liz—and the experience has spoilt me for all other designers. Liz, you have a magical way of tapping into the very heart of my writing and bringing it to creative, colourful life, and I count my blessings every day that we work together.

Liz Harfull

Right: Image by Genevieve Cooper.

First published in 2018

Allen & Unwin
83 Alexander Street
Crows Nest NSW 2065
Australia
Phone: (61 2) 8425 0100
Email: info@allenandunwin.com
Web: www.allenandunwin.com

Cataloguing-in-Publication details are available from the National Library of Australia
www.trove.nla.gov.au

ISBN 978 1 76029 104 4

Designed and typeset by Liz Nicholson, DesignBite
Printed and bound in China by Hang Tai Printing Company Limited

10 9 8 7 6 5 4 3 2 1

Credits

Page 80: Copha advertisement from *What Shall I Cook Today?: 100 copha recipes*, c. 1950s.
Page 81: Dried fruit advertisement from the *Sunshine Cookery Book*, c. 1930s.
Page 122: Arnott's Nice biscuit advertisement from *The Woman's Day*, 1962.
Page 123: Gay Ware advertisement from *The Australian Women's Weekly Cook Book* supplement, 1958.
Page 154: Empire Tea advertisement created by Troedel & Co., Melbourne, c. 1880s (State Library of Victoria).
Page 155: Vegemite advertisement, 1942 (courtesy Bega Cheese Limited).
Page 180: Sunbeam Electric Frypan advertisement from *The Australian Women's Weekly Cook Book* supplement, 1958.
Page 181: James Northfield (1887–1973) Gratify your wish for health: demand quality guaranteed Board eggs, c. 1940 (© James Northfield Heritage Art Trust).
Pages 206–207: Golden Circle advertisement from *The Australian Women's Weekly*, 1963.
Page 252: Illustration from a Davis Gelatine supplement in the *Green and Gold Cookery Book*, ninth edition, 1938 (Pembroke School Archives).
Page 253: Nurse's Corn Flour advertisement from the *Green and Gold Cookery Book*, seventh edition, c. 1933 (Pembroke School Archives).
Page 290: Bushells Instant Coffee advertisement from *The Coronation Cookery Book*, ninth edition, revised, 1963 (CWA of NSW archives).
Page 291: Bushells Tea advertisement from *The Coronation Cookery Book*, ninth edition, revised, 1963 (CWA of NSW archives).

STOCK LIBRARY CREDITS
Page 22: Scotch broth image from Shutterstock.
Page 147: Cumquats image from Shutterstock.
Chapter-opening pages: Tea towel image from iStock.
Image of note paper used on recipe pages from iStock.
Image of butchers' paper used on recipe and montage pages from Shutterstock.

Unless otherwise stated, all photographs were taken by the author and original cookbooks sourced from the author's private collection.

A note about the recipes

The recipes in this book have all been carefully modified to make them more user-friendly for today's home cooks. While some of the quantities and methods have changed, the intent has been to stay true to the intentions of the original recipe and achieve a similar end result.

The recipes have all been converted to Australian standard metric measures: that is, a 250 millilitre cup for measuring liquids, with dry ingredients given in both grams and cup equivalents where appropriate; and tablespoons with a 20 millilitre liquid capacity. Please check your tablespoon measures as some brands sold in Australia are based on the American tablespoon, which is only 15 millilitres, or the British Imperial measure, which is 18 millilitres.

Following the standard Australian approach, the recipes use eggs with an average weight of 60 grams.

Oven temperatures are given both as a description, and in degrees. The degrees given in parentheses are based on a conventional electric oven. As with all recipes, it is important to remember that ovens vary enormously, and the temperatures and cooking times are intended as a guide only.

JOLLY JUMBUCK!

a mutton cookbook

INGELLIC

Centenary
COOK
BOOK

1879   1979

c Public School Centenary

Appetising
RECIPES
BY
THORNDENE KINDERGARTEN
MOTHERS' CLUB

Fathers'
Delights

Recipes of the Wives of Anglican Priests
in the Diocese of Brisbane

Echuca Branch
Country Women's Association

COOKERY
BOOK :: of
Tested Recipes

- Price 1s. 6d. -

AFTERNOON TEA

with the "PHE"

HOME-TESTED
RECIPES

COPYRIGHT

The Everyday
and Everyday

RECIPE
BOOK

Price Two Shillings

FAMILY
FAVOURITES

RECIPE BOOK, No. 3
(1963 - 64)

Compiled by Members of the
LADIES' OVER 21 CLUB
of
St. Stephen's Presbyterian
Church
CANNING BRIDGE

THE
CORONATION
COOKERY BOOK

Compiled by
THE COUNTRY WOMEN'S
ASSOCIATION
OF N.S.W.

PRICE 12/6

Chairo Christian
School
Family Recipe Book

THE
COOK'S HANDBOOK

TARA
TUCKER
BOOK

The Joy Of Eating

CWA
ESK VALLEY
COOKERY BOOK

NEW EDITION

I LOVE TO EAT
JEWISH

The
21st Birthday
Cookery
Book
of The
Country Women's
Association
in Tasmania

C W A
EATON — SOUTH-WEST
COOKERY BOOK

COOKERY
BOOK

Compiled by
Royal Flying Doctor Service
WOMEN'S AUXILIARY OF THE AIR BRANCH
ALICE SPRINGS

Bulyee's
Beaut
Bakes

Flour

GUIDE DOGS for the
BLIND ASSOCIATION

Miscellaneous &
Luncheon Snacks..Blue
Fish..............Green
Meat & Chicken...Buff
Cakes, loaves, biscuits
and slices......Pink
Deserts..........Gold

100
RECIPES FROM

THE
TATIARA
NEW HALL

RECIPE
BOOK
1960

THE AUSTRALIAN
FISH
COOKERY BOOK

Edited by LAURIE BRUCE STEER
for the Country Women's Association of N.S.W.

East Torrens District Kindergarten
COLLECTION OF RECIPES

THE
CORONATION
COOKERY BOOK

COMPILED B'y THE
COUNTRY WOMENS ASSOCIATION
OF NSW

[COPYRIGHT]

ALL IN ONE

Price
2/-

Recipe Book
AND
Household
Guide

Published by
The Disabled Mens Association
of Australia

RECIPE BOOK

TESTED RECIPES
COMPILED BY QUEEN'S METHODIST LADIES. BOULDER. W.A

THE
P.W.M.U.
COOKERY BOOK
OF VICTORIA

PRACTICAL
HOUSEHOLD RECIPES
1/6
COMPILED & ISSUED BY
E PRESBYTERIAN WOMEN'S MISSION
UNION OF VICTORIA

COOKERY

Price 1'-

THE
DISCRIMINATING
HOUSE – WIFE'S
DAILY COMPANION

Entire proceeds for the
N.S.W. Methodist Mission

By over Fifty Australian Hostesses

SOMETHING
DIFFERENT
FOR
DINNER

THE
Coronation
COOKERY
BOOK

GREEN
and
GOLD

Compiled by
The Country Women's Association of N.S.W

DROUIN
PRIMARY
SCHOOL

HAYDAYS
PLAIN
& FANCY